Sherman Tank Crewman

Sherman Tank Crewman

Sharpshooter Snapshots: From D-Day to the Defeat of the Third Reich

John Fisher

Frontline Books

SHERMAN TANK CREWMAN
Sharpshooter Snapshots: From D-Day to the Defeat of the Third Reich

First published in Great Britain, as *Sharpshooter Snapshots*,
by Portway Publishing in 1996. This edition published in 2026 by
Frontline Books,
An imprint of Pen & Sword Books Ltd
Yorkshire – Philadelphia

ISBN 978 1 03618 679 1

A CIP catalogue record for this book is
available from the British Library.

Typeset by Mac Style
Printed in the UK by CPI Group (UK) Ltd, Croydon, CR0 4YY.

The Publisher's authorised representative in the EU for product safety is Authorised Rep Compliance Ltd., Ground Floor, 71 Lower Baggot Street, Dublin D02 P593, Ireland.
www.arccompliance.com

For a complete list of Pen & Sword titles please contact:

PEN & SWORD BOOKS LIMITED
47 Church Street, Barnsley, South Yorkshire, S70 2AS, England
E-mail: enquiries@pen-and-sword.co.uk
Website: www.pen-and-sword.co.uk
or
PEN AND SWORD BOOKS
1950 Lawrence Road, Havertown, PA 19083, USA
E-mail: uspen-and-sword@casematepublishers.com
Website: www.penandswordbooks.com

This book is dedicated to the memory of Trooper John Peter Cotton, 'C' Squadron, 4th and 3/4th CLY, who died on 28th March 1945, and is buried with other Sharpshooters in the Reichswald War Cemetery, near Cleves in Germany.

Contents

Foreword

Anyone who has been in the army will find here many vivid pictures of army life as it was lived from 1943/1945. Those of us who have 'messed about in tanks', whether in peace or war, will taste again the meat and veg, get that benzine smell of a brew-up, remember with thankfulness the comradeship in tank and troop, realise what dangerous piles of metal and machinery formed our home, at risk from armour-piercing shell and bog alike. But there also is one man's honest account of the confusion, bewilderment and grief of war. He is eloquent about his own mistakes, and his account, to our cynical and in many ways selfish days, will seem innocent, honest and full of self-sacrifice. No doubt the Sharpshooters of the County of London Yeomanry will get special pleasure from this book, but the rest of us soldiers, veterans and tank people will make tracks through familiar and remembered places.

The Bishop of Bath and Wells,
The Right Reverend James Thompson

Preface to the Original Edition

The title of the book, *Sharpshooter Snapshots*, was suggested by my publisher, Terry Delaney, who has guided me through the many pitfalls and traps which lie in wait for the inexperienced writer. To him I owe a great debt of gratitude.

My memories of what Jack Geddes names 'those difficult years' are like snapshots as I recall incidents seen through periscope or telescope from the tank gunner's position, and of other incidents in a short army career. I hope that these memories will be of interest to those who took part in the campaign in North-West Europe in 1944, and to others who are interested in the events of that time.

Acknowledgements

The Rt. Rev'd. James Thompson, Bishop of Bath and Wells, for writing the Foreword.

Dr. P. Boyden and the National Army Museum for permission to reproduce photographs from the 'Sale' Collection.

M. Jean-Paul Marchal for permission to reproduce the 'Kruishoutem' account from his book *Gent – September '44*.

Major Boris Mollo, T.D., and Brian Mulcock, B.E.M., for help in tracing Wireless Operator's Codes at the Sharpshooter Museum.

Harry Gell and Roy Cawston for their help and encouragement.

Terry Delaney of Portway Publications, Wells, for his help and guidance in the production in the first edition of the book.

Samantha Delaney, who drew the maps and helped with proof-reading.

Glossary

Astrid	Queen of the Belgians. Died in automobile accident, 29th August 1935.
Auster	High-wing monoplane used for artillery spotting (Air Observation Post). Made by British Taylorcraft.
Baby	Code for armoured fighting vehicle.
Baker Roger	Code for bridge.
Bazooka	Rocket-propelled anti-tank grenade launcher used by US Forces but also used by the British as the name for the German 'Panzerfaust'.
Belly	When a tank sinks in soft ground until the hull rests on the ground and the tracks can find no purchase in order to move.
BD	Battledress. Introduced for wear by the Army in 1938.
BESA	0.303 calibre machine-gun on British tanks. Made by the Birmingham Small Arms Co – hence the name.
Blue	Refers to a river or canal so marked on a map or to the feature on the ground.
Brassing up	Engaging an enemy with machine-gun fire.
Buzz, Buzzed	When low-flying aircraft, friendly or hostile, flies low over a target.
Char and wad	Tea and a bun. Conventional refreshment in a canteen.
Churchill	British heavy tank used mainly to support infantry.
CSM	Company Sergeant Major.
Cymbalum	Stringed instrument played by hammers held in the hand.
DAQMG	Deputy Assistant Quarter-master General.
DD	Duplex-driven Sherman tank fitted with equipment which enabled it to float.

DR	Despatch rider motor-cyclist.
Dressed	Ranks of troops lined up on parade.
Feet	Term for infantry.
15-cwt	A medium-sized lorry.
Firefly	Sherman tank with a British 17-pounder gun.
Fiesler-Storch	German high-winged monoplane used for artillery spotting and reconnaissance, as was the Auster (qv).
Flak	General term for anti-aircraft fire.
Flimsy	A petrol can made of light metal, as opposed to the more robust jerrican.
Frog	Code for 'road' – rhyming slang 'frog and toad'.
Funny	General term for an AFV which was adapted to carry out special tasks. These included 'Crocodiles' (flame-throwing Churchill tanks), 'Crabs' (mine-clearing Shermans), and 'Ark' (a bridge-layer).
Griff	Information.
GSC	General Service Corps.
Hard	Solid landing or embarkation place on river or sea shore.
High port	Rifle canted across the body in a position of readiness.
Iron horse thing	Code for railway track.
Jankers	Being confined to barracks, or some other punishment, for a misdemeanour.
KRR	Kings Royal Rifle Corps.
Leaguer	Derived from Boer 'Laager' – AFVs drawn up in a defensive formation for the night.
Locals	Civilian population.
LCT	Landing Craft, Tank.
LST	Landing Ship, Tank.
Maquis	Armed French civilian organisation – guerrilla organisation.
Mairsi dotes	Words of a popular song: tr. Mares eat oats.
Mother Riley	Music hall artiste Arthur Lucan, who appeared in the character of an old woman.
Motor	Travel a distance without any enemy opposition.

Nebelwerfer	Literally 'Fog thrower' – a German multiple-barrelled mortar used to lay a smoke screen or high-explosive shells.
New friends with the funny hats	Canadian infantry who wore a new pattern of steel helmet introduced in 1944.
Old friends with the funny hats	8th Hussars, 7th Armoured Division Reconnaissance Regiment. The officers' dress hat was tent-shaped and had a small tassel on the front. This head-dress dated from the Peninsular War.
OR	Other Ranks as distinct from Officers.
Prof. Joad	A radio and TV pundit of the 1940s and '50s.
PTI	Member of the Army Physical Training Corps. A PT Instructor.
Q	A Quartermaster.
Red Shield	Salvation Army canteens or vans.
RHA	Royal Horse Artillery.
RHQ	Regimental Headquarters.
Rocket	A severe reprimand.
RTO	Railway Transport Officer.
Sabot	Armour-piercing shot. An outer shell was discarded when the round left the muzzle of the gun. This device increased muzzle velocity.
Scrim	Camouflage material.
Sharp end	The front line. Also used to denote the bows of a vessel.
Skins	The Inniskilling Dragoon Guards.
Spandau	German machine-gun with rapid rate of fire and distinctive sound.
Spuds	Additional plates fitted on the outer end of a track plate to give increased traction.
Spider's Boys	'A' Squadron Fitters. Sgt. Webb was the Fitter Sergeant.
SSM	Squadron Sergeant Major.
Stag	Sentry duty.
Stand and be still	Reference to a Kipling poem. The Birkenhead was a troopship which foundered off the coast of Africa on 26th February 1852. Troops aboard lined up in ranks

	on deck, thus allowing women and children into the lifeboats.
Stonk	A short concentration of shellfire on a target.
Sunny Jim	A character on the packaging of a popular breakfast cereal.
Swan	Proceed into unknown territory.
Tear off a strip	Being reprimanded.
Typhoons	Fighter, carrying rockets and armed with cannon. Made by the Hawker Aircraft Co.
Umbrellas	Used sometimes to keep out rain from a tank turret.
Volkssturm	German equivalent of the Home Guard.
Wire pickets	Metal stakes, with an end which could be screwed into the ground to hold barbed-wire entanglements.

List of Maps

List of Plates

Chapter 1

'Gone for a Soldier'

When I enlisted at Derby in 1943, the Recruiting Officer, Captain Jacques, told me that those who volunteered could choose to serve in whatever branch of the army they wished.

"I would like to go into tanks," I said.

"That's just what I had in mind," was the reply.

So, I volunteered, ignoring my mother's advice that I should not go into those "stinking tanks", as she called them, and also dismissing the remark of a friend who informed me that those who went into tanks had to have nerves of steel!

So, to Bovington to join the Royal Armoured Corps.

I went by train from our local station 'Stapleford and Sandiacre', accompanied by my mother and father to as far as Nottingham, where I took the train to St Pancras. A companion from Junior School was also travelling to London to join the Royal Artillery at Woolwich and his father was coming with us, so I had company on the first stage of my new adventure. My travelling companions and I parted with mutual good wishes at St Pancras, and I took the tube to Waterloo, finding the right train without difficulty. As we rattled along, a uniformed member of the WAAF who was sitting opposite me asked if I was "joining up". I said I was, and she said that I would soon get used to the life. I was grateful for that remark. I suppose that the small case I was carrying gave the game away. In it were toilet requisites and brown paper and string to parcel up and send back home my civilian clothes when a uniform was issued.

Waterloo then and the train to Wool, Dorset, the station for Bovington.

In the carriage were two people I took to be civilians, also a soldier and, sharing a bottle of beer, two girls in the ATS. When the train moved off, they proffered the bottle to the other occupants of the carriage in a most friendly way. We all refused – one or two with hurt dignity I thought. One of the girls asked me where I was going.

"Bovington," I said.

"Poor young bugger!" she replied as she applied her lips to the bottle again.

My heart sank! To what kind of a place was I going? Only slightly reassured by hoardings which told me that I was 'Going to the Strong Country', I gazed out of the window as the train chuffed on its way south.

It was pleasant to travel on a bright sunny afternoon through unknown country, as all our holidays before the war had been taken on the east coast of England, except for one holiday in Blackpool in the summer of 1938. That was a great break with tradition.

Now we drew up at a small station just outside Bournemouth. The station had been bombed, perhaps in 1940, and the waiting-room had only one wall, dazzling white in the sunshine and standing out against the intense blue sky, like something from a stage set about war.

We then travelled through pine woods and heathland and arrived at Wool Station.

A number of us got off the train and we were approached by a suntanned corporal who wore the black beret and badge of the Royal Tank Regiment (RTR). He came up to me and asked, "Are you for the Primary Training Wing?" I said "No!", for I had been told to report to the Primary Training Centre. Being slow on the uptake, I had not realised that the PTW and the PTC were one and the same place.

The corporal shepherded the others into the back of a three-tonner and they drove away, leaving me alone, so I set off to walk to camp as there did not seem to be any transport. In the station yard, a soldier who was driving a pick-up truck asked me where I wanted to go and said that he would take me to my intended destination.

We drove off, pausing at the level-crossing to let a Cruiser tank rattle away up the road ahead of us. At last a 'stinking tank', and I already imagined myself riding along in such a vehicle.

Deposited in Amiens Square at the top of the hill, I made my way to the unit office and reported in, handing over documents I had brought with me. I was then directed to one of the wooden huts which lined one edge of the Square. These had been erected for soldiers in the 1914-18 conflict, but for World War Two an addition had been made in the shape of chest-high concrete blast-walls on the sides of the huts and across one end. Two huts formed one unit, being joined by an ablutions section in the middle.

In my hut were assembled the group which had come up in the three-tonner, and the RTR corporal. To my relief, his eye passed over me without recognition.

We shambled off in some sort of order for tea, having been given large white mugs. ("Don't break it! That's the only one you'll get!" said the Trooper who was giving them out). As we waited outside the mess hut, we heard the sound of many marching feet striking the ground together as one. A column of bronzed young men in shirt-sleeve order marched up to the mess hut and halted with a crash, filing into the hut before we could do so. We were awed by such swank, little thinking that we were looking at a picture of ourselves as we would be in a few weeks time. We followed them into the mess hut.

Over tea, introductions were made and we got to know our companions a little. Introductions, in the form of saying who we were and where we came from, continued in the barrack hut after tea. Then we were marched away to the bedding store with our palliasses to fill them with straw, pillows too, getting ourselves ready for our first night in the Army. After the excitement of the day, I think most of us spent a peaceful night, being roused by Reveille, an infantry call on a bugle.

After breakfast we were issued with our equipment – webbing belts and packs, rifles, uniforms, denim overalls, boots, 'drawers cellular', as it was summer, and other gear. The webbing equipment was as yet unblancoed, a delight to come. Anklets, we discovered, could be put on back to front and one of our companions had to be re-adjusted amid howls of laughter. Braces, holding up our trousers, were of unyielding webbing and some trousers had metal buttons. The consequent strain on the thread made buttons fly off at frequent intervals. One of the lads, Boxford, was particularly prone to this condition. When we had been on leave and had got into the same carriage at Waterloo, one of us said, "Hello Boxford. How's your trousers?" "Alright, Ray," said Boxford, stretching up to put his pack on the luggage rack. A button instantly flew across the carriage, and we all hugged ourselves with glee!

But that episode lay in the future. Now, we were all lined up on our first parade in one long line, tallest at either end, shortest in the middle.

We numbered off, odd numbers fell back one pace and turned right, even numbers turned left. We 'quick marched' to form three ranks, pushed into place by the NCOs. By means of this magic, we found ourselves in three ranks, tallest at either end, shortest in the middle. "Look at the men on either side of you. Always fall in between them in the same places."

The next task for the NCOs was to form us into a well-oiled drill squad, and of course we began with basic drill movements. We gathered round to watch the NCOs demonstrating. We were told that the medical profession was concerned about the way in which the army stamped during drill, so we were told: "Don't stamp. Place your feet firmly on the ground – like this" (STAMP!!), as Sergeant Mackenzie demonstrated.

Some of our instructors had taken part in the 1940 debacle in France and Belgium in 1940. Sergeant Mackenzie was one of these exalted beings. He wore the badge of the Border Regiment in his field service cap, and it was also in the form of a coloured painted badge, on the front of his steel helmet. Perhaps this was a Border Regiment speciality. I envied him his denim trousers, which had been washed to a delicate shade of pale pink.

Another sergeant, long jawed and with long, yellow teeth, told us how to march and showed us how. "Feet straight forward and with toes turned neither in nor out and dig your heels in. Dig, dig, dig!" I enjoyed foot-drill and I think all of us got satisfaction from gradually seeing an improvement in 'getting it together'.

When Sergeant Mackenzie showed us the rudiments of rifle-drill, we noted that his rifle seemed to hover in mid-air and wait for him to catch it with his left hand in the first movement of 'Slope arms'. Before long, we too were able to perform the drill movement in the same way, expending just enough energy to throw the rifle up to the right height for it to be caught. So, we grew in confidence in foot- and rifle-drill.

One day there appeared in our midst a Grenadier Sergeant. If Sergeant Mackenzie could make a rifle hover in mid-air, this man could make a rifle all but sit up and beg. It was a plaything for him as he demonstrated to us how to drill. Foot-drill under his command was different too, and we had to become used to the executive word of command being given in a high-pitched yelp, like the sound of a dog having its tail trapped in a door!

Another Guards custom seemed to consist of barking "Sah!" at regular and frequent intervals when being addressed by an officer. I happened to be within earshot of the Grenadier and our CO, a Coldstream Major and heard the voice of the officer droning on, while the sergeant interjected "Sah!" at what seemed to be counted intervals.

We drilled on Amiens Square, and as we paraded after lunch, the men of the REME and other Corps troops, who had been enjoying a cup of tea in the Red Shield Club on the other side of the square, always turned out to watch our parade, no doubt with a critical eye. Then they paraded before marching off to their afternoon work, carrying out all their movements to the beat of a side-drum. Rather superior I thought.

Our first parade of the day took place under the eagle eye of the Sergeant Major, RTR, one 'Tiny' Rowlands. The Company Officer, Lieutenant Cadogan, was also on parade but never that paragon, the Coldstream Major. We were 'got on parade' on our markers (Corporal Instructors) and when we had been 'dressed' and were at attention, Sergeant Mackenzie and the Lieutenant marched toward each other, saluting as they passed and marching on for a few paces more before turning about at the same moment, marching toward each other again, halting and saluting. Then the sergeant reported that we were on parade and ready for inspection.

The parade I dreaded was the physical training parade. I had never been any good at PT at school.

I always incurred the wrath of the PT master, who was a sarcastic bully anyway. This Army PT was going to be worse, I was sure. I had missed the first of the PT parades as I had to go to the dentist. My companions had spotted the best (i.e. the more pleasant) instructors on the first parade and so when we fell in next to the instructors, I found myself to be the only one beside the instructor I had chosen. Foolishly I said, "You don't seem to be popular." He looked at me and retorted, "I am with a razor. See the Sergeant-Major." So, I trotted across the parade-ground and got a rocket from that worthy for not shaving properly. I suppose that he was in a good mood, or I might have found myself on a charge.

Nevertheless, PT parades were always a misery while I was in the Training Regiment and worse was to follow when we were marched up to the swimming pool, which was in the open air on the edge of the tank training ground. It was fed from a fresh-water spring and was icy cold, as I discovered when I lowered myself into the water. Others had dived in with enthusiasm but, after gasping to get my breath for a few moments, my nose began to bleed rather severely and one of the PTIs told me to come out of the water, 'If I was not enjoying it'. Indeed, I was not!

Foot- and arms-drill were enjoyable, however, and so used did we become to the feel of our own rifles that we could distinguish them as ours without looking at the number stamped on them.

Now we learned to shoot on the 30-yard range. The No. 4 rifle, the successor to the short Lee-Enfield, the best rifle ever made in my opinion, was sighted to 1,300 yards, with fixed 'pig-sticker' bayonet. Then, still with bayonet fixed, we fired off our rounds. When the turn came for my detail to fire, I made a mistake in trying to take first pressure and shot off a round without orders. "Who was that?" asked the long-toothed sergeant. I put up my hand. "Don't worry, lad. We're teaching you to kill Germans." That remark pulled me up sharply.

The firing continued and it was a noisy affair, the firing point being enclosed on three sides and roofed by corrugated iron. The sides of the shed rang with the noise of rifle fire. When the time came to fire Bren-guns, I became deaf for three days as a result. This was fun for the others, who bellowed out instructions like "PASS THE JAM, JACK!" at teatime; but the day after firing the Bren, I was given the job of raising and lowering the red flag to show that the 30-yard range was in use. Instructions were shouted from the firing point. "Flag up" and "Flag down", to indicate that firing had ceased or was taking place. The person in charge of the flag repeated the shouted command and raised or lowered the flag accordingly.

I could hear no shouts because of my deafness, though of course I had reported my condition. Irate and baffled instructors removed me from my post and gave me the job of counting spent cartridges in one of the nearby huts. This was quite a simple task as all one had to do was to place the cartridges in holes in a plywood board. There were 100 holes and so, when they were all filled, that was 100 spent cartridges, and they were tipped onto an ever-growing pile and the total chalked up on a board. A simple task, which even the dullest (or most deaf) could perform.

Instruction in gas precautions came our way. The Gas Instructor was a Scot who rejoiced in the name of 'Phosgene Pete'. Phosgene was a gas which had been employed in the First World War and there was still a risk that the combatants would use chemical warfare.

Our respirators were of the box type, carried on the chest when worn in the 'Alert' position.

Failure to don the mask properly resulted in it riding up over the chin and the wrath of 'Pete' descending. "Ye're in a hell of a mess, aren't ye, lad!" I heard him say to one unhappy bungler.

Our chemical warfare experience was completed by being subjected to a gas known as DM. We entered a gas chamber, and a quantity of DM was released. We did five minutes PT, breathing the fumes of course, for our respirators were not worn; we then put them on and marched back to the barrack hut. The effect of the gas was to make our sinuses ache and our noses dribble mucus, but we marched onto the square, red-faced, aching and dribbling for some time after we had taken off our respirators.

Sometimes, if we were not on fatigues, the NCOs would sit in the hut and talk to us about life in the army. We heard a little about the 1940 affair which ended at Dunkirk and other ports in Northern France and Belgium, the efficiency (or not) of weapons (the Boyes anti-tank rifle was only fit to be thrown over a hedge to lighten the load!) and 'what it was like' in tanks and life in the peace-time Army. This seemed ideal. Work in the morning and an opportunity to learn a trade, sport in the afternoon, and walking out with a girl in the evenings.

We made a trip to the rifle ranges at East Holme, taken there by truck and then marching back after we had fired our course. The distance was about seven miles. I had developed hard skin on my heels as a result of all that 'digging' on the square, and as we marched, bloody blisters developed under the skin. Soon I was hobbling and had to drop out, even though others carried my kit (battle order) and rifle. There was a Red Shield van selling tea and buns and here we halted by arrangement. After this break, I was able to totter back to camp with the others, where I flopped on my bunk. Some kind soul put a blanket over me, and I slept an exhausted sleep.

Next day, I went sick. I tip-toed behind the parade as we made our way down to the main camp where the medical quarters were situated. There I was examined and the blisters were duly admired. I was told to kneel on a chair, heels and blisters exposed. "See how many poppies you can count in that field," said the Medical Orderly as he set to work. Painful excavations followed, but then I was repaired with sticking-plaster and marched back to our barracks with the rest of the Sick Parade – a new man.

A second visit to East Holme a few days later ended as we hurried back to camp, alternating between 'double' and very 'quick march'. No trouble from the heels this time. No doubt the NCOs told every squad that they had broken the record marching from East Holme to Bovington, but when they told us that we had done this we felt very pleased with ourselves.

We had seen news-reels of soldiers in the Eighth Army, as part of their toughening-up programme, leaping from the back of trucks as they sped through the desert. Now we, too, took part in this activity and three-tonners motored along on the moors at 30 mph as we hurled ourselves off the back. I suppose that this was to test our nerve as well as our fitness in this new form of PT.

Though the threat of invasion by the German Army had long since passed, there was still the possibility of some kind of raid on the south coast by enemy forces. Round the camp were the hulls of old tanks placed at strategic points on the perimeter. These were dug into the earth for use as strong-points. We were taken on a tour of these one day and were allocated one of the points to man. I well recall seeing one tank which was dug into the side of the bank that lined the road to the station. I think that it was a Vickers Mk.VI.

Earlier in our army career we had the inevitable injections for tetanus and other ailments which might strike us down in our prime. No-one fainted but we all had aching arms after these 'jabs'. "Swing your arms!" bellowed our NCOs as we marched back up the hill to Amiens Square. Swing we did, and the circulation soon disposed of the ache.

I was blancoing my kit one evening when I had a welcome visitor in the person of a young man who was in the Training Regiment. He had worked with my father in Nottingham, having been evacuated from London early in the war. He reassured me about life in the Training Regiment, and we spent a pleasant half-hour chatting. Later on, in 1944, his father was killed by a V rocket. He had compassionate leave, of course, but was himself killed when he returned to his unit in the Netherlands.

The time drew near for us to move down to the '58th' and become Troopers in the Royal Armoured Corps, shedding our designation as Privates in the General Service Corps. We had a rehearsal, marching behind the band of the 'Skins' (Inniskilling Dragoon Guards) and wearing our best battle dress uniforms. I stood out from the crowd, for not only had my BD blouse a fly front, as opposed to the newer more utilitarian model worn by my companions, but the uniform itself was a vintage creation in other ways. There had previously been a trial to make BD more resistant to gas attack, and uniforms had been impregnated with same chemical. This gave the uniform itself a lighter hue than the others and gave the whole thing the texture of soapy cardboard. Very good for retaining creases.

Wearing the 'cardboard' BD, I marched with the others behind the band as we made our way through the camp, and as we marched 'to attention' received a 'Present Arms' from one sentry we passed on our route. There was something uplifting marching behind the band and the 'Present' lifted our spirits even higher.

A concert was arranged to mark the end of our time at the PTW and there were rehearsals in the evenings in our hut. The squad comedian seemed to have but one idea, to our disappointment. He kept insisting that if he came onto the stage and pretended to trip up, this would bring the house down. Something more original was demanded, we thought. Several ideas from Scout concerts of the past were suitable and memory was dredged for turns we had seen on stage. I wrote a little sketch for myself and Kay Shewell to perform. He was to be a *BBC* interviewer, and I was to be 'The Oldest NAAFI Girl', giving my reminiscences of the Boer War and subsequent conflicts in which I had provided comfort for our lads.

The concert began on the appointed evening, and I watched the efforts of the others before I went backstage to put on my 'costume', comprising two army blankets, one as a skirt, held up by my belt, and the other a kind of 'Mother Riley' type shawl. Some time elapsed and no call came for me to enter on the scene. I noticed that the NCOs on the Staff had joined in the proceedings and the songs they were singing were of a ribald, if not obscene quality.

Disappointed, I took off my costume, for our innocent sketch had no place in this company. I went back to our hut, where I expected the others to arrive at the end of the evening. To my surprise, all the squad were already there, having left the concert when it became obvious that the Staff were going to take over. We hoped that they would have thick heads in the morning.

The Passing Out parade was held on the camp square, scene of so much 'bashing' and then we marched down the hill, once again led by the 'Skins' band, ending our training in the General Service Corps and becoming Troopers in the Royal Armoured Corps at last.

Chapter 2

58th Training Regiment

We settled into our new home, a larger barrack hut of more recent vintage than the ones we had left, being built for the Training Regiment. Our bunks were more substantial and larger in that the occupant of the bottom bunk had more headroom. We were issued with new badges for our berets, discarding the GSC badge of the Royal Coat of Arms and substituting the badge of the Royal Armoured Corps, again a plastic one but a pinkish hue instead of the brown GSC one. A mailed fist formed the centre of the RAC badge, with arrows encircling it, reminiscent of the diagrams one saw in newspapers, which indicated the progress of advancing armies.

We had made the acquaintance of that focus of much activity, the barrack square, when we had come down the hill for our PT parades. Now we fell in at the front of the regiment on our first parade with our new comrades. Chaos reigned at first, for we had up until this moment observed a pause of 'two – three' between each of our drill movements. The rest of the regiment had discarded this definite pause and so their drill movements were quicker than ours. After a disastrous start, the old hands were told to observe the definite pause to synchronise with the new boys. One could almost feel the waves of resentment and irritation as they made the adjustment. Within a day or two, it was we who had changed our ways and so all was harmony on the square once more.

Our immediate superiors were styled PULCs, or Provisional Unpaid Lance Corporals. These lads had been selected from previous intakes for officer training and so were getting practice in the arts of command, and we were the guinea-pigs.

Sometimes we would see these officers-to-be running exhausted round the assault course on the southern edge of the camp. They had already run cross-country and this was the final, killing stage. At the time, part of the officer training course involved running up and down mountains in Wales and this training at the Regiment was to prepare them for the agony to come.

Some of our intake would be recommended for commissions, going on to the Officer Cadet Training Unit (OCTU) but most of us were destined to stay in the ranks.

When Robert Graves was commissioned to write a book about the RAC, the title being '*The Black Beret*', he wrote about the 58th, mentioning 'Phosgene Pete' and giving the CO the name of 'Jock Scotland' instead of 'Paddy' Ireland, which was his real name. Most of the characters in Graves' book become officers and fight in the Western Desert, commanding tanks.

I doubt that many of us had our eyes fixed on commissions. Surviving the Training Regiment life without getting into trouble was the aim of most of us. The guard room was a place to be avoided, for instance, for this was the lair of the Provost Sergeant, Hayter by name, which seemed appropriate. It was from his lips that I first heard the colourful threat, "I'll have your guts for garters!" said, not to me, but to an unfortunate Pioneer, who was doing time for some misdemeanour.

The guard room did play an important part in our routine, however, for we now had guard duties to perform. To begin with, guard mounting took place on the square, for it was summer and the evenings were light. We drew our rifles for guard from the arms store. They were not the Lee-Enfield No. 4 rifles we had used before but were rifles similar to the long Lee Enfield and were made by licence in America. The bayonet was a 17- inch sword bayonet and when the bayonets were fixed and we marched along, the empty scabbards swung at our sides in a swanky manner.

We marched off guard parade to our respective posts. Some to the guard room at the main gate, some to a 'log cabin' type structure made of railway sleepers, which was located at a track to the west of the camp. This post was the quieter of the two, for most of the activity took place at the main gate.

As the nights closed in, the mess hall was cleared of tables and forms, and guard mounting took place there. Placing our feet firmly on the floor here caused a tremendous crash in the enclosed space. Normal cook housework went on, of course, as preparations for next day's meals were made. I remember seeing a lad 'margarineing' bread. On one side of a pile of cut slices was a basin of melted margarine; the slice of bread was seized; a shaving brush was dipped into the basin and 'painted' over the bread – *voila*! An ever-growing pile of bread ready for breakfast! No wonder the margarine cracked when we sank our teeth into the bread in the morning.

Powers of observation were tested one evening as the orderly officer and the guard sergeant walked round one man several times, inspecting him.

Something, they could tell, was wrong – but what? A Trooper in the next rank behind had spotted it, "No respirator, sir." Sure enough, the respirator was missing.

On main gate guard, one dark, windy and wet night, I had an unfortunate encounter with the orderly officer. A Utility truck drove rapidly toward me as I stood on sentry; I brandished rifle and bayonet and shouted "Halt!" several times, to no avail. The truck was driven right up to me, and it was obviously done to unsettle the guard. The orderly officer got out and began to question me about various officers in command. I could tell by the indrawn breath of my fellow guard that the answers I was giving were the wrong ones. My mind was a blank after the encounter with the truck. A ticking-off from the officer and another from the guard sergeant when my 'stag' was over. I wish I had bundled the occupants of the truck out at bayonet point and doubled them down to the guard room. That would have caused a stir.

There was the story, true or not, of a keen young officer who had sneaked up behind the sentry and grappled with him, only to be nearly bayoneted for his keenness. Never fool around with an armed man!

One night we had to stop and make a record of all vehicles passing along the road past the main gate. We had a hurricane lamp which we swung to stop the vehicles, and we had to ask questions about journey and destination. One irate American driver had been stopped by the pair we had relieved and he was not pleased to be held up on his return. "These so-and-so Limeys, etc., etc!" "We had," we said, "our orders." He drove off, still grumbling about his allies.

There was a tale told about one of our NCOs who had been halted by the sentry and then told to "Advance and be recognised", which he did. When he had given his name to the sentry, he added "And the woman behind", and out of the shadows tottered a high-heeled figure, dressed in an Army greatcoat and beret. The pair vanished in the night in the direction of the sergeant's billet.

When the guards' supper came along, we had our introduction to what seemed to be a universal menu for men on this duty – scrag-ends of cheese and offcuts of loaves. I enjoyed the cocoa, which was sweet and strong.

We slept when not on 'stag'. In the 'log cabin' there were bunks, but at the main gate one slept on the floor or balanced on a form. Unlaced boots and the removal of 'specs' seemed to ensure a sound sleep for me. Despite the others coming in after their turn on guard, and the droning voices of the guard sergeant and corporal who had to stay awake, I always managed to drop off. Not always an asset, as I was later to discover.

If one was on last relief, it was inspiring to hear Reveille sounded on bugle and trumpet in the early morning light as the various sections of the vast camp area were roused. I always enjoyed the infantry call but found the cavalry reveille tediously long. The trumpeter cycled up to the guard room, did his bit, mounted his bike and rode off to another part of the camp to wake the dead there.

As the guard fell in for the last time at the end of the duty, there was an air of liveliness. We marched back through the camp to hand in our rifles and ammunition and disperse to our barrack hut. No matter how long the queue in the ablutions section, we always seemed to be ready for breakfast, washed and shaved. Once in the dining hall, tables and forms now replaced, it was a matter of eating and leaving quickly as there were so many to feed. The cook sergeant, a rotund figure in the tradition of his calling, moved among the tables intoning a litany – "Hurry up! Eat up! Get a move on!" One of the lads swore that he had been in the mess hall when it was empty and the cook sergeant was still muttering these words among the deserted tables!

There were other personalities, too, among the NCOs and members of the Troop.

Sergeant Burt was a lean man who had the jowls of a bulldog. He was a kindly man, who showed me how to come to attention with a movement of the whole body – which proclaimed alert soldierliness. Corporal Drynan was a handsome Irishman who had the habit of walking up and down in front of the Troop, softly intoning the words of command and then loudly uttering the executive word. It kept everyone on their toes, as they had to listen very intently for the instructions.

The Regimental Sergeant Major was named Pike – a lean whippet of a man with his own eccentric pronunciation of 'About'. "AbUout turn" he would shout. There was no mistaking what we were expected to do. To him, everyone was 'Sunny Jim'. "Now, Sunny Jim! What are you doing with that rifle?" The Troop (57 Troop, 'C' Squadron, 58th Training Regiment, RAC, for the record), had luminaries of course. Ginger Richards had been an RSM in the Army Cadet Force and so had the edge on us all, at first, in matters of foot drill and weapons training. His name was coupled with Bill Tough, a fellow Londoner. ("What is your name, lad?" "Tough, sir." "Well, I hope you are!"). I think Bill got tired of this witty repartee after a while.

There was 'Kay' Shewell, so called because he bore a faint resemblance to Kay Kyser, an American band leader. "My God!" he exclaimed, when the real K.K. appeared in a film we saw at the Garrison Cinema, "do I look like that?" We went to the cinema as often as we could and waited for the tune 'Getting Sentimental' to be played. That was the signal for the lights to be tuned down and the performance to begin.

Ray Warnes was older than most of us and so was known as 'Granny'. He had led an exotic life before joining the Army. He had been a tin-miner in Cornwall (despite coming from Streatham) and, being a flute-player, had tried to join the Royal Air Force band. His other claim to fame was that he was a communist. He had a heated discussion with one of our instructors, Lieutenant Lewis, who joined 4th CL Y in time for the Caen battle, about the possibility of Infantrymen being carried to battle on the back of tanks. Mr Lewis was not impressed by the idea, "But" said Ray, "the Soviet Army do it!"

Vic Steeden was a vigorous, noisy young man who told us how to get our berets to the right shape. "Put a small plate inside and soak 'em overnight in water," was his advice. His own neat beret was a good advertisement for this drastic treatment. Bob Sawtell had a remarkable hat which came to light when we did the 'Marathon March' from Axminster to Dorchester at the end of our training. The hat was a superior Balaclava with a peak, and the sides could be folded up so that it became a large, peaked woolly hat. It gave a vague air of polar exploration to the proceedings.

Ned Daley was a dear, gentle lad from Tyneside. He had been a police cadet before joining up. It was difficult to think of him arresting anyone, as his tall, spindly frame oozed kindness. If the Tyneside police were all like him, criminals would give themselves up in droves, assured of fair treatment. He was once reprimanded on parade and replied, "But it wasn't my fault, Sergeant, man!" to the amusement of the rest of us and, it must be said, the sergeant.

'Taff' Evans was one of several Welshmen, and I was to meet him again, in the Netherlands, at a place called Stramproy, when one of Hobart's 'Funnies', a 'Crocodile' flame-throwing Churchill tank, came to demonstrate its terrors to us. "Oh!" said Taff, "you're on a gun-tank." I thought it was an odd, if accurate, description of the Sherman 75mm tank I was on. Jimmy Nunn I last saw at Bovington in the 1960s. He was then a sergeant instructor and his tank stopped near us as we paused on our way to the coast. I regret that neither of us had the confidence to say "Hello!"

I once did a guard with a lad from Luton, who had a consuming interest in the 'Dawgs'. "When I go on leave, I'll pick up the girl and we'll go to the Dawgs," he said. I thought his knowledge was very limited, as he claimed not to know anything about Robin Hood. His real claim to fame lay in being discovered at inspection, before a CO's parade, to have brown boot laces in his best boots. He was practically carried by the NCOs into the barracks, where he was hurriedly fitted up with a pair of boot-laces belonging to Sergeant Burt.

That was not the only excitement at CO's parade that Saturday morning. The 'Skins' band was in attendance, for there was to be a march-past at the end of the parade. As we were inspected, the band played suitable music, and the bandmaster had decided on something a little different. The strains of 'I'm for ever blowing bubbles' wafted over our heads. This was too much of a good thing and it only needed one snort of stifled laughter from someone to set the whole Troop quivering with suppressed mirth. The RSM hurried over to the bandmaster and a muttered word in an ear soon brought that masterpiece grinding to a halt. We recovered our composure and prepared to be inspected and march past in line, to the tune of the regimental march 'Claire's Dragoons', one line of which runs 'Hurrah! Hurrah! for Ireland's right', which seemed an appropriate tribute to our CO.

Looking at the photograph of the PTW intake posed on Amiens Square, I cannot put names to many of the young faces. One face, however, does stand out and that is of John Cotton. His face is swollen and looks lop-sided as he had been to the dentist and had picked up a bug of some kind. Coming from (he emphasised Great) Yarmouth, his career and mine were to be linked, for we were both to join the same regiment in the end. I stand out in the photograph by virtue of my 'gas-proof' BD.

Once we had transferred from primary training to our new unit, and had settled in, we had a few days of field-craft and map-reading under Sergeant Burt. We endured our first CO's parade and inspection and then marched down to Wool Station for our first leave of 60 hours.

As we drew near Waterloo Station, my companions astounded me by taking out of their small packs; webbing equipment, valises, water bottles, the lot, finally arrayed in marching order for their first leave home. How to impress parents and friends, I thought.

When we returned from leave, our real training began. We were divided into groups to learn about driving and maintenance, wireless and gunnery. By this time, I think, we must have made our choice whether to be trained on British tanks or American ones. I had chosen British, knowing nothing of the sorry story of British armour. We were divided into three groups and took each of the subjects in turn, beginning in the case of my group with wireless. There were Nissen huts ranged along one side of the square and here were the indoor training schools. We learned about the 19 Set, which was used on tanks. This part of our training lasted for about three weeks and then we were given seven days leave. We marched down to Wool Station singing our songs, in one of which, I remember, we thanked goodness cows didn't fly in Mobile!

Leave ended with a final session of a few more days on the 19 Set, being transported about the countryside in 15-cwt trucks and communicating by wireless with other members of the Troop.

I was not really at home with wireless, especially after a disaster with procedure, replying "Out" to Mr Lewis after he had closed his conversation with me by the word 'Out'. We were passing under high-tension cables at the time, but I could hear his voice getting more agitated at my replies.

We made our way to Swanage on that exercise, and we stood by the famous Globe which is a feature of one part of the town. I felt rather down after my foolish mistake and was brooding over the miseries of army life. Below us in the little valley stood a small car and standing beside it a couple, obviously the driver and his wife, perhaps on holiday. I felt I would like to go and talk to them and restore my spirits in conversation with someone who had no connection with army life at all, but of course I dismissed these thoughts.

We drifted into town, looking at what few shops were open, and I bought a postcard and sent it off to my parents. My father took the card to work when it arrived home and showed it to the people in his office. Included in the number was a friend who noticed the postmark. He and his wife had been on holiday in Dorset and had been in Swanage on the day in question, noticing soldiers from the tanks, judging by the berets they wore, who were gathered round the Globe just up the hill from where they had parked their car!

I felt that I was not cut out to be an operator and it was with relief that we next moved to the Gunnery Wing Nissen huts. There, our squad learned about the 6-pounder tank gun and the faithful Besa Calibre 7.92 mm machine gun, used on British tanks. Had I chosen to go for American Sherman tanks, I would have learned about the 75mm main gun and 0.300 Browning machine gun.

In one of the Gunnery Wing huts there was the 6-pounder mounted on a steel frame, and here we learned the intricacies of firing-pins and hydraulic recoil systems. We loaded the gun, dealt with simulated emergencies, and wrote down details about muzzle velocity and other gunnery specialities.

The faithful but heavy Besa, made by Birmingham Small Arms Co., hence the name, was stripped and assembled and we learned about 'Immediate Action' procedures.

"Gun firing alright," droned Corporal Jones, our moustached Liverpudlian instructor, "Gun firing alright – GUNSTOPS !" he yelled. "First IA!" (Immediate Action) "Recock! Gun firing alright – GUNSTOPS!" "Second IA!", and so on. And thus, we worked through the Immediate Action procedures we had learned, light years away, it seemed, on the Bren at the PTW.

The good corporal had difficulties with the letter 'R', so instructions to 'Wub the working parts with gwaphite gwease' were a bit difficult for him.

There was a pellet range up the hill, where we learned the basics of shooting from a moving turret. The indoor mock-up of a tank turret was equipped with a main armament gun, but, for the purpose of the exercise, firing was by means of an air rifle, fixed to it and calibrated to a tank telescope through which the gunner looked. One was able to traverse the turret in the normal manner by means of a 'spade grip' (a handle shaped like a spade handle, which one twisted to left or right to bring the turret onto the target). To simulate movement over uneven ground, moving cams mounted under the base of the turret, lifted it as they moved round. In front of the turret was a large sand-table and, on this, three lead weights (the targets) moved, towed round on a wire which passed over three pulleys. It all seemed fairly straightforward, and I enjoyed shooting at the targets as they moved along, 'aiming off' and waiting for the roll of the turret in order to shoot on a smooth bit, so I didn't shoot on an upward or downward roll.

This seemed to be fairly simple stuff, but the elevation and depression of the gun was controlled by a large leather-bound stirrup in which the gunner's shoulder rested. Riding over the moors and trying to control the elevation and depression of the gun was very difficult. The gun could be locked in position as the firing-trigger mounting was moved sideways, but when this mechanism was released, the gun moved up and down and the gunner was pressed into his seat or lifted up towards the turret roof. I did not know how I was going to struggle with this monster while trying to shoot at real targets. The system was probably good for the 2-pounder, but it seemed impractical for the 6-pounder gun.

Whatever the difficulties, though, we were eagerly anticipating our move to Lulworth to fire tank guns on the ranges there. We duly moved into our accommodation, Nissen huts, of course, which were built on land up off the road which ran behind the ranges. One had a magnificent view of the hills backing the ranges and, through a gap, a glimpse of the Channel.

One of the lads had a relative who lived in Dorset and this aunt had given him a book entitled '*Dorset, Up-along and Down-along*'. Among the stories of smugglers and other goings-on, we discovered a story about Lulworth. On the left-hand hill of the gap could be seen the outline of earthworks. The remains of a Roman fort. According to the story, a Roman Legion (had they been out on the town?) had lost its way in the fog and plunged over the cliffs to a watery grave. 'Still', the narrative continued, 'on nights when no rabbits run and no dogs bark, the ghostly Legion marches up the hill.' Just the thing to keep nervous young sentries on edge during their 'stag'.

For sentry duty there was! I was fortunate in that I did my guard duty with a lad from a previous intake, who had to go into hospital. This was his second time at Lulworth and so he knew the form. One of our last duties at the end of our 'stag' was to wake the cookhouse staff for them to prepare breakfast. The cookhouse was 'manned' by ATS personnel and when the time came to wake them up, we made our way to their hut. My companion unfixed his bayonet, the 17-inch kind, and hammered on the door of the hut with the hilt. A shriek of "Alright" from inside the hut assured us that someone was awake. My hopes of catching a glimpse of a scantily clad female form were dashed!

Daytime brought the opportunity to fire real guns. First, the Bren in an anti-aircraft role. We stood in the turret of a tank, where a large tarpaulin had been draped round and inside the hatch to form a large sack. This was to catch the empty cartridge cases as we fired. When it was my turn, I stood in the hatch, grasping the Bren waist high. A silhouette model of an aircraft hurtled before me on a horizontal track, my tracer pursuing it. 'Aim off! Aim off!' cried the instructors, but I had the feeling that any Luftwaffe pilot had nothing to fear from my Bren.

Someone had thought about this matter of shooting at aircraft and also the possibility of being shot at in return! One solution was a curious affair called a Parrish-Lulworth Mounting. It looked like an arrangement of bicycle frames, cycle brake levers and Bowden cables. It fitted through a hole in the top of the turret, mountings for two Vickers guns (aircraft type) outside the turret and the controls were inside, where the tank commander could engage the enemy aircraft sheltered by the turret, in reasonable safety. I was to meet this device in other circumstances later on.

Pistol shooting and firing with the Thompson sub-machine-gun followed. We were told to hold the pistol, crouch forward, body supported by the left hand on the left knee and then shoot. The Thompson had to be fought like a fire-hose as the rate of fire was such that the gun was easily thrown off target unless held very firmly to counteract the torque.

The humble Sten gun was then in a primitive form, with no safety device as I recall. There was a definite danger of the thing going off if dropped on the ground when it had a magazine fitted.

Six-pounders and Besas were the main armament for British tanks and we fired these. Exotic things like Thompson sub-machine-guns were extras.

Lulworth was the place for experimental weapons too, and I remember seeing an armoured car rocking gingerly over the range with two large glass cylinders on the back. They looked like outlandish test-tubes from the laboratory of some mad scientist. Perhaps they were experimental hydraulic systems for the turret. If we had asked, we would no doubt have found that the system was very 'hush-hush'.

We saw a new gun being tested one day. A Sherman drove up to the firing point, and it had a very long gun mounted in the turret. We who were watching were told to put our hands over our ears in case they should be damaged by blast. The gun fired one round and then the tank drove away again. I think the gun was a 17-pounder and we had seen our first 'Firefly', the name given by our Army to this Sherman type.

We returned to Bovington and a change of barrack room and began our Driving and Maintenance (D and M) course.

The course consisted of a day of theory and then a day of driving on 15 cwt trucks. Three or four of us were allocated an instructor and we careered round the Dorset and Hampshire countryside, taking it in turns to be driver. Double de-clutching I found very difficult and there was much grinding of gears on the part of the driver, and teeth on the part of the instructor. I wondered why he was so bad-tempered!

Our truck had a small glass screen for protection against the rain, and I dreaded rainy days, for, as I wore spectacles, the screen was quite inadequate. Being unused to driving, I envied my companions who had probably learned on the family car, despite petrol rationing. I could hear them double de-clutching like mad as I struggled with the gears.

We drove to Shaftesbury, Axminster, Seaton and Yeovil in the truck. I had my first sight of Maiden Castle, outside Dorchester, as we drove past one day. A drive along the coast towards Bridport took us past St. Catherine's Chapel on a little hill, and a sight of Chesil Beach, stretching away to Portland. A brace of Spitfires flew down the coast below us as we motored along the hillside road towards Bridport.

Another week-end leave and then back to camp to learn about and drive Crusaders. There was a week of theory in the classroom. We celebrated

Cambrai Day (20th November), the Officers waiting on us at an excellent lunch and one or two becoming slightly the worse for wear on beer which was available.

Our first drive on tanks was to Clouds Hill, home of T.E. Lawrence. I looked to see the house, but it was surrounded by rhododendrons, and we drove past and went onto the moors. This was exciting, as the tank bucked and rolled over the terrain. I had the unfortunate experience of being 'tank sick', which was something like sea-sickness, and I hung over the back of the tank among the petrol fumes feeling quite ill. When in the driving seat of course, these feelings disappeared as my mind was wonderfully concentrated on other things. I enjoyed myself, as I had always been fascinated by the sight of vehicles rolling along, regardless of obstacles, something like ships at sea responding to the waves.

Our driving instructor had a claw-like hand, with little flesh on the bones of the fingers. His ears were devoid of tops and his nose was pinched. The skin on his face had a stretched appearance and, had I recognised the signs, I would have known that he was a tank fire victim.

We had a change of instructor and made the acquaintance of the 'Big Dipper', a man-made heap of earth up which we drove, then balanced delicately on the top and drove gently down the other side, when the balance of the tank tipped it over and forward.

We ended our Crusader driving instruction with a two-day 'scheme' driving to Blandford, Salisbury (a glimpse of the Cathedral spire), and into the New Forest. There we slept under the bivouac tents secured to the side of the tank and then drove back to camp in time for tea.

Our task next day was checking the tank equipment and cleaning the beast. One of our crew annoyed me by throwing the kit from the tank, jacks and so on, onto the tarpaulin which had been laid out on the hardstanding. When I remonstrated with him, his reply was, "When I want your advice, Fish, I'll ask for it!" – words I hurled back at him a few days later, complete with Dorset accent (he came from Dorset), when he was telling me what to do one day. I didn't feel at all guilty!

The final stage of our training consisted of working as an armoured squadron with tracked personnel carriers and Bren carriers as 'tanks'; ourselves as crew of four acted in turn as commander, operator and driver.

A period of instruction began our training on the carriers. During one class, an NCO came into the lecture room and had a few muttered words with the instructor. When he had left the room, the instructor said, "Well, you might as well know, because you'll find out anyway. A carrier has overturned and one of the other intake has been killed." The carriers, it seemed, were not as safe to drive as we had imagined.

The Marathon March drew nearer and so mixed in with our time on the carriers we had to endure the Assault Course and enjoyed an exercise in battle-drill, a way of using Infantry in a tactical way to attack the enemy. Basically, it meant sending out a Bren team on a flank to engage the enemy position, while the rest of the squad carried out an assault. For the moment, then, we became Infantry and carried out the drill in the countryside surrounding the camp.

We were expected to carry out the battle drill on the Marathon March for we were to be split up into sections and expected to do battle with any other sections we encountered on our march to the objective and employ the drill if a rival section was on the objective before us.

We were taken to Axminster in trucks and spent the rest of the day battle drilling up and down in one of the hilly fields near the town. The officers and NCOs had a great time throwing thunder-flashes about.

These fireworks exploded with an enormous bang, much louder than any November 5th festivities. We charged up and down, section against section, firing off our blank ammunition like mad to add to the mayhem. We were carrying the same type of rifle as that issued for our guard duties. This was the Enfield pattern '14, later adopted by the United States, who named it the Enfield '17. Thousands of these rifles were leased back to the UK and issued to the Home Guard.

Our billet for the night was an empty isolation hospital near Axminster and here we prepared our supper in the grounds. Bob Sawtell, I recall, making tea over a smoking fire, wearing his polar explorers' hat and smoking a 'Sherlock Holmes' pipe. Perhaps that is why we elected him to be our Leader for the March.

In the morning, we set off for our destination, which was a cluster of tumuli outside Dorchester. Dressed in battle order, less steel helmet, with rifle and blank ammunition, we plodded out of the grounds, having left our bed-rolls to the mercies of the staff, who would bring bedding and rations to us at the end of the day. We would ring up camp and give a map reference for our billet. Camp had a wireless link with the truck carrying bedding and food and the truck would bring us our stuff, picking it up again in the morning.

We tramped along roads and field-paths, Bob being our map-reader. Towards the middle of the afternoon Lieutenant Lewis appeared in the 15-cwt truck and we were commended for marching to attention as we approached the vehicle and halted. On the outskirts of Beaminster, we found a friendly farmer who would let us sleep in his barn overnight – "But no smoking!" he stipulated. With the exception of Bob and his pipe, I don't think any of us smoked anyway.

Bob and one or two of the others set off to find a house with a 'phone, the farm not having one, and they returned shortly, having found a house with 'phone, a map-reading ex-army type and a cup of tea. Fortunately, both the ex-army map reference and Bob's agreed. The truck arrived at our barn very shortly and we got our food and bedding out of the back. It then drove off and left us to get our beds ready, and we surveyed the tinned goods and bread.

Someone made the suggestion that it would be a good idea if we could find one of the friendly inhabitants of Beaminster who would cook our breakfast for us. We were too hungry to cook supper, so had bread and jam. We split into two parties and set off on an exploration, agreeing to return to the barn in an hour. By now it was quite dark and our party walked through the silent town.

An imposing house on the left of the road looked promising. Perhaps there was a servants' kitchen with a friendly cook. We knocked at a side door, and a young girl opened it. We explained our plans to her, but she rather nervously explained that the house was occupied by an evacuated girls' school. There was, however, a similar establishment for boys across the road, which would be more suitable for soldiers. We knocked at the door of an equally imposing house and soon found ourselves in a warm kitchen, with cook and other female staff bustling about making us a cup of tea. This, we decided, was just the job.

If we appeared in the morning, it was agreed, cook would boil eggs for our breakfast. We explained about our Marathon March, suitably embroidered, as we related the hard life of young soldiers. A small boy appeared. He wanted to see us but was bundled out of the kitchen unceremoniously. Perhaps it was his bed-time. Full of tea and agreeing to report for breakfast, we set off for the farm again.

When we got back to the barn, we heard that our other exploring party had found a US Army Camp (Field Artillery). They enquired at the cookhouse about our rations being cooked there. The cook sergeant was summoned from the kitchen. He was, in girth, equivalent to the cook sergeant at Bovington. "How many of you are there?" he asked. "Eight of us." "Aw hell! Eight men don't make no difference to the US Army. There's no need to bring your raytions!"

We duly reported for breakfast, thinking guiltily of our school friends and the eggs.

We were each given a metal tray, divided into sections. "Just keep going round until you've had enough," they said. Good advice to give to healthy young men on the Marathon! Bacon, eggs, flapjacks, fried potatoes, maple syrup, all were eaten with gusto. What a contrast to our breakfast at Bovington!

Staggering away from the table, we washed our utensils and trays. Several large dustbins stood there, filled with yellow fruit segments. What could it be? Of course, grapefruit! But why so much? "Most of the boys don't get up for breakfast on Sunday mornings, but we have to open enough tins in case they do," we were told.

We lined up, sloped arms and marched out of the US Army Camp at attention. It seemed the right thing to do out of gratitude for our breakfast.

We climbed a hill away from the town and marched on. A remote field provided cover for the answering of what had become an urgent message from our 'innards' – now bursting with American 'raytions'.

We marched hard all day to get ourselves into a position for a good jump off to the objective outside Dorchester on Monday morning.

Again, a friendly farmer. This time we were to occupy a stable, but with no horses in it. We could sleep in the hay-loft above, there was a gap between the loft floor and the wall where hay could be fed down for the animals to eat.

The truck arrived by arrangement as before, with food and blankets, and we made a supper of sorts before creeping into bed, weary after our march.

I half woke in the night to hear the voice of the driver saying 'It's alright. I only want to get their rifles', and I turned over to sleep again, because we had locked the door to the hay loft and no-one could get in. Then I heard the unmistakable sound of rifles rattling together! The driver had climbed through the feeding gap to steal four of our rifles. Bob and I ran downstairs to see if we could stop the thieves, but to no avail. There was not even the sound of the truck driving away with the loot. The night was quite still, and the hills loomed dark in the starlight. We agreed that we should have posted a sentry. Too tired to think about that. A hard lesson for us, and when the truck came in the morning to collect our bedding and return the rifles, caustic comments came our way.

Worse was to follow, for we still did not keep a look-out for the other section. Suddenly, as we were finishing our tea and toast, they burst in upon us!

"Bang! Bang! I'm a Bren gun. You're all dead" shouted one keen type. "Jolly good! Have a piece of toast," somebody said. The Bren gunner was disgusted by such flippancy on the part of a corpse.

Our attackers vanished. We thought that they were keen because they had with them a subaltern fresh from Sandhurst.

We set off in pursuit when we had finished our breakfast and thanked the farmer for the accommodation. Before long, as we topped a rise, we saw our objective before us. We had no binoculars with us and so could not see whether the 'enemy' was in occupation or not. The thing to do was to assume that the other section was already there and proceed.

We did things 'by the book', linking arms to dash past gaps in hedgerows and crawling along hedge bottoms, not crossing fields, as we neared our objective.

Two of us, who had foot problems, were detached to act as the Bren team and were sent out on the right flank. We waited for them to begin firing before we made our move. Using a hedgerow as cover, we began to get nearer to the tumuli. The Bren gunner of the morning, who had mown us all down in that encounter, saw us on the other side of the hedge and scuttled off to report our presence. We could still have managed to surprise the others if we had crept up the hedge which ran right up to the tumuli, but we threw all caution to the winds, as we had been spotted, and rushed in the open across some newly sprouting wheat.

"Not supposed to run over there," bellowed the subaltern, then, "OK, might as well carry on!"

Of course, what we had done was sheer folly in tactical terms and we would have been mown down in reality. We were commended on our approach from the high ground, when the other section had spotted us on the sky-line. Then they had lost sight of us until we had been spotted by the Bren gunner scout, for no-one had seen us until we had popped up right under the noses of our opponents.

We marched to our pick-up point and flopped into the back of the three-tonner, The Marathon March was over!

At Bovington, assault courses, lectures and guard duties were the pattern for the next clay and night, followed by a carrier exercise to Poole. Notable because we had topped up with oil before we moved off from our overnight halt and someone had not screwed on the oil-can cap properly. There was a dribble of oil across the floor of the carrier and out of the back. This was spotted by one of the NCOs as a trail on the ground. Panic stations! Someone had a cracked sump! When the real cause was discovered, we were fortunate not to be put on a charge.

Sunday of next week was spent in preparation for an exercise which was to last for several days. We set out on Monday, camping out and on guard the first night. The next day was very wet. We spent the day on Troop tactics ("Send your Troop Corporal round that bend to see if there's an anti-tank gun there, Troop Leader!"). It was very like the real thing, with lots of waiting about while tactics were sorted out. The rain continued at night, so we slept, not under bushes as we had previously, but in a local school hall, on the floor. I had no idea that floor-boards could be so comfortable. I was very refreshed by my sleep when 1 woke in the morning. Moving next clay to Ringwood, we returned from there to Bovington on Friday in time for Christmas Day, which was on the Saturday.

Christmas Day 1943 was a bit of a disaster for me! I had intended to go to Church, but to my dismay, I was put on a fatigue. (What a discouraging name for these necessary duties!) Kay Shewell was a kind soul, and he had not been detailed for fatigue, so he volunteered to take my place. His father was a canon of St Albans Cathedral.

The fatigue party left and I got myself ready for church. Let it be said that I am the worst when it comes to finding things! I put on my best battledress and then looked for my best boots. They were nowhere to be found. I searched high and low. The time for the service came and went, and after mooching round miserably for some time, I went to the NAAFI. The fatigue party came in, and Kay sat at my table, making no comment. When I got back to the barrack hut, I found that my boots had been under the bed all the time.

A few days later, we were cleaning the ablutions block, and I was sent to get cleaning materials from a cupboard where they were kept. I looked everywhere for the cupboard, but the corporal had given me vague directions, and I could find no cupboard anywhere. I should have noticed it in the normal course of events, I suppose. I gave up searching and went back to the barrack hut. To my dismay, the other members of the Troop had not returned. Soon, they came in and Kay spoke to me. "You're getting too sharp, Jack," he said, "First I do your fatigue, for you to go to church, and then I find you in the NAAFI, then you dodge the fatigue this morning!" He was quite right from his point of view and I had no defence. One could hardly plead stupidity, but I felt dreadful as I had not intended to dodge the fatigues and it seemed, with justification, that was my intention.

We spent our time, as the year drew to a close, driving in carriers, both personnel and Bren. I believe that the personnel carriers were designed for the transport of tank crews. They had tiller bars for steering, something like a tank. The Bren carrier had a steering wheel and the tracks bowed in the middle to give direction.

The first Bren carrier ride was not a success. We were bowling merrily along when we began to slow down and then jerkily speeded up again. We had some water in the petrol and so it was a matter of turning round and making our way back to camp by fits and starts. The next time out, we were given the task of driving up a steep, muddy hill in a field. Some managed to get their vehicles to the top, but I could not coax my carrier to get there.

At the end of every afternoon, we had to take out the batteries from the carriers to immobilise them. We had to carry the heavy batteries across the tank park to one of the huts where they could be kept secure and recharged if necessary. I remember carrying a battery at the end of the day, when an NCO looked at me and said, in sneering tones, "I suppose you're one of these officer types are you?" I was amazed. I had never, to my knowledge, seen this man before and his remark came out of the blue. Perhaps he had fallen foul of one of the young officers we had about.

One of us who was an officer type, much to his consternation, was our Communist, Ray Warnes. Later on, when we had been posted, I got letters from him, still at Bovington, where he kept badgering the authorities to release him from officer training and let him loose on the Germans.

The time was running out, and we had to decide in which unit we wanted to serve. I was asked by George Rowan to go with him to one regiment but changed my mind at the last minute and decided to go to the 15th and 19th King's Royal Hussars, with John Cotton. The '5 and 9s' were stationed in Northumberland.

Cameo: Trooper – to sleepy figure in bunk, "Ay, Bill, the XXXs (where they were to be posted) are at Newmarket." Bill: "Don't be a fool. Newmarket's a card game."

We had a parade wearing full marching order. An outgoing Troop had parade dressed in FMO a few weeks before. We had seen them on the square and each man was leaning forward to balance the weight of his kit. They looked as if they were all facing into a howling gale. A strange sight!

Soon, it was our turn to be driven to Wool Station on the first part of our journey, north for some, including John and me, the others scattered about other parts of the country. As we passed the guard room, somebody said, "Let's give three 'Boos' for Sergeant Hayter!" He was told to shut up. I really think we believed that Sergeant Hayter would rush out and clap us in the guard room even as we went on draft to our regiments.

We got out of our train at Waterloo and changed stations to go north. Our train left late at night, so we went to the cinema, leaving our kit at the station, then we 'entrained' and set off on our journey to the '5 and 9s' in the 9th Armoured Brigade.

Chapter 3

The 'Five and Nines'

It was early morning when we arrived at our destination, Morpeth. There had been overnight rain but now the sun was shining, pale and watery, as we got on the 3-tonner which was to take us to the regiment.

The 15th and 19th Hussars had been amalgamated in 1922 and had been occupying outposts of the Empire for several years since then. Egypt from 1924-1928, India from 1928-1933. They were home-based from 1934 until the outbreak of war, when the regiment was sent to France as division cavalry for the 3rd Division.

Caught up in the Blitzkrieg, they were in action from 10th to 30th May 1940, when they were evacuated from Dunkirk. The regiment had 7 officers and 27 other ranks killed in that short time and 6 officers and 100 other ranks taken prisoner.

From November 1940, the regiment had been part of the 9th Armoured Division and were still part of that division when John and I, the only members of the draft to join the '5 and 9s', came to the regiment.

There were detachments at Acton House, a manor with Nissen huts in the grounds, Longframlington, Swarland and Weldon Bridge. I believe we were taken to Longframlington, picking up on the way a 2nd lieutenant in the Royal Scots Greys. He was wearing cut-down leather boots, and I thought that they looked very unmilitary, but there was a lot of mud about and so they were quite sensible wear, despite their appearance.

We were deposited at the regimental canteen, empty apart from two ORs, one obviously 'in charge' and the other evading duties by concealing himself in the canteen. I found this out when I visited the WC, which was outside the building. When I returned, the door was locked but as there were voices coming from inside, I knocked for admittance. "Who's there?" asked a voice, to which I replied, "Me!" Fortunately, John recognised my voice as I gave this strange answer, and I was admitted. The 'lead swinger' then told me, in no uncertain tones, how I had frightened him when I had knocked on the door.

We were then taken to our squadron and installed in different Troop huts. The Nissen huts stood beside the road in a small village. The school was the mess-hall and there was a church, I know, because we went to Evensong and I fell asleep and snored during the sermon.

There was no word of welcome, or even of advice, from anyone. We just fitted into the squadron routine as best as we could, finding our way by trial and (mostly) error.

There were traditions, of course, which were observed in such old regiments. One of these dated from the Peninsular War, when the 15th Dragoons (Hussars) had been roused from slumber to attack and defeat a Brigade of French Dragoons at Sagahun (pronounced Sagoon).

As a result of this it became the tradition to have a pre-Reveille parade to wake up the troops. No matter if boots were unlaced and braces dangling, sleepy Troopers lined up in front of their huts to answer their names as the squadron sergeant-major (a replica of the Bovington warrant officers) called them out. Of course, in the rain and the dark, you could, by mutual arrangement, ask a friend to answer for you while you had an extra few minutes 'charp'. This was slang for bed or sleep, being short for 'charpoy', a remnant of service in India.

SSM to Trooper: "Brushed your hair this morning, lad?"

Trooper: "No Sar' Major."

SSM to Trooper: "Should do, lad. Brushing your hair is worth an hour of charp!"

After the pre-Reveille parade, I trudged across the field in the dark to the ablutions hut. Usually, I was the only person there. Whether the others retired for an extra hour of 'charp' I do not know. What I do know is that a bucket of water was brought into our hut at night and all the chaps washed in it in the morning. The grey, scummy water was more than I could face. Whether the chaps had a proper wash later on I never discovered. We were supposed to be living in active service conditions, and I discovered that we ate out of mess-tins. That was one thing, but sharing a bucket for washing was quite another.

It was not long before the newcomers were sent on courses. I left my new companions and went with a number of others to a gunnery course at Acton House. John Cotton also came but his course must have been on wireless as he was an operator.

Gunnery was straightforward, and it was simply a matter of brushing up on stuff I had learned at Bovington. There were differences, however. On the Cromwell, the 6-pounder had been replaced by a 75mm gun. The gun was elevated and depressed, not by the dreaded 'stirrup' but by an elevating wheel. There was a refinement here as the wheel was marked off in degrees and half-degrees. When firing high-explosive shells, it was now possible to 'bracket' a target as in conventional field artillery shooting.

There was a small range which we used on the course. A Sten gun was mounted on the main gun, and earth and sand made hills and other features on the little range. Pieces of wood were used to simulate anti-tank gun emplacements and other targets. By lining up on a target and raising and lowering the gun under the direction of the commander, one was able to bracket and then hit the target, using the divisions on the wheel. It was all very simple, and I wondered why no-one had put this method of tank firing into operation before.

The nearby village had a cobbled square set off from the main road. Here, the guard was mounted and defaulters paraded 'behind the guard' ("You'll be parading behind the guard, lad!" was the cry of NCOs).

The view from the square was splendid. We looked from our range of hills on which the village stood, and gazed over the flat plain below, where pit head-stocks could be seen. Some of the coal seams, we were told, went under the sea in this part of the country. Beyond the pits and the fields, the North Sea shimmered in the grey winter light. A mill stood on one side of the square. Here, wool was woven into fabric and here, too, we paraded for baths in large wooden vats, used for dyeing perhaps.

Our time on the courses was short-lived, for in the higher echelons of command, decisions were made which would change our fortunes.

One afternoon, John Cotton came into our hut and said excitedly that we were on a draft "To the Seventh Armoured Division, the Desert Rats!" he announced with gleaming eyes. I scanned the notice-board and found my name on the '5 and 9' draft. There were to be ORs from our regiment and the Fife and Forfar Yeomanry going to the 7th Armoured Division.

We found ourselves parading with our kit once more. We had one extra item to carry and that was a pistol. Asked if I wanted a Webley or a Smith and Wesson 0.38 revolver, I plumped for the Smith and Wesson. I thought that it was a better-looking weapon and probably of better quality, too, if all those cowboy films were anything to go by. I soon discovered that I had made a good choice; the Smith and Wesson had a hair-trigger – a refinement the Webley did not have.

As we waited for the trucks to take us to the station, an officer rode toward us on his horse. He addressed us and wished us well for the future. He ended by saying, "I don't know which of us will meet the enemy first!" (Inevitable voice from rear rank, "I bloody well do!").

I think that we got on the train at Alnwick. By a strange coincidence my father had journeyed from Alnwick in 1915. He, too, had been on his way to a new regiment. There was, at that time, an army camp in the park of Alnwick Castle, where wounded soldiers were sent to regain their fitness after recovering from wounds. My father had sustained a bad leg wound at the Battle of Loos in 1915. He was then serving with the Rifle Battalion of the Sherwood Foresters, the Robin Hood Rifles. To his dismay, after Alnwick, he was drafted into the King's Shropshire Light Infantry and sent to Salonika. When I next went on leave, we compared notes on that rather odd coincidence.

Down the east side of England, we clattered on the train, and it was in the afternoon that I noticed we were passing through stations in the north of Nottinghamshire, some known to me. It was no surprise when we drew in at one station and discovered that it was Lincoln – the city basking in the February sunshine, with the Cathedral, with green nave and transepts roof, looking down from the hill on which it stands.

We set out again, and it became evident that East Anglia was to be our destination. The train began to slow down, and the distinctive smell of a sugar-beet factory assailed our nostrils as we crawled past and drew into Brandon Station.

Chapter 4

The 4th County of London Yeomanry

The first sight which met my astonished gaze was that of a figure on the station platform wearing a khaki field service cap and gleaming white webbing equipment. This was the Provost Sergeant of 4th CLY. Though we had not as yet been allocated to regiments, it seemed as if some were going to this new mob, in which berets were not worn and white blanco was the order of the day!

When we were lined up in the station yard, I discovered that this was to be my regiment. The draft also included 68 others from the 9th Armoured Division. Loaded onto trucks, we set off on our journey along straight roads through pine wood plantations.

Passing one plantation, one '5 and 9' said gloomily, "This is Shakers Wood." The regiment had been stationed in this wood in 1943. That name seemed ominous, but we motored on up the road and turned into the tank park (no tanks there as yet) of another Nissen-hutted camp. This, we came to know, was High Ash Wood. The huts were hidden among the trees, and concrete paths wound about among the huts.

We dismounted and were taken to our respective Troop huts. With me were two of the reinforcements, Briggs and Hopkins. I did not know either of them but soon discovered that Hopkins was a Scot with a caustic wit and Briggs was a true Yorkshireman with a downright view on most subjects.

The first person I encountered as I entered the hut was Ginger Williams, who was sitting on his bunk cleaning some equipment. "How old are you?" he asked without any preamble. "Eighteen," I said. "My God!" he exclaimed, "They're sending us babies!"

I was directed to a top bunk at the far end of the hut, next to the door. The bed was neatly made and on it were placed two plates and a mug. No mess tins here! I assumed that the members of the regiment, having been on active service for so long, applied the old maxim 'a good camper never roughs it' if conditions could be made more civilised.

Over the next few days, we got to know each other. I certainly felt more at home with the CLY than I had with the '5 and 9s'. Perhaps in the Hussars, being a regular army regiment, the attitude was not the same. I felt as if I had not left the training regiment. With the Yeomanry, 'baby' though I was, it was obvious that the men were 'warriors for the working day' and had been in civilian jobs before the war. Some had wives and children.

Hopkins made himself popular by observing, during one discussion we had about our service in the Army, that the Desert Rats would have been better occupied, like him, in getting to know their own country first, instead of gallivanting half-way round the world! On another occasion, Hoppy described shooting from a tank as it drove through the surf when making a landing on shore. Ginger asked when that was? "On a 'scheme' with the other regiment", said Hoppy! Ginger addressed the hut at large: "Cor! These chaps have only been on schemes."

As I had never been on a scheme, I kept my mouth shut before these seasoned Desert Warriors.

The white 'blancoed' equipment which had filled my heart with dismay when I observed it adorning the body of the Provost Sergeant turned out not to be 'blanco' at all. The kit had been scrubbed and then buried in desert sand. This had bleached the webbing to the white shade which all 7th Armoured Division units favoured. We newcomers were provided with a packet of bleach, and we set to scrubbing our kit with this and were gratified to note that our webbing became gleaming white too.

The regiment was issued with berets and so we did not have to convert to that most impractical of headgear in tanks, the Field Service Cap. We had two berets, of course, best and second-best. Our best berets were taken away and shortly returned to us, having had a dark green ribbon sewn into the headband. This distinguished CLY from any run of the mill tank unit. A cap-badge could not be found for me and so for some time I made do with a collar-badge. This was a home-made version manufactured in Egypt, and the '4' in the centre of the badge was slightly skewed.

The divisional sign, the Desert Rat, appeared on the sleeves of the battle-dress blouses of the desert comrades. It was a red rat on a khaki background.

To me, it looked home-made, but authentic. I was dismayed when we all got our new 'rats' to sew on our blouses. The rat looked more like a kangaroo and the back legs were not nearly long enough. Nevertheless, this was to be our new divisional sign.

I was in 'A' Squadron and in 1 Troop. Hugh Stanton was Troop Corporal, and he soon became something of a hero to me! Johnny Owens and Ginger Williams came from Liverpool. The other Williams, Bill, was an inhabitant of the East End. Aked, known to all as 'Naked' of course, came from Leicestershire and was in the stocking manufacturing industry. Granny Swales, though not the oldest member of the Troop, was in the opposite corner of the hut to me. He was a quiet man I never really got to know. There was a fitter in our company, and he came from Gloucestershire and rejoiced in the name of 'Wim-wam'. If shown a piece of machinery, he would at once declare that it was a "Wim-wam for a mustard mill!" (A real 'Whim wham', I found out years later, was an architectural feature of a medieval window).

Ernie was a lad with a big smile who had, so he said, a reputation as a lady-killer. A small driver who had a bunk near the other door, was reputed to need blocks on the foot pedals of the tank because his feet did not reach them, his legs being so short. Our Troop Leader was Lieutenant Hurley, a South African, who wore orange strips on his shoulder straps.

Johnny Owens, I was to discover, would always announce his intention of getting into his bunk by saying, "Yokking time for Yokkers!" before getting into the blankets. When the time came for him to seal up a letter he had written to his wife, he would sing a little popular ditty about 'hoping with every message, she would soon be in his arms again!'

Ginger tried to start an argument with me about the inefficiency of soldiers who wore spectacles. "What would you do if you broke them?" "I'd put another pair on!" "Well, what would you do if you broke *them*?"

Bill Williams astonished me. Knowing he came from London, I said to him, "Of course, you've been to the Tower?" "What for?" he asked. I could think of no reply! I expect that I thought he was an habitué of the historic places of London and spent a good bit of the time hanging around Buckingham Palace and the Mall, hoping for a glimpse of Their Majesties!

In the winter evenings we huddled round the Tortoise stove, hearing the 'Do you remember?' accounts of the Desert and Cairo. The officer who was heard over the air during a tank battle to say, "My arm's off and so am I!" The driver who used to stick his head out of his hatch and shout to the desert air "Eee-aye-ipo!" Mostly, though, there were amusing accounts of incidents away from the battle-field in dubious watering holes in Cairo or fighting off the attentions of passionate Italian ladies.

'Wim-wam', I remember, livened up the proceedings one night by reciting an epic poem of Rabelaisian content, set in an English countryside.

My boots began to take on a more polished appearance, for at the Training Regiment we were not allowed to use polish, but only dubbin. Naturally, this directive (it was an Army order) did not apply in the CLY, so when I first appeared on parade, I got a gentle 'rocket' from the Squadron Leader, Major Peter Scott, for my scruffy boots. I was pleased when my boots became presentable, for one Saturday morning I was detailed for escort duty for someone on a 'charge'. All the other members of the Troop had gone home on week-end leave.

The Trooper who was in trouble, I discovered, was my 'Mystery Man'. He inhabited the bunk below mine. I knew that it was slept in, but he was not there when I went to bed and was not there when I got up in the morning, and I had not set eyes on him until I stood beside him – he with beret and belt off, on this occasion. What his misdemeanour was, I now have no idea, but I discovered that his job in camp was to light the cookhouse fires. That would account for his early rising, but his absence at bedtime? Who knows? My next encounter with him was during a Troop Leader's inspection. This officer was having a 'blitz' on mugs, inspected mine and then bent down to examine the mug of my bunk companion. Naturally, tannin stains coated the inside of the mug. "Disgusting!" said the officer. "It should be as clean as this!", holding up my mug as an example. How embarrassing!

The day came when the drivers went to collect the Cromwells. Ginger stamped angrily into the hut. "So that's your Cromwell, is it?" he declaimed, throwing his driving gloves onto his bunk, "Armour bolted on! What happens if a shot hits the bolt? It'll fly off round the turret!" I didn't understand his concern until I discovered that this had happened with Grant tanks and riveted armour in the desert battles. The rivets had been hurled round the interior of the tanks when they had been hit.

Some of the Cromwells which came to us were not new, having been used by other units for training. Some were quite battered and shabby. One had been used by Guard's Armoured and was painted completely black. Another had a brass plate screwed on to the storage bin, which proclaimed that the money to buy the tank had been raised during a 'Tanks for Attack' week by an English town. No doubt the good people of the town thought that 'their' tank was even now attacking the enemy in Italy or somewhere and had not simply been relegated to a training role in this country.

Some of the tanks had on the turret our old friend the Parrish-Lulworth Mounting, which was instantly removed, as was the co-drivers' seat, for the extra space so gained to be used for the storage of ammunition. I don't know what the drivers thought about this arrangement!

It was Gus Watson, who excited my admiration, for he had a green and yellow Field Service dress cap which he wore on Saturdays, who pointed out the folly of the exhausts which pointed up into the air at the rear of the tank. He asked us to imagine tanks concealed by dense foliage. When they started their engines, plumes of exhaust smoke, as was common with the engines, would shoot up into the air, giving away the position of the vehicles. I don't suppose it was his protest which had some tank boffin invent the Normandy Cowl which directed exhaust smoke down onto the ground, but it gave us even less confidence in the tank designers that such a modification had to be made.

On a more personal level, when we had been issued with violent yellow gauntlets and I said how conspicuous they would be, it was Gus who said "Well, you won't be doing this" (waving his hands in the air), "and shouting to Jerry, 'Look at my new gloves!'"

About a week after we had arrived as reinforcements, the division was inspected by Montgomery at Didlington Park, a few miles from High Ash. The old hands were singularly unimpressed by the opportunity to see the great man, but I was quite eager to see this legendary figure in the flesh.

The division was assembled in a great hollow square for the inspection. Flakes of snow whirled through the air as we waited. Were we early or was he late? After a mug of hot tea for breakfast, and standing in the cold of the morning, discomfort was felt by many of us, so when the order was given 'Fall out!', naturally the opportunity was taken to relieve our pressing need. In the middle of the hollow square was a large clump of trees, and at that strategic moment, out of the trees chugged a tractor with a Land-girl driver. Eyes fixed on some distant point on the far horizon; she disappeared as quickly as she had come upon the watery scene.

We resumed ranks again and Montgomery arrived.

As he walked round inside the square, I was struck by the intense blue of his eyes. They seemed to be piercing and quite unusual.

We were told to gather round his Jeep as he stood on the bonnet and talked to us. He removed the flying jacket which he was wearing and revealed a fruit salad of medal ribbons. This sight provoked wolf whistles from the assembled soldiery and, to quote a fellow Sharpshooter, the great man was not pleased.

I suppose he wished us "good hunting" and promised us that we would "Knock Rommel for six", but I have forgotten his exact words.

We had a visit from His Majesty the King one sunny day. To my dismay we were confined to our huts but were to emerge as HM drove away and give him three hearty cheers. There was a crowd of people round the window at the end of the hut as people peered out, trying to see the King. I tried to push forward. "He wants to see the King", said Bill Williams, in mocking tones. Undeterred, I got to the window and looked out to catch a glimpse of a figure clad in a British warm, wearing a red-banded cap and highly polished brown riding boots. When HM drove away, we rushed to the side of the road and gave three cheers. To my surprise, when I was nearly deafened by someone cheering beside me, I turned round to see Bill. There was a Guard at the 'Present' too, with short magazine Lee-Enfields with 17-inch bayonets fixed. I was disloyal enough to think that, if a Guard had been assembled made up of ex-58th personnel now in the CLY, we would have been smarter!

The grapevine rumour was that Bill Cotton had told HM what he thought of the Cromwell, in no uncertain terms.

The GOC 7th Armoured Division paid us a visit. We were told that we would not be in the 'chorus' when the time for the invasion came, but we would be in the first row of the stalls. He also said that the countryside in which we would be fighting would be very like the countryside where we were, the Brecklands of Norfolk!

Training continued apace. I joined a party who were pistol-shooting on the small range. I adopted the posture I had been taught at the training regiment: feet apart, left knee bent, with the left hand on the knee, body in a semi-crouching position. The SSM pulled me up, "Hasn't anyone told you how to shoot with a pistol?" he asked and put me in a more conventional pose, standing, feet apart and sideways-on to the target. I wasn't taught satisfactorily how to shoot with a pistol until after the war was over – and then by a Danish officer seconded to the regiment in which I was serving at that time.

We had a session driving Cromwells backwards and forwards round a row of empty, flimsy petrol cans, guided by a companion indicating turns from the front of the tank, trying to judge the space between the cans to avoid crushing them.

There was a small 'mock up' range of earth and sand with pieces of wood to represent enemy positions, and the Sten gun once again held on the barrel of the 75mm by brackets. Here we practised the 'bracketing' procedure I had already become familiar with in the '5 and 9s'. Perhaps for this reason, I was detailed to give a demonstration for the Colonel. I made a bad start, because of stage fright, and corrected down instead of up when directed by the tank commander. I soon recovered my composure, however and a successful demonstration was the outcome.

A large theatre, constructed like a giant Nissen hut, stood at the end of one of the wider rides between nearby woods. This was named the 'Desert Rat', and we could walk there to see shows. The one I remember was given by a company run by Devine and King. There were pretty girls in the chorus, of course. 'Showpiece' was the name of the concert. One item was a comedy in which a wedding party and the vicar all lost their voices. A hilarious scene unfolded as there were misunderstood gestures when they all mimed their way through the ceremony and roars of laughter from the audience as the bawdy humour unfolded.

Local concert parties came to entertain us in our small 'theatre' in one of the Nissen huts. I was surprised at the remarks made by the hard-bitten (I thought) soldiery after one show, when a young man sang Formby songs, accompanying himself on a ukulele. Naturally, the verses were 'Formbyesque' and my companions expressed dismay that one so young should be so vulgar.

But we were all amused by the stories of land-girls and cows and bulls, when told by the leader of the party as he related stories of unfortunate misunderstandings in the Norfolk countryside. There was a 'policeman' who did the obligatory 'knees bend' routine and then looked round to see if the coast was clear before taking off his helmet and producing a bag of chips that he had hidden inside. He ate the chips with great delicacy and then licked his white-gloved fingers.

I discovered the secret of the lightning cartoonist when I was clearing up after the concert next day and found his cartoons already outlined faintly on the sheets of paper he had been using. One of the party 'played' the violin, imitating the sound so expertly that we were all amazed when he finished bowing yet the violin sound could still be heard.

What brought the house down was the song *Pistol Packin' Momma* which was sung with gusto by a vigorous young lady. We all joined in the chorus as we roared out the words with her.

A more serious note was struck when we were shown the film *The Next of Kin*. This was really a film about security and the necessity to guard against careless talk. The story line concerned a raiding party which was to land on the French coast. A young subaltern was befriended by a dancer in the local theatre. Needless to say, she was a spy. When the raiding party landed on the coast, the Wehrmacht had laid on a reception committee. Amid the sounds of machine-gun fire could be heard the sounds of Stukas bombing the troops. Very tense moments. But when the Infantry CO heard the sound of these aircraft and said, "My God! What's that?" the room exploded in howls of laughter and the rest of the dialogue was drowned in the hilarity.

The response of the more staid of the troops to the young ukulele player was matched when some of the lads went to a local dance where 'Jitterbugging' was allowed. "The girls didn't care!" said one astonished Trooper, "You could see their knickers!" Obviously, standards had slipped during his time overseas.

An incident at another dance was reported with great glee. Tich Brown, always good for a laugh, had lit a cigarette lighter and placed it in the middle of the dance hall. He and another CLY chap stood watching it with folded arms. Within minutes, the dance had ground to a halt, with excited people pushing to see what was going on in the middle of the hall.

The conspirators then pocketed the lighter and exited, leaving the dancers bewildered and jammed solid by the crush. Tich continued to amuse us as, in the canteen one break-time, he produced a box of Captain Webb matches and showed us a trick he could work with them.

The canteen was manned by a couple of older civilians and was a welcome refuge for our 'char and wad' sessions at mid-morning. There was a loud-speaker system which we were able to enjoy. I remember John Cotton and I listening to a performance of '*Dance Macabre*' which I had first heard at school, when a music master had broadened our musical knowledge by playing classical records to us in morning assembly. "Listen to that violin weep!" said John as we listened intently.

More training was due for the regiment, and the tank ranges in Scotland (Kirkcudbright) were the proving ground for the 75mm tank guns. I did not accompany the tank crews but was sent on seven days leave. I walked in at home, much to everyone's surprise, and spent a week of unexpected leave visiting friends and then returned, via London, to Norfolk. I chummed up with another member of the regiment at Paddington Station, and we set off on our journey. Night fell and we both dozed off, to wake up in the early morning at Norwich, having slept through our station. We had to take the first train out in the morning to Thetford, where we found one of the regimental trucks going back to Camp.

The time came for us to prepare to take part in our own 'schemes'. To this end, wireless procedures were re-emphasised by a young officer who gave us a talk on this subject. Security was paramount and so at no time was the procedure and form of words used by 4th CLY to be used over the air. Discontent was in the air. How would the enemy not be aware of our presence in the invasion forces? Even the dockers had known who the regiment were and that 7th Armoured Division had come home from Italy at the beginning of the year.

The 'schemes' went forward, however and we drove into the battle area for our manoeuvres. At one point on one of the roads, there was a Calvary and it was easy to imagine, as we passed it, that one was already on the Continent. I had bet Hoppy half a crown that we would land in France. He was sure we would land in the Netherlands as it was nearer to Germany. I thought that the rivers and canals would hamper our armies and so I turned down that idea.

I was very surprised on a day 'scheme' when the driver and commander said that they were "Fed up with this" (the exercise), and so the driver did a skid turn in a ploughed field and had a track off. Immobilised, we had a brew and waited for the fitters to arrive!

We had no PT parades but went out on short route marches round the countryside. One day, as we marched away from the Camp, two tank transporters appeared, driving toward us. All eyes followed them as they drove past. They had Shermans on board and as they passed us, we saw that they had long guns mounted in the turrets, though both tanks were sheeted down. There was a murmur of appreciation from the column. I remembered the Sherman at Lulworth which had fired such a weapon – we had seen our first 'Firefly' tanks being transported to their regiments.

We had our own Fireflies to collect from Chilwell later on. How I wished that I had been able to go with the party, for my home was just over the hill from the Ordnance Depot and my mother worked there. The detail returned, somewhat dismayed. One of the tanks had hit a telegraph pole and the pole, in falling, had killed a man in his front garden. The driver was very upset by this sad accident.

Another 'scheme' and we spent the night under the stars. As we got ready to 'leaguer' in the late afternoon a number of Flying Fortresses flew overhead, returning from a raid. One of them had an outer engine stopped. They were all flying very low and we wondered if there were casualties on board some of them.

After we had enjoyed a night's sleep and had our breakfast next morning, we heard the roar of engines from behind the ridge near us. As the sound increased in volume, DR outriders appeared. One of my companions said, "You won't see anything like this again." There passed before us an Armoured Regiment (RTR) in what was essentially a desert manoeuvre, in box formation, taking advantage of the broad heath land.

The evenings were getting lighter and there was opportunity to explore had I wished. Grimes Graves was nearby, and the hamlet of Hilborough where Nelson stayed sometimes as a boy, when his uncle was Rector. My expeditions were very limited in scope, however I do remember walking back from Swaffham, where there was a canteen in the Market Hall, and seeing two sinister figures approaching me on the otherwise deserted road. I eyed them with apprehension as they looked so ragged. I need not have worried. They turned out to be two very polite Irish labourers who were working on a nearby airfield. Like me, they were out on a walk enjoying the spring sunshine. Unlike me, they had lost their way. I was not able to direct them, for, though aircraft were regularly flying overhead, I had not seen any signs of an airfield.

I went further afield on Saturdays, always to the pictures in some nearby town, but John Cotton was more adventurous. He once went to Cambridge and came back with tales of going on a punt and seeing the girl undergraduates sitting on the bank of the river, with their skirts pulled up onto their thighs, "As Bohemian as you like!" said John. 'Bohemian!' How innocent it seems now.

If there were no trucks making a trip into towns, we thumbed a lift. I once got a lift into Swaffham in an artillery 'Quad' – a vehicle used for towing 25-pounder field guns. There were seats inside for all the gun crew and I found it a bit like a family saloon with seats for every member of the family.

Coming back from Swaffham one night, we got a lift with two RAF officers. As we drew near camp, they asked if there was any chance of getting a can of petrol. Fortunately, my companion said he could arrange it as he knew the guard. Being a new boy, it was no use my asking.

There were the inevitable fatigues, of course. I was detailed to join another newcomer in sawing up wood for the officer's mess. We worked with a double-handed saw, in fits and starts. In fact, there was more jaw than saw. "Oh! Here comes the CO," said my companion, Richard Dipple, "We'd better make some vague working motions!"

A most unpleasant task was that of cleaning out the grease-trap outside the officer's mess. I found that a sick-making job. A more attractive prospect lay in accompanying the regimental butcher on a journey to fetch meat from the nearby depot. This was a treat, as I saw a new part of the countryside.

Apart from the log-sawing episode, my next encounter with the CO was when I was sent to light the stove in his office. It was the usual 'Tortoise' stove – we all had them in our huts – and I could not get the thing to light, although I tried every combination of wood, coal and paper, damper in and damper out.

As I was on my knees blowing fruitlessly at my dead fire, the door opened and the CO came in. I knew it was him, because he wore leather gaiters like the Home Guard. As I was at ground level, I noted them, but could see nothing above the knees. Should I stand and come smartly to the salute or keep blowing? I kept blowing and the gaiters and knees withdrew! I was relieved of my fire-lighting chore at once. That evening, I was having a shower and heard Ernie Ridall remark to a companion that he had been sent to light the CO's fire that morning. "One of these new lads couldn't do it," he said, "they haven't a clue."

Ernie surprised me one morning when I was reading a leaflet urging the wisdom of counting rounds as one fired them. The thing was presented in story form and told of an unfortunate soldier who had not counted his rounds and so had an empty magazine when an enemy soldier came round the corner and surprised him. "Don't worry," said Ernie, "when they get that close, I'll put my hands up."

I was rather horrified at that statement, being brought up on death or glory deeds at the cinema and not forgetting the BBC and the morale-boosting plays and factual programmes about gallant acts of bravery in the defence of democracy.

In contrast to the '5 and 9s', conversation was larded, not with Indian slang, but Arabic. I never knew how to spell these words except by writing them phonetically, but 'bar din' (later on) 'stanaswyia' (wait a little), 'alakeefak' (easy, as in 'I'm alakeefak'), and 'malaish' (never mind, or ignore, as in 'Malaish the cabbage, let's have another helping of chips'). I apologise to any Arabists who read these words!

It was these and other words and phrases which, I had been told, should not be used over the air when we landed. As I remember, Cockney rhyming slang and Arabic phrases still tickled our ears and, we were sure, baffled the enemy as we spoke over the air.

So, the 'Baker Roger over the blue' meant a bridge over a stream or river. Baker Roger being the first two letters, BR, of the word 'bridge'. 'Frog', 'Frog and Toad', Cockney rhyming slang for 'road!' 'Baby', tank; e.g. 'My baby has got up to the corner of the frog'. 'Iron horse thing', railway.

'Our friends in the funny hats', the 8th Hussars, who were the Reconnaissance Regiment in 7th Armoured Division. The officers wore green and gold 'tent hats' dating from the Peninsular War. These were of Spanish origin and had gold tassels hanging from the front. This description fitted well until we worked with Canadian Infantry in the Caen battle. They had the 'improved' but unbalanced steel helmet, and the camouflage netting over the helmets was padded out with shell-dressings to give a broken outline. We then had reference over the air to 'Our new friends with the funny hats' as opposed to 'Our old friends with the funny hats'.

We went to Boyton tank ranges to fire our guns once more. I think it was there that the 95mm Howitzer Cromwell was tried out. We fired at a hillside across the valley, through the bottom of which ran a road. Strangely, it was still in use, and we had to wait until a small van had driven down it and out of sight before the tank could open fire. I wonder if the driver knew!

There was an invitation from Sergeant Ken Weightman for someone to drive a tank back to camp. I accepted the invitation, though I had not driven very much except for the practice at High Ash Wood with the 'flimsies'.

Getting into the driving seat, I started up the engine. The first thing to do was to get out of the line of stationary tanks and so Sergeant Weightman beckoned me forward to give some room to do this. He walked backward toward the next tank in the column, and I continued to creep forward. I only just remembered the clutch in time to avoid squashing the Sergeant against the tank in front!

We set out on our journey, despite this mishap, known only to me of course. My shortcomings as a driver were to come to light more dramatically when we descended a small hill. I foolishly tried to change to a lower gear as the tank rolled forward. Of course, all the revs I could muster were not enough to get the tank in gear again and we rolled ever faster downhill, in neutral, with no steering.

At the bottom of the hill, the road took a sharp left-hand turn. What I could not see, but those in the turret could see all too clearly, was a very wet-looking lake on the other side of a little bank edging the bend. Two of the lads were sitting half out of the operator's hatch. They said later that each had tried to push the other inside the tank in order to escape when the tank mounted the bank and hit the water. Fortunately, Sergeant Weightman was the one who kept calm. "FOOT BRAKE, FOOT BRAKE, FOOT BRAKE!!!" he called down the microphone, and I duly stood on the foot brake. We hit the bank, breaking a concrete fence post and came to rest.

After a pause for all to regain their shattered nerves, we set off again. By this time, I had lost all confidence and negotiated a traffic island by going round it in skid turns. "That was not necessary," said Sergeant W., wondering by this time, no doubt, what idiots the reinforcing regiments had got rid of! We reached camp safely, to the relief of all.

To my dismay, I found that I was not to be in a tank crew, but was to be on an ammunition truck, with Alf Grey as driver. So, I was to invade Europe on a lorry. When the time came to leave High Ash, therefore, I travelled in the back of the lorry to Orwell Park, Nacton, beside the River Orwell, where grey vessels could be seen lying at anchor.

I remember little of the journey, for my nose was buried in a book, but I do recall going through a village where one of the shops was owned by someone called 'Gotobed', which seemed an amusing name.

We arrived at our new camp.

Beside the entrance to the camping area, there were several mock graves, which were rather startling at first sight. On the crosses at the head of the grave-mounds were written cautionary phrases – for instance, 'He didn't keep his head down!', and other warnings for the unwary soldier.

Orwell Park itself was rolling and sloped gently down to the river where there was a small cliff, about ten or twelve feet high. The river was tidal of course. There was a Hall to the left of the gates and one of the rooms had stars on the ceiling. An outer wall of this room had collapsed outward, so one could see inside.

There was a NAAFI outside the gates, with real girls in attendance, though the NAAFI itself was a temporary wooden construction. To my surprise, I saw a group of firemen sitting in there one day. Were they to accompany us to the other side, or were they there as a fire precaution in the camp? On reflection, perhaps they had just made a trip from Ipswich for a 'char and wad'! (tea and cake).

Our main task was to waterproof the tanks which were lined up in a nearby field. The Fireflies were hidden away from the rest of the tanks, concealed in a small copse.

I made the acquaintance of Bostik and balloon fabric. The fabric was for sticking round gun mantlets and other parts which moved – periscopes for instance. Storage bins were sealed and all the tanks carried boxes which had held ammunition at one time or another. Personal possessions were in these boxes and so they were sealed too, as were tins of cigarettes. Metal chutes were fitted round hatches and exhausts, and the turret ring was sealed. The underside of the vehicles was sealed too, and I well remember Hoppy seizing the foot of Lieutenant Hurley, the Troop Leader, who was working with him underneath the tank. "Seen this, Sir?" said Hoppy, and twisted the foot, drawing a cry of pain from the lieutenant as he could not roll over in the confined space under the tank. We all, including the tortured one, burst into laughter.

I walked up one clay with Ernie to the 'Firefly' copse. The long 17-pounder guns had been camouflaged by the expedient of painting, from halfway along the barrel to the muzzle, a pattern of shading from green on top of the barrel to white underneath. From a distance, then, the guns would look like 75mm weapons. This type of camouflage was credited to Rex Whistler, artist and officer in the Guards Armoured Division.

As we walked back to the Cromwell park, someone, who for some reason had loaded a two-inch mortar which all the tanks carried in the turret, fired the thing. I heard the mortar bomb whistling through the air and flung myself on the ground. Ernie, who hadn't moved, roared with laughter and related to the others how 'bomb happy' I was.

I had found a skylark's nest in the ivy which covered the ground in the 'Firefly' copse, but when I searched for it again, it had been destroyed by an uncaring boot. It was like a symbol of the suffering war brought to innocents; I told myself.

No leave was allowed from the area, but the camp was not yet sealed, and we could go into Ipswich. I saw the film *The Drum* there, starring Roger Livesey, Valerie Hobson, Sabu and Raymond Massey (as the villainous contender for the throne of the little state on the North-West Frontier). There were pipes and drums and lots of action – real good British hokum. After this, I scrounged a lift back to camp in one of our trucks, riding in the cab. As we motored along, we saw a figure lying in the road. Someone else was after a lift. The driver revved the engine and the truck roared forward as the inert figure sprang to his feet and shot over the hedge.

Some stalwarts did go on leave, however unofficially. We woke one Monday morning to the sound of words of command being shouted. Looking to another part of the camp. we saw the RHA in full marching order doing foot-drill. As one gunner, they had all agreed to go home for the weekend. This was their punishment.

At this time, there was a discussion in Parliament about punishment in the Forces, and the troops had caught some of the feeling of the futility of some of the punishment imposed. Therefore, when Bill Williams was on 'Jankers' and was drilled in his kit by the provost sergeant, a band of 'A' Squadron gathered round to watch and pass comments, loudly, on the proceedings. The performance was not repeated, but I was told to guard Bill and remember sitting with him in a bell tent in the field where the tanks were being waterproofed.

From the outset of our stay in Orwell Park, I had decided to sleep out under the stars. I didn't fancy the cramped quarters of a bell tent and the weather was fine. I put my gas-cape over the blankets and crept into bed, snug in the warm spring weather. There was a thunderstorm one night and Ernie rushed out of the tent to see if I wanted to come in with the others. It was kind of him, but with my gas-cape cover I was warm and dry.

My 19th birthday came. My mother had sent me a parcel which contained a fruit cake, home-made sweets and other goodies. I should like to be able to say that I was generous and shared the treat with my comrades, but I fear that I ate the lot myself and was ill in consequence. "Just like a greedy schoolboy," said Hugh.

In the Hall belonging to the Park, we saw the film *In Which We Serve*, with Noel Coward, Richard Attenborough, John Mills, Bernard Miles and other luminaries of the British silver screen. Many stood at the back to see what I still believe to be an excellent film, despite the cut-glass accents of some of the cast. All was viewed in silence until the Dunkirk episode, when the destroyer docked, carrying a Battalion of Coldstream Guards picked up from the beaches. The camera panned along the faces of the troops as they were drawn up on the quay-side. Many were asleep on their feet as the Regimental March *Milanollo* played softly in the background.

The RSM, rifle at the slope, marched up to the CO and gave a cracking salute. Given permission to march off, he gave the words of command, "P'rade!" and every head jerked up, "Shun!" A crash of boots on the quayside and a roar of laughter from the audience as the Battalion marched away to the strains of *Milanollo* forte! More laughter from the audience. I still find this episode in the film a moving moment and felt then that the lads had spoiled it for me. But I was young, and they had seen men coming out of action. Yet my father had told me that he had seen the Guards coming out of the trenches, covered in chalk from head to foot. As the first Guardsman reached the pavé road, he marked time and the other Guardsmen, as they fell in, picked up the step before they marched off. I think David Lean captured something of the spirit of the thing in his film, and I got a frisson of pride, despite the laughter.

On guard at the tank park, I was engaged in conversation by one of the local inhabitants. I understood not one word of what he was saying. I contributed nothing to the conversation but non-committal grunts and smiles. It might have been Swahili as far as I was concerned, and not the English tongue at all.

I recall marching down from the tank park after a day of waterproofing and seeing the lush green elm trees as we marched along. I resolved to imprint that scene on my mind as a picture of the English countryside, and it has remained with me to this day.

A day came when we had to draw clean underclothes, "In case you're wounded," somebody said. I got into minor trouble for not seeing the notice about drawing extra rations, but I was not alone, for Alf Grey had also missed the extra ration parade, so we each got our share in a sandbag. The next day saw us moving out of the camp. The trucks were drawn up outside the camp, along the road. I staggered along the line of trucks, with bedroll, kit and my sandbag of goodies. Somebody I didn't know gave me a hand with all my stuff, which I thought very kind. After all, he was much older than I and I was touched that he should help a younger soldier. But this was the CLY.

Alf found, and my kit stowed on board, we waited for the 'off'. There was a third member of the party, a Welsh lad I didn't know. He was to ride in the cab with Alf. The afternoon found us creeping along the road into Felixstowe. As we waited to get onto the 'hard', preparatory to boarding,

I looked at some infantrymen who were kicking a football around. They were fully kitted up with rifles slung and I thought how professional they looked, hung about with all kinds of stuff, and helmets covered with 'scrim' camouflage netting.

There was the 'hard' and our Landing Ship, Tank (LST), bow doors open and ramp down waiting to receive us all. We reversed on board and were taken 'topsides'. It was an American ship, so I suppose the lift which took us up was an 'elevator'. We then drove to our allotted space on the deck. Once the truck had been secured to the deck by chains and turnbuckles, we leaned over the rail at the bows and watched as the tanks were loaded onto the lower deck. A sailor asked me if the tanks had been in action. I could see what he meant. As they came on board, we could see where mud-guards had been scraped and bent on various exercises. Brackets had been welded onto turrets and sides according to the wishes of the crew, and these now carried bed-rolls. Altogether, they looked a purposeful lot! I had to say that, though the tanks had seen no action as yet, the men had seen much.

Another sailor made me move away from the bows, for there were wire cables holding the ship against the 'hard'. "Move away from there, soldier," he said, "If one of them wires breaks, you'll have your legs cut off!" I moved!

The ship loaded, we moved out into the river to await the order to go. History tells us that Eisenhower delayed starting the invasion and certainly we spent one night aboard in the river. In the morning, when we woke, I saw that the Blue Peter was at the masthead. We had a final visit from a launch crewed by WRNS, who brought large sacks which were hoisted on board. We slipped our moorings and crept down river.

There were many craft moored beside the river bank and all the crews were lining the decks. As we passed each one, a Bos'n's whistle rang out in salute. We too were standing to attention, facing outward from our deck. We passed one small vessel which was deserted and silent. "Wot! No whistle!" said someone, and a snort of laughter came from the others, breaking the silence. "Take that man's name, sergeant!" said an official voice.

One barrack-like building stood on the hillside away from the river on the Shotley shore. Perhaps part of the naval establishment, 'H.M.S. *Ganges*'. A balcony ran the length of the building and on it stood a WRN, feet astride, slowly waving her arm from side to side in farewell. It struck me then that we were really off on a perilous venture and some of us would not be seeing these shores of home again.

Eventually, we felt our ship lift to the swell of the waves and knew that we were nearing the sea. We looked at our life-jackets (tubes of balloon fabric, inflated by blowing into them and tied on by tapes). We had been given sea-sickness pills and also vomit-bags, items which seemed to cancel each other out. If you needed one, would you need the other?

Though the LST was American, we did not enjoy the breakfast fare we had eaten at Beaminster. The cooking for the troops was done by our army lads. I am sure the crew had their own cooks and kitchen. Galley, of course!

One unexpected dish was potatoes cooked in their skins. After I had inspected them with suspicion, I was surprised at how tasty they were.

The touch of luxury was provided by our allies. A tap, dispensing hot coffee all day, was fitted beside the galley door. Nearby were two large bins. One contained tins of evaporated milk, already punctured, and the other was full of sugar. We helped ourselves!

There was plenty to see. Other ships sailed ahead and behind us. Many now had small barrage balloons hovering over the stern as a protection from low-flying aircraft. Destroyers hurried about and, because there was now a heavy swell, smaller craft were making a rough passage.

In front of our truck was a three-tonner loaded with Bailey-bridge sections. When we were in the river all was well, but now the ship had begun to roll, the sections, which had not been lashed to the sides of the truck, began to move and thrash from side to side of the truck. It looked as if the sides would be bashed out by the punishment they were getting. The driver and his companion spent some time stalking the sections and had several narrow escapes from injury before the sections were secured to the side of the truck. It was a bit like roping a wild steer.

Soon we saw, out at sea, three constructions on spindly legs, like H.G. Wells' 'Martians'. They were platforms for anti-aircraft guns; they were also forts protecting the estuary. Looking at the constructions, I knew that I would not like to spend the war stationed on one of those forts.

So, night began to fall and, with it, instructions through the loud-hailer. "Now hear this! Now hear this! No smoking top-sides after dusk! It's for your own good. I can swim!" We turned in, sleeping on the boxes of ammunition in the back of the three-tonner.

I was wakened by Alf, who wanted me to see The Needles as we sailed past them in the early dawn. The day passed in sleeping and chat and in exploration of the ship. We looked in lockers and found them full of steel helmets. Did the American sailors not have their own helmets, or did they just grab one from the locker and put it on? Other lockers contained sleeping bags of excellent quality material. We were forbidden to take these, but some found their way on shore, and I inherited one from a companion who brought two away with him.

Over the ship's loud hailer system, we heard of the landings in France and were given a printed message from Montgomery, some French money and a phrase book on France and the language. The message from Montgomery contained the following:

'He either fears his fate too much,
Or his deserts are small
Who dares not put it to the touch
To win or to lose all.'

There was also a wish for 'Good hunting on the mainland of Europe!'

Chapter 5

A Landing at Sunset

There was a fire on the surface of the sea ahead of us and after a time we passed the blaze but could see the flames for hours afterwards flickering in the twilight.

Ahead of us, then, land. France! The evening of D-Day.

There were planes about after darkness fell, and tracer shells began to climb into the sky. Our sailor gunners had taken up their posts and now swung to and fro in the gun harnesses, steel-helmeted and wearing life jackets. "A pity you can't have a go!" I said to one gunner near me. "Uh, uh!" he replied unenthusiastically. Perhaps he was thinking about the cleaning he would have to do if he had the misfortune to be ordered to open fire himself.

So, the evening of D-Day drew to a close and night came on, with more wondrous pyrotechnics from the invasion fleet. After a night spent on top of the ammunition boxes once more, dawn saw us up and about again. This time, after ablutions and breakfast, all eyes were turned to the shore, where beach parties were working clearing mines, and German guns from inland put down shells. I believe that the balloons helped the German gunners to range on the beachhead, so after a time they were cut adrift. Same LSTs were nearer the beach than we were, and as the tide went out, they sat on the sand, giving their vehicles a dry landing, we thought.

In the afternoon, a battleship went into action to the west of us. The concussion of the guns could be felt long before the sound of firing carried to us. The *Warspite* (was it?), or the *Rodney*, made an impressive sight as, half hidden in the smoke, she went into action.

We had to wait all day to get ashore. The sun was low in the west when we drove onto the lift and descended into the bowels of the ship and onto the Landing Craft, Tank (LCT) which would take us to the beach.

There was a strong current running in the Channel, and we had watched from 'topsides' as the LCT had juggled first one way and then the other to

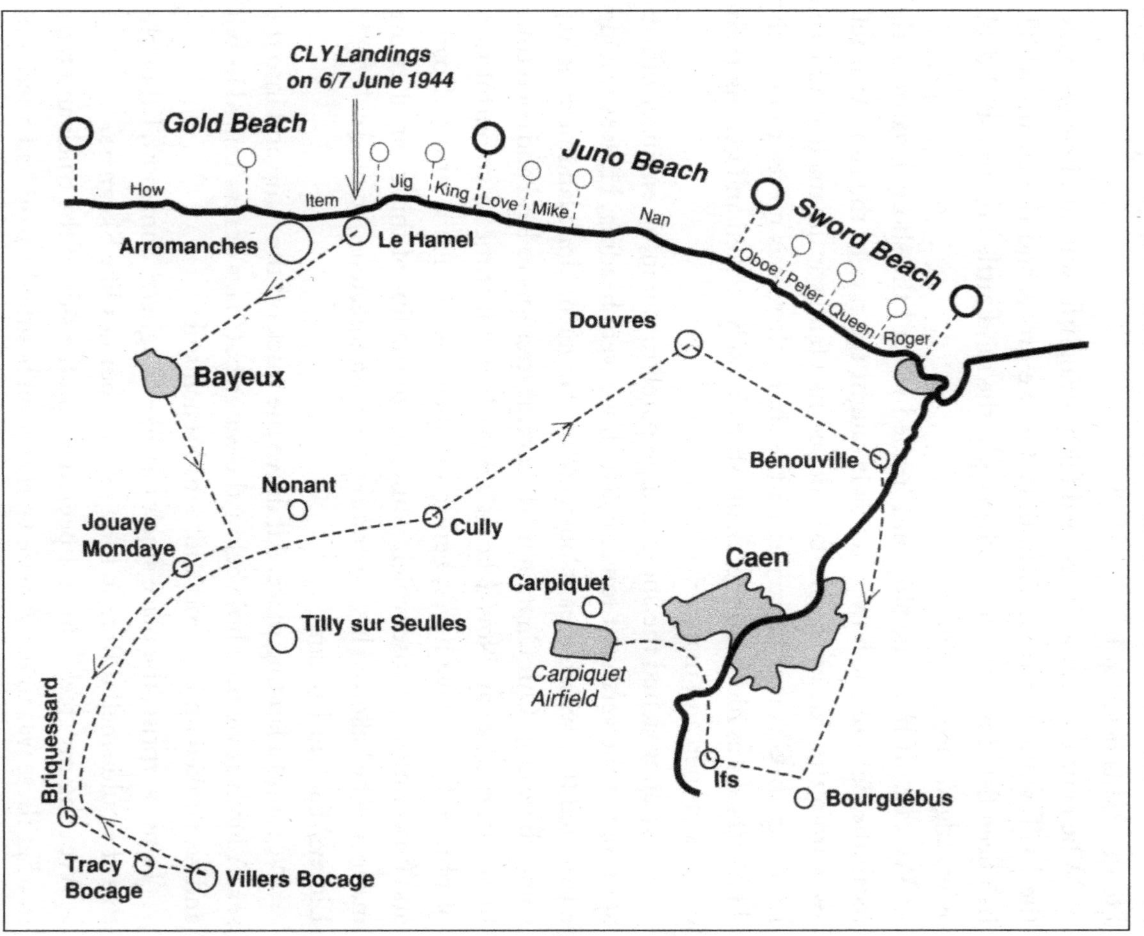

Map 1: The 4th CLY's movements from 7th June to 29th July 1944.

load her precious cargo of tanks. The ramp of the LCT had to be aligned with the bow-ramp of the ship and this took some time. "Call this a Navy?" said one of our lads to an American sailor who was watching the proceedings. He shook his head sadly.

When aur turn came, it seemed fairly straightforward and we got onto the LCT without too much trouble. On we drove, and the chains which had been fitted on the tyres to help grip the sand rattled on the steel deck as we edged into position.

We cast off from the ship and headed toward the shore. I particularly recall the sight of the bow-wave as it caught the rays of the sun. As it fell away from the side of the craft, it looked like fantastically made gold lace. Looking up-Channel as we neared the shore, there was no sea to be seen. The surface was hidden under many ships, closely packed and getting their cargoes of men and material ashore.

As we approached the shore and prepared to run in, an engineer officer appeared at the very spot towards which we were heading. He was waving a large red flag, which meant 'obstacle' or 'danger' or 'don't land here' or 'try somewhere else'. Our Captain made several attempts to land and each time he was turned away. Now I knew sailors had sometimes a colourful turn of phrase, but I have never, before or since, heard such a string of oaths and obscenities as those which poured from the lips of this cigar-chewing mariner as he bellowed his frustration. He even threatened to take us "****** Limeys" back in England!

We found a landing place. Alf drove the truck off the ramp and into the sea. A lurch as we hit a hole below the water, but 'bags of revs' pulled us out and we clinked up the sand and onto French soil.

To my surprise, the place smelt just like Skegness! Somehow, I thought that it would smell different, foreign even, but not like Skegness.

Wearing my steel helmet, I peered round the side of the truck and took in what there was to see. A wired-off section beside the road had a series of triangular yellow signs which said 'MINEN!'

A large group of German prisoners was being herded along, presumably to be taken back to England. There was a large grey concrete bunker, with grey, white and red objects along one wall. As we drew nearer, these objects resolved themselves into German dead, lying in all attitudes in the sand.

The driver of the truck behind saw that I was wearing my steel helmet, which was like a paratrooper's except that it had only one chin-strap. "Take that helmet off," he shouted, "you look like a Jerry!" (or even "It looks like a jerry"). I took off the helmet and put on my beret. Helmets, obviously, were not *de rigeur* in the CLY.

Now we turned off the beach road and drove inland. A vignette of a 17-pounder gun team getting the gun into position behind a wall, in which they had knocked a hole. One of the crew draped over the end of the barrel as a counterbalance and the rest swinging the trail round to bring the gun to face the possible approach of the enemy. Once again, in the fading light, I was struck by the appearance of the soldiers, as if they had been on the ground and preparing for battle for years.

We turned into a field and drew up, our journeyings over for the day. What a remarkable feat of planning to get us onto the ship, disembarked and get us to the right field in France without any mistake. I took it all for granted, then, content to be part of the British Expeditionary Force, as we were initially known. An honourable title, I thought. Shades of 1914 and 1939!

We found that we were near a battery of artillery. Perhaps RHA, they were certainly tracked vehicles. A voice, loud-speaker assisted, surely, bellowed things like "Angles of sight" and other mysterious jargon known only to gunners, and the guns hammered away at a target. It was not going to be a quiet night if this kept up. We had a brew and prepared for bed. I elected to sleep in the back of the truck again; Alf and the Welsh lad decided on the open air.

Waking in the night, I heard the familiar unsynchronised drone of a Heinkel and then the explosion of the dozens of anti-personnel bombs it dropped. Quickly, I rolled off the ammunition boxes into a gap in the middle of the load and spent the rest of the night sleeping on the floor of the truck. The others laughed when I told them that I thought I would be safer there.

Breakfast was made from 'Compo' rations, a form of diet long known to my two companions. Making tea successfully was the main difficulty. Each of us had our own method. The brew came in an almost powder form, with tea and milk powder mixed together. If they were mixed first with cold water, I found, and then boiling water added, a fairly palatable brew was the result. Carelessness could mean that cither tea or milk floated to the top of the mug.

The rations were packed in a box and were designed to feed 'Eight men for one day'. Sweets and chocolate bars were carefully shared among us. At first, we had biscuits to eat, and these came in the pack. I found that biscuits and a bar of chocolate filled a hole if one was not able to have a proper meal. Biscuits pounded up and mixed with hot water made a hot filler to start the day. People called this meal 'burgoo' (dictionary gives: Naut. 'porridge', so it is obviously a Navy term). The bacon came out of the tin in a rather greasy form and there were soya-link sausages and the famous tins of 'M and V' (meat and vegetable stew).

Cooking facilities improved as tins became available. An empty biscuit tin made a useful kettle if a hole was knocked in one corner for pouring, and a wire handle fitted. Stoves were made out of 'flimsy' petrol tins. A square hole was cut in the end of the tin, but only on three sides, the fourth being left attached so that a flap was formed to regulate the flow of air. The tin was laid on its side and a hole cut out of the top. This is where the pot or kettle was placed. A few holes driven in the other sides with a pick, a spadeful of earth placed in the 'stove', a dash of petrol, a match and, *voila*, cooking could proceed on the blazing fire. Naturally, these culinary aids soon became blackened by fire and they were carried, dangling from bits of wire on the back of vehicles.

I wrench myself away from these culinary arrangements and recount my first few days in Normandy.

One of our people came across two German soldiers who wanted to be made prisoners, and brought them into our vehicle lines, so I hoped that they would be given a hot drink and a cigarette to show them we were a civilised crowd.

Our Welsh friend disappeared and came back after some time, declaring that he had found female company. I looked round at the fields and trees, which was all I could see. Had he hitched into Bayeux? Had he knocked at the door of the nearest farmhouse and found 'accommodation' there? He gave the impression that this was the only reason he had come to France! Perhaps, I thought, it was an idle boast after all.

We moved to another location, just outside a village named Nonant, and parked on what in England would be called a bridle path, the truck tucked in on the verge beside a tall hedge.

By this time, I had chummed up with Mike Geer ("Hello, Mike. Still in bottom?") and we strolled out together sometimes. We encountered the locals for the first time in the shape of two farm labourers. I readied myself to greet them with '*Bon jour*' but they got in first with '*ça va*?' of which I had never heard. I compromised with a feeble "Good morning!"

Mike and I walked down the lane, intending to make a short circular tour. As we walked along, we saw a rifle stuck in the high grass verge and looking through the hedge, we saw a grave. The hedge had been broken down and the rifle, upright and with no bolt, had been a marker. We stood at the grave-side in silence. There was a wooden cross and, over the grave mound, webbing equipment arranged as if on a body. Flowers had been placed in an empty food tin. A private of the Norfolk Regiment lay there. I wondered if, later on, the graves would be tended with as much care when casualties became more commonplace, as they were bound to do.

We walked on and saw a German helmet in a hedge bottom. It was filled with clips of ammunition and small egg grenades. I dearly wanted a German helmet to hang in our hall at home. Our Vicar had one hanging in his hall at the Vicarage, from World War 1 of course, and I remembered looking at this with envy. I tied some German telephone wire round the chin strap of the helmet, looking carefully for booby traps, stood some way off and pulled the helmet out of the hedge and onto the road. All the contents spilled out, and I was left with 'my' helmet. The rest of the stuff we left in the hedge bottom.

Looking at our antics were two French women, mother and daughter perhaps. They had come into the field to milk a cow which was there. We walked over to them and, in stumbling French, began to talk. The young woman was named Marie – no surprise. I wanted to give her a bar of chocolate. "She won't take it the wrong way?" asked Mike. "No." The bar was received with thanks by Marie, who had a scar, the result of some accident, on her face.

My next 'French encounter' was with a farmer, who conversed animatedly when I spoke a few words of French to him. He was as incomprehensible as the Norfolk farm labourer! He was railing against the depredations of "The Boche", who had stolen his prize bull. At least that is what I think they had stolen, by the way he clutched part of his anatomy.

A Focke-Wulf fighter came hedge-hopping one day. I was sitting on the tail-board of the truck and rolled sideways and off onto the ground. As I did so, my clasp knife, which was on a belt round my waist, clattered on the metal of the truck. Taff Evans (not our female-hunting friend) was given the fright of his life as he thought that it was bullets hitting the vehicle.

If that was an amusing episode, another was much more solemn. We saw one of our tanks coming along the track. Stan Dovey was standing on the back, outside the turret, directing the driver through his microphone. The tank came to a halt in front of us. Stan jumped down from the back of the tank and the driver got out.

The crew of this tank had sustained casualties, said Stan, and it was our job to clean up the inside of the tank. We climbed aboard and looked inside. There was nothing to do but conquer one's feelings and set to work. We used tin lids as scrapers and petrol-soaked cotton-waste to mop up. Even the turret floor had to be lifted to clean up the floor of the tank hull. I smoked my first cigarette and noticed the raw smell of tobacco smoke when it was mixed with petrol fumes. We put our blood-soaked cotton waste in a hole we had dug for the purpose, together with the tin lids. A young French couple came by, and the youth picked up one of the tin lids, dropping it hastily when he discovered how it had been used.

The trucks moved to another location. More open country here, where the field we were in sloped down to a meandering, slow-flowing river. By this time, I had deserted the ammunition boxes and was sleeping outside under a 'bivvy'. Wakened one night by an unusual noise, I listened. A very noisy motor-cycle seemed to be getting nearer and nearer. The noise stopped and a moment later there was a tremendous explosion which rocked the ground. I wondered, in a half-asleep way, what the explanation could be and drifted off to sleep again.

When we woke in the morning, we discovered an enormous crater in the field next to the one we were in, and a small barn had been tipped back, in its entirety, from the crater's edge. We had heard our first V1!

In the field where we were, there was another large hole, caused, we thought by a naval shell. One of the lads decided that he would fire the Bren gun he had been cleaning into this hole. He had not taken account of someone else who was standing on the other side of the crater. I saw a couple of tracer rounds zip past him and there were various comments on the carelessness of some people as he skipped nimbly out of the way.

On this day, 13th June, a drama had been enacted at Villers Bocage which was to decimate 4th CLY and lead eventually to our amalgamation with our parent 3rd CL Y.

It was late in the afternoon when we heard the news that HQ, 'A' Squadron, which was my squadron, a Rifle Brigade Company and artillery spotters among others, had been trapped and defeated at Villers. We had no news of casualties of course, so did not know the extent of killed, wounded and prisoners. Almost coincidentally with the arrival of the news, Hugh Stanton, Ernie Ridall, Briggs and another member of 'A' Squadron drove into the field in a Cromwell. They had left the rest of the tanks at an earlier stage that day for some reason. Hugh kept saying how lucky they were and Briggs and Ernie told me about some of the action they had seen since they had landed on D-Day+ 1.

Hugh had a brother with 'A' Squadron, so I felt for him as he must have been wondering what had happened to the brother.

There was a sense in which I took the news of Villers philosophically enough. My yardstick seemed to be First World War casualties, on which I had been brought up, so as I walked beside the quiet river, I thought of the casualties in my father's battalion on the Somme, where, of 27 officers and 600 ORs, only 90 men were left after the 1st July 1916. With my lack of experience and the naïveté of youth, I thought that this was the inevitable price of war. Casualties there were and would have to be accepted. It was with great relief that we later heard that the majority of CLY were prisoners. An added incentive to push on and finish the war!

Rebuilding 'A' and 'HQ' Squadrons began. 'A' was re-formed on a two-Troop basis at first, and when the new tanks arrived, I achieved my ambition and became a member of a crew.

I was gunner on the tank of the Troop Leader, John Philip-Smith MC. The operator was Eric Shone, like me, a reinforcement from 9th Armoured. The driver was little Taff Evans, whom I'd scared with my clasp knife when the Focke-Wulf hedge-hopped. Taff was a desert veteran, as was the commander.

All the tanks of our Troop were tucked into the overgrown hedge on the east side of the field. Over the hedge was a wide track we had driven down to get into the field, and on the other sides of the field and beyond were the other members of the regiment with their tanks. An addition to our force was an anti-aircraft tank carrying Oerlikon cannon. Cliff Pace was a member of the AA crew. They had only just come ashore and were shocked to find half the regiment gone. We had a new RSM seconded from the Rifle Brigade and Sergeant Stan Dovey got promotion to be our squadron sergeant-major.

Across the track, near the field gate where our tank stood, was a small barn. The upper room of the barn served, suitably enough, as a Chapel, and Holy Communion was celebrated there on at least one occasion. There must have been a monastery near at hand, for a deep-toned bell sometimes tolled, though the buildings themselves were not visible through the trees.

The crew next to ours, of which 'Darby' Darbyshire was a member, had 'found' a very large tarpaulin in a railway sidings. Stout pieces of wood had also come to light, and a cabin-like structure was built with these materials at the side of their tank. Around this 'cabin' sported 'Wilfred', a large white rabbit. Alas, someone from another crew threw a stick at the poor creature and killed him. (Had he invaded with us?). Dismay among the crew! I don't know whether they got over their grief and skinned and ate him, but I doubt it.

One day the fitter's truck came round to each tank and deposited a large wooden crate beside each vehicle. "Water-proofing kit. We're going home," the Fitters said when we asked, "What's in the boxes?" Not so. Each box contained a new commanders' batch, with periscopes mounted all the way round for better vision.

The MO, Captain MacLean, M.C. was just across the track from us and sometimes the sound of his bagpipes could be heard. I thoroughly enjoyed this music, but I remember a Frenchwoman walking past as he was playing and she smiled at me as if we were sharing a joke about the habits of these mad foreigners.

Camembert cheese, Calvados and rich Normandy butter made their appearance.

Eric Shone was an inventive cook, producing fish-cakes out of sardines and the ubiquitous biscuits pounded and mixed together. I was less successful in my preparation of breakfast. Because of my usual inability to find things that were under my nose, we were reduced to M and V for breakfast one day. Mr. Philip-Smith was a bit disgusted and took me to the food locker at the side of the tank, where he instantly pointed out the tinned bacon which I had been unable to find.

Regimental Headquarters was in the next field, so duties which we had to perform included that of telephone orderly on the exchange. This duty came my way with dire results. First of all, I woke up late and had to brave the wrath of the RSM. Then, when the mechanics of the exchange were explained to me, I could not grasp how the thing worked. Then there was understanding what the people at the other end of the line were saying. I did not realise that all the units in the brigade were on the exchange. There was a message for all, about a film show. I listened horrified, as all the other units acknowledged that they had understood the message, for I had not. Sighing heavily, the speaker repeated the whole message again for me.

A caller wanted to speak to Lieutenant X in the officer's mess, so I got through and told him that 'a bloke' wanted to speak to him. A listening NCO was shocked, "You should say 'a gentleman'," he said, "not (scornfully) 'a bloke'."

Repercussions from my late arrival on duty. I was on a charge! My escort was another member of the Troop who had been the last man on guard and who would have woken me up had I put in an early call with the guard commander. He told me that he had gone to sleep again after he had been called for his turn on duty. This could be serious and he asked me to help him out if I could. This was easy, all I had to do was tell the truth and say that I had not put in an early call. When I was paraded at the tail of the 15-cwt truck and I told the squadron leader what had happened, saying that I had not put in an early call "For I was sure I would wake when the guard woke the operator", he looked at me in disbelief. "You must be mad!" he said. "Three extra telephone duties!" This was punishment indeed!

"Thanks, Fish," said the Sleeping Guard, for all the world as if I had fibbed to save him. I had to explain that my excuse was a genuine one.

Ironically, the next morning I was again not woken up, though I had conscientiously put in for an early call. Another failed guard? I rushed to get dressed and down to the exchange before my second misdemeanour could come to light. Trotting up the hedge to the gap where the exchange was situated, I ran into our new Squadron Leader, Major I.B. 'Ibby' Aird.

"Good morning," he said, so I said, "Good morning, Sir." Then he said, "I think you're supposed to salute me. Should we try that again?" So, we tried it again and I threw up my best salute for such a courteous gentleman.

I never did get the hang of that telephone exchange.

One cloudy afternoon, the sound of an aircraft could be heard. I stood outside the 'bivvy' and watched as a Focke-Wulf fighter dodged in and out of the clouds. Suddenly, a Bofors anti-aircraft gun opened up and shot off a wing with the first shell of a clip of five. In a second, the aircraft plunged behind some trees.

Later on in the day, Mike Geer and I decided that we would see where the plane had come down. We found the spot not far away. There was a field with a taped-off area in the middle. There was a quite small hole with a glimpse of shining metal at the bottom of it, and tinkling, crackling noises could be heard, presumably as the metal cooled. We could hardly believe that this was all there was to see and decided that the rest of the wreckage had been cleared away.

Tich Brown continued to live up to his reputation as a comic. A member of the 'Tarpaulin' tank crew was clearing up after a meal and was throwing empty food tins over the hedge. Along came Tich and began to help, but he threw over not only used tins, but cooking pots and other kitchen ware! Much to the annoyance of 'cook' and the glee of Tich.

The people who came to build up the strength of the regiment came from the supply echelons, like me. I think that some new reinforcements came too, maybe from other armoured regiments, or even straight from England. One of the chaps who came along to join us was a young man who brought with him a repertoire of stories and a long poem, all in rhyming couplets, about a seduction. He worked through the sordid tale, using the letters of the alphabet, beginning with A and ending with Zest 'as they start again!'

Another quieter older man was an 'old' CLY member who entertained us with accounts of his travels in Germany before the war, Youth Hostelling. All was well until the late 1930's, when any British Hostellers risked having the door of the Hostel slammed in their faces, and 'Keinplatz' was the order of the day.

Not all our time was spent yarning, going for walks and mounting guard. We carried out an exercise with Canadian troops in which a method of dealing with anti-tank guns was tried out. The Canadian infantry spotted the gun, fired a Very pistol in the direction in which it lay, and the tank, taking direction from this indicator, then spotted and dealt with the gun. That was the idea. I don't know whether this method was adopted, but it seemed rather desperate.

Mr. Philip-Smith had given me permission to sit outside on the turret to see how the operation was carried out. The squadron leader jumped on the back of the tank and said to me, "What would you do if I said, 'Traverse left'?" "It's alright," said my commander, "I've told him he could stay outside to watch." "Get inside!" said the squadron leader. So, I did. All was not lost, however. "I'll have him off!" said our driver, Taff Evans, to me, not over the intercom but speaking over his shoulder from the driving compartment. He then sought out the lowest apple tree he could find and drove the tank under it. I watched with interest as the boughs scraped along the back of the tank and the squadron leader had to jump for it! Honours even!

The time came for our departure, and we rose while it was still dark. When we had packed up, Eric thought a brew would be a good idea. He made the necessary preparations, intending to put the 'kettle' on the stove and mask the flames. He applied a match and flames shot up into the air. Very annoyed shouting came from across the field: "Put that fire out!", but we were observed and, despite prompt dousing of the flames, in a moment or two enemy shells began to thunder nearby. We hopped into the tank very quickly and waited until the fuss had died down.

Then we were on the move. Daylight found us in a more open field. There was a small copse to the north but open country lay to the south. An artillery battery of 25-pounders had occupied the field before us and gun-pits had been dug for them. There was a Bofors anti-aircraft gun in one corner of the field and while we were there, with startling suddenness, a dog-fight erupted overhead. Two Spitfires and a Messerschmitt 109 chased each other in tighter and tighter circles, trying to get a shot in. I was surprised at the appearance of all the aircraft – they looked more like huge models than real planes. Then, for some unfathomable reason, at any rate to me, the Bofors crew opened up. Shells began to burst in the middle of the combatants. The gunners stood a two-to-one chance of hitting a 'Spit' and it seemed a very strange thing to do, to fire at the aircraft. The German machine broke off the fight and fled south, pursued by the Spitfires, and all three fighters disappeared as quickly as they had come.

I had to hand in my Smith and Wesson and got a Sten gun in place of it. To my mind a poor bargain, but all the gunners were being so equipped. At least some thought had been given to safety, and a hole had been drilled into the side of the gun. The cocking handle had been extended slightly, and the end could now be pushed into the hole, held there by the spring. Now there was no danger of the gun firing if it was dropped with a magazine in place.

I saw one accident caused by a Sten gun, and this happened when we had attended Church parade. A three-tonner was our transport, and we all piled in after the service. A huge column of smoke shot up some distance away and an aircraft flew towards us, fast and low. Everyone jumped out of the truck and felt rather foolish when the aircraft, as it roared past us, was seen to be a Spitfire. The column of smoke was nothing to do with the plane. To our surprise, though, one of our number was reeling about clutching his head. Blood could be seen coming from his scalp! Someone, in his eagerness to vacate the truck, had hurled out his Sten gun. Our 'wounded' comrade had been hit on the head by the hurtling weapon.

I was under the 'bivvy' one evening when Mike Geer called out, "Hey, Fish, come and look at this lot!" I scrambled out and gazed skyward. Flying overhead were bombers making for an enemy target. There were about 250 bombers, four-engined Lancasters and Halifaxes, flying over en route to bomb Villers Bocage, of unhappy memory. Soon they turned westward and the thunder of bombs could be heard. There seemed to be an extraordinary amount of 'flak' put up and shells could be seen bursting among the aircraft. I thought of these guns being directed at us in future when the time came to do battle once more, but I suppose that not all of it was 88mm fire. Dust and smoke rose in the air and then, with a tremendous thump, an aircraft blew up. A whole wing fell earthward in a series of swoops, like an autumn leaf falling. Then the other aircraft flew home, leaving the dust and smoke to rise as a funeral pyre for aircrew and town.

I wanted to try out my new Sten gun, so Mike and I walked along looking for a suitable spot to fire off a few rounds. We came to a small pond and that seemed to be a good spot. I could shoot into the pond, and the water and mud would smother the bullets. I saw some other tank people coming toward us, including Jimmy Nunn, who had been in my Troop at Bovington. He had heard about the Villers affair and was very sympathetic. When he and his companions had gone, I loosed off a few rounds. Next to arrive on the scene were three American soldiers. They had not seen a Sten gun before and were very interested. I let them have a go and then changed to 'automatic', rattling off several shots. They were quite impressed by this and asked if we had any spare 9mm ammunition for a Luger which they produced for our inspection. I emptied my magazine and gave the remaining rounds to them, then suggested they came back to our field where I could get some more ammunition. We bounced back 'home' in the Jeep, where I found some more rounds for their pistol. They appeared to be quite impressed by the Cromwells!

One evening there was a glorious sunset. Out of the east flew an aircraft, American I think it was. He was ablaze, smoke and flames trailing in the sky behind him, a golden red cloud in the rays of the dying sun. Flying beside the stricken plane was another, his companion. They flew west, out of sight behind the trees. Was the pilot of the blazing plane wounded? Why did he not bale out? I wondered what his fate would be.

A note of normal army life was introduced by a unit not far away sounding bugle calls. I wondered how far away the unit was and if the calls carried to the Germans.

We had already tested the 75mm main armament guns. A drive to a secluded valley and the guns and telescopes were aligned. A white fencepost was the target I had to shoot at. I applied a foot to the trigger. Misfire! We ejected the round, but the shell-case parted company from the shell, and cordite spilled out into the breech of the gun.

The shell was left in place and the armourers were called. They returned with a cut-down charge, which we loaded and fired, fortunately on target. Later, the time came to test the Besas. We were given a compass bearing and lined up the guns. We were all given the same elevation on the wheel and got ready to fire off a belt of ammunition. In preparation for this affair, I had tried to move a nut which operated a device to hold the gun in place. I had lost the spanner down the gun mantlet; there was no time to retrieve it before we had to fire. I shoved the gun up against the mounting with one hand and pulled the trigger with the other, hoping that no bullets were falling short.

Chapter 6

Tracks in the Wheat – Caen

Now the time came to move to another location to prepare for the attack across the Orne.

The scene was set on the edge of a cornfield where the regiment was drawn up in lines. A road ran across the rear of the field, and beyond that an airstrip where 'Typhoons' roared away on take off amid a tremendous cloud of dust in the dry weather.

As evening drew on, this cloud of dust, with the sun behind it, became a golden, glowing backdrop for an endless procession of vehicles moving along. They were all in black silhouette and the effect was quite striking. Most odd-looking were the half-tracks and motor-cycles, which had front wheels seemingly detached from the body of the vehicles.

I was on guard duty, the last relief of the night. Sunshine and peace, for no sound of gunfire disturbed the air. I could see many tanks and trucks around our lines, a mighty army of men sleeping. My duty was to wake the operators, but where to begin? Was I guarding the whole regiment or just my squadron? No-one had said. I woke our own squadron people and left it at that. No-one complained, so I supposed it was alright.

A little later on, the bombers came. We watched as the aircraft flew through a gigantic smoke and dust cloud, which drifted seaward in the light breeze. We had seen the raid on Villers, but this bombing was much more intense and went on for much longer, as many more aircraft were involved.

On, then, to begin our approach to the bridges which would take us across the Orne. There were, I believe, six Bailey bridges which would carry the Armoured Divisions over the Odon and the Orne. 7th Armoured was the last Division to cross over to the east bank of the Orne and so it was a matter of creeping forward in the columns of armour and other vehicles and waiting, creeping forward and waiting, once under the muzzles of a battery of medium artillery which was firing as rapidly as it could. Very noisy!

Looking south, now, as we crossed the rivers and turned to face the line of the advance, we could see in the distance the districts of Caen which lay on the east side of the city. Fires blazed in tall, grey factory buildings, and high-tension cables drooped almost to the ground, looking like the liquorice 'bootlaces' we used to buy as children. Such was the effect of the bombing raid we had witnessed earlier.

There seemed to be a vast plain before us, devoted to the growing of wheat. We drove forward through the wheat but, because we were the last division to come onto the scene of the action, there seemed to be a lot of hanging about for a time.

We halted and tore up handfuls of wheat to place round the tank and on the hull to disguise the shape. Later on, we moved about on the plain below Bourgebus Ridge, halting at intervals and waiting to be called forward to action. A motor-cycle was found in the wheat and Eric Shone, who had been a motor-cyclist in the Auxiliary Fire Service at home, tried to start it up. He did not succeed, but our SSM, Stan Dovey, started it and roared up and down on it for a few moments. There were slit-trenches about in the wheat and I thought that this was a hazardous business because they could not be seen and I had visions of Stan vanishing into one as he rode about.

There is nothing in my memory to distinguish the sequence of events at first in the Caen affair. One of my recollections is of a summer mist in the morning and hearing, over the wireless, communication between the tanks of one of our squadrons, (was it 'C'?), as they brought back our Infantry, on the back of the tanks, from a sticky situation? It may have been units of the Rifle Brigade which had got into trouble. Through the mist there came the sound of a Nebelwerfer firing somewhere. I had not heard one before and thought at first that it was the dying tones of a French air-raid siren. Just about on a par with the CO in the film, *The Next of Kin*, though I did not betray my ignorance by exclaiming – "My God! What's that?" It was probably during this action that, as John Cotton related, a group of German soldiers was seen under a tree, apparently enjoying a game of cards! The command to fire, he said, was given as, "Traverse left. At card school under tree, one round, fire!"

There were some knocked-out tanks – Cromwells – nearby and I went to have a look at one of them after we had eaten a meal. I wandered round the burnt-out wreck. When I got back to the crew, someone, it must have been Taff Evans, said, "Did you notice the smell?" Indeed, I did, a pungent, throat-catching reek. "Once you smell it, you never forget it!" he said, and I can recall the smell to this day.

Later on, someone came across the body of an officer from this tank and a couple of the lads assisted at his burial. "Did you see him?" I was asked. I was pleased to say I had not, for he had been run over by another tank. It was impossible to avoid these corpses in the corn, unless they had a marker of some kind – a rifle stuck in the ground, for instance.

As night came on, the question, 'Where to sleep?' arose. We chose already-dug slit-trenches; this seemed the sensible thing to do. The commander and I slept in a long trench which allowed us to sleep feet to feet. There was a frisson of the macabre in being a blanket-wrapped body in a grave-like hole in the ground.

I woke up to the sound of a tremendous racket and looked up to see tracer flying over the top of the trench in both directions. I was concerned in case an attack was being mounted and tried to wake my slumbering companion by kicking his feet. All to no avail. He was sleeping like the – er – dead! Perhaps he was dead! Surely no-one could sleep through that noise! With the thought that morning would reveal all, I drifted off to sleep again.

Morning came (sans corpse) and there were no fresh signs of battle around and one was tempted to believe that the racket during the night had been a figment of the imagination. What was not a figment was the evidence of mosquito bites which covered my face, which felt very strange and lumpy. Bill Williams was very sympathetic and gave me his mosquito-net, a relic of the Desert Days, to sleep in next night.

Our services were required at last, and so we found ourselves facing rising ground, moving against the enemy! For me, the first time, for many others, yet again, as in Africa and Italy.

I once asked my father what it would be like, "You'll be too busy to be afraid," he said. That was true, mostly. I felt uncomfortable without the others around me and so tanks was the right choice for me.

There was a sense in which I did not have to decide. To be part of a crew, under the direction of the commander, was to be carried along. There was no individual decision on my part about whether to go into that house, or round that corner, as there would have been if I had been an Infantryman. We were all together in one small unit of four or five as a crew and, though the sentiment was rarely expressed, relying on each other as members of a team.

So, when things began to explode outside the tank, and earth and stones began to rattle against the sides, I took comfort from the words of my dear old Dad, about being busy, and the closeness of my companions, Mr. Philip-Smith, Eric and Taff.

We reached ground higher up on Bourgebus Ridge. I could see knocked-out British tanks as I looked through my periscope. In front of us was an abandoned Sherman, a hole drilled neatly through the barrel of the 75mm gun. A call from someone over the air: 'Do not fire! You have a hole through the barrel of your gun!' (Did he say that? Was the message not coded?). At any rate, the reply came: 'Not me. A knocked-out baby!'

I was keeping an eye on the goings-on, looking through my periscope, when I heard behind me the clink of glasses. Then Mr. Philip-Smith's voice, "Would you like a gin and orange, Fisher?" I had never had a gin and orange in my life, but I said, "Yes please!", and so we sat in the tank and sipped gin and orange. It seemed a very CLY thing to do and I felt like an experienced soldier, drinking gin and orange in a battle.

In front and to our left was a Firefly. I saw it fire at a target, unseen to me. As I watched, figures tumbled out of the tank. Though I had not seen a tank knocked-out before, I knew instinctively what had happened. "They've got the Firefly, sir!" I shouted to the commander. He told Eric to load a round of smoke-shot to fire and cover the escape of the crew as they scuttled for cover to the rear. Though I fired this round and another in the direction of the escaping figures, my aim was not good and afterwards the commander explained, in the most polite way, where he had wanted me to place the shots.

Jack Geddes was the gunner on the Firefly which had been knocked out. The tank was hit by three shots fired by the enemy. The crew baled out, as I saw, but I did not realise that Jack was still standing on the hull of the tank, trying to guide the commander, Sergeant Lancaster, out of the turret as he had been wounded and was disoriented. My smoke shots, the only contribution I made to the Caen battle, were no help to the escaping crew at all, as they exploded too far away to give cover.

How large the cornfields were! We moved to another part of the battlefield, where more Cromwells were standing in the grain. They were all abandoned, some 'brewed up'. They appeared to be tanks of the Northants Yeomanry, and they had come under fire from 88mm guns, tanks and anti-tank guns, firing from the ridge which we could see ahead of us. Stan Dovey had a look inside some of the abandoned tanks and stood on our tank afterwards, saying, in an amazed tone, "Some of these tanks have still got their wirelesses switched on!"

We were able to wheel our Firefly 17-pounder Shermans in among the abandoned Cromwells and, under cover of these, shoot up several German tanks which we could see milling about on the ridge ahead.

One of the things to remember about firing the 17-pounder was the pressure of blast from the gun when one was inside the turret. In this instance, when the enemy was being engaged, I saw one of our reinforcements being led away, having had his ears damaged in this way. Later on, when I was working with the 17-pounder, I was always careful to keep my mouth open when firing; this minimised the pressure on the ears. Our casualty had clenched his teeth as he fired.

The gun designer 'boffins' had developed a round for the 17-pounder which was known as a 'sabot' round. The armour-piercing shell was encased in another round, which disintegrated in sections when the whole left the barrel of the gun. The armour-piercing shot then went on its way to the target, with flatter trajectory and increased muzzle velocity. The gunner's telescope had an additional set of markings or 'graticules' for the gunner to aim accurately when using the 'sabot'.

Another location and, as night fell, we took shelter in a hut which was surrounded by a high earth and brick wall. Outside and some distance away, flames from knocked-out tanks flickered in the gloom. We were shelled during the night, and earth and stones rattled on the roof of the hut. I remember thinking that if a shell landed on the roof, the walls would confine the blast, and we would all be killed. Sleep overcame me before I could pursue that line of thought.

We were engaged by enemy tanks when we were lined up in a ploughed field. All of us were dismounted and I took refuge with others in a good slit-trench dug into a hedgerow. The Germans were firing armour-piercing shot but it must have been at extreme range for the shooting was poor and no tanks were hit, though we did have one man wounded, perhaps by a shell splinter from an armour-piercing/high-explosive shot (AP/HE).

Both the Royal Air Force and the Luftwaffe put in appearances to liven things up. We were attacked by Typhoons – cannon only, thank goodness – they had used their rockets on more legitimate targets. Eric was not in the tank when the planes swooped on us, but he leaped into the turret, shutting the operator's hatch firmly on his headphone lead and chopping it in two.

We were sitting around enjoying a cup of tea one morning when the German planes came over. I was the only one facing toward them and saw these aircraft flying low over the wheat field. "Watch it!" I called, and everyone dived for cover. Eric and I found ourselves under our tank, in a bunch of thistles, having a fit of the giggles while the Luftwaffe swooped and roared round us. But one of our number had been wounded and we watched him being carried away on a stretcher, his face the livid 'wounded' colour. We heard that a cannon shell had hit his legs, so the wound was bound to be serious.

Jack Geddes, too, was outside his tank on urgent personal business when another attack came from the air. He leapt on to our tank when the attack was over and showed us his tobacco pipe which he had been smoking in 'contemplation'. In the excitement he had bitten off the mouthpiece!

Compared with the air attacks which the regiment had undergone in the desert, where the Luftwaffe was in great strength, these attacks were small beer. Here in France, there were no Stukas to scream out of the sky and dive-bomb the tanks and troops.

We moved to another part of the battlefield. Late in the afternoon a column of German prisoners walked up to us, under escort on their way to the rear. The leaders of the group muttered something incomprehensible to me. "What do they want?" said someone. "Water," was the reply; but our water cans were empty, as someone demonstrated by rattling one of them. One prisoner had an 88 mm gun crew medallion pinned to his breast. One of us tried to bargain for it, but the proud owner refused.

Stan Dovey, I remember clearly, as he had stuck his head in our turret one day and surveyed the sweet-papers Eric and I had left about. "This turret is like a pig-sty!" he boomed at us.

As I recall it, the Regiment formed itself into a 'box' for the night, on the wide wheat-covered slope below Borgebus Ridge. I was on guard one evening as the light faded. To our front, somewhere, were the Germans and, I supposed, our screening Infantry. From that direction a figure approached – tall, with one of the new steel helmets on his head and equipped with a wireless. I thought it strange that a solitary figure should be walking about at dusk. He came up to me and asked if I knew where the Rifle Brigade were. I said that I had no idea and suggested that he asked one of the officers around our tanks. He walked toward them and, I supposed, obtained the information; but it was very strange, and I wondered if I had let a German soldier of courage and enterprise, spying out the land, slip through my fingers. I gather from an RB Officer that they wore berets and not steel helmets!

Later on that evening, I was standing in the turret watching some German shelling, which seemed to be some distance away in the near dark. I felt a tremendous blow on the chest and dropped down instantly into the turret. Turning on the turret light, I examined myself carefully: I would not have been surprised to find a tear in my blouse, or even blood! To my amazement, not a sign of anything, and an examination of the turret floor revealed nothing which could have been the cause of my scare. It was a warning not to treat even distant shelling too casually.

The attack southward seemed to have ground to a halt, and our next location was near the village of Ifs.

This small place is mentioned in a book by Richard Collier, entitled '*Ten Thousand Eyes*', which tells the story of French endeavours to gather information about German fortifications, not only on the shore-line, but inland, too. The Mayor of Ifs advertised for a man to travel round farms in the area, recording milk production. Under the cover of this legitimate work, M. Leon Dumis, the man so employed, recorded the strength of fortifications and batteries round Ifs and other villages round Caen. He used a system of matches broken into different lengths to indicate distances, strengths of fortifications, number of batteries and other vital information which was fed back to London.

Facing north, then, we looked across the plain, sloping away from us to Caen. To the left, the still burning factories and chimneys of the Faubourg de Vaucelles district of Caen. To the right, Ifs.

Standing high in the wheat was a complete tail unit of a Stirling bomber, with the rear gunner's turret still intact. No other wreckage of the aircraft could be seen. Near at hand, beside a wall of a farmhouse on the edge of Ifs was a US Airforce fighter aircraft. I approached this plane with some trepidation, wondering what I might find in the cockpit, but there was no dead occupant. I was baffled by the fact that all this metal could get itself airborne.

The Canadian infantry were engaged with the enemy further up the slope to the south and beyond our sight, but a road ran past Ifs from east to west and down this road came the casualties from that fighting. Sometimes a Jeep would come down the road, carrying a figure being rushed to a field dressing station. Sometimes a Jeep would bring the shrouded form of a dead soldier to his burial place in the small war cemetery next to the village. The burial service took place then, with the men grouped round, heads bowed, as the Chaplain read the service at the graveside.

I wandered over to inspect the burial-place one afternoon. A bullet-holed and blood-stained high boot of the Canadian pattern, a mess-tin, a litter of webbing equipment, newly-dug graves and new crosses – and all so far from Canada.

Shells were plopping round as I made a brew at the rear of the tank one afternoon. The bangs were not too near (had I forgotten my 'turret' experience?) and my father's words came to me 'You don't hear the one that gets you!', so I continued making the tea. A Canadian hurried past. "Tea time?" he asked, somewhat amused.

Another golden evening and we had the wireless tuned in to London, a Promenade Concert, and a lovely contralto voice drifted over the wheat from the head-set which dangled outside the turret. "Listen to that!" said our tank commander, in appreciation.

We drew further back to more level ground and awaited events. One feature here was a nightly 'raid' by chafer bugs. They were a great nuisance as they emerged from the wheat in the evenings, and figures could be seen flailing away at them with frying-pans or anything which came in handy to drive them away. I discovered that they would not fly under the 'bivvy' so I used to retire under there when 'bug time' came. It rained at one stage, and the ground became sloppily muddy and not the best for camping out as we were doing.

We left the slopes of Borgebus Ridge and withdrew through Caen to the airfield at Carpiquet. There was the debris of battle still around, of course. We were still in the wheat and Bill Williams discovered the body of a one-legged German soldier at the back of his tank when he went round to get materials for a 'brew'. "I had to lean over him to get the stove," said Bill. "Dunno where the other leg was. Hoppin' about on its own, I suppose."

They had difficulty in persuading Bill's lieutenant to move the tank forward and away from this grisly sight, leaving the corpse in the wheat. Some of the large shell holes had been filled in and notices stuck in the earth proclaimed that here were buried 'six German soldiers', or other numbers of bodies.

An exploration of a collapsed wooden hut, sunk in the ground, yielded the photograph of a group of soldiers on a beach somewhere, with a number of girls in bathing costumes. Germans on leave, perhaps on a French beach? There were clips of cartridges which had wooden bullets, dyed pink, in them. Practice rounds or a Secret Weapon? – was the dye poisonous? Who could tell? The most useful acquisition from the hut was an orange-coloured screw-top container in which I kept soap for some years.

Someone found a cupboard from one of the huts or buildings nearby and three neat holes were made in the back. It was then placed face down over a slit-trench and communal 'contemplation' was advertised for anyone who wished. I think most still preferred a solitary walk in the wheat, carrying a spade.

Chapter 7

Amalgamation at Carpiquet

A senior officer from the division came to address us. He referred to a Sunday in the desert, which had become known as 'Black Sunday': "Now," he said, "another Black Sunday looms. 4th CLY is to leave 7th Armoured Division." I later was told that the regiment was to amalgamate with 3rd CLY and join 4th Armoured Brigade. This amalgamation was to take place over 29th to 31st July. 30th July was a Sunday.

The quartermaster began to issue new clothing: 'drawers cellular', socks and new battledress trousers; it was a free-for-all as kit was traded in and new stock dispensed to the troops. I could think of nothing I wanted to exchange and so sat and watched all this going on. I was wearing a pair of khaki shorts, civilian style, and I remember being told not to wear them in action in case I was captured, when I would need trousers to stand the rigours of a PoW Camp. As I watched, someone came up and said, "You were in the desert, then?" but I had to confess that my shorts were a product of the local Co-op!

We took our tanks to the 5th Dragoon Guards, who were to replace us in 7th Armoured. Now I know that, because of casualties in men and tanks, a number of regiments were amalgamating or being disbanded at this time, so we were not alone in our misfortune, though it felt like that the time.

Personnel vanished to other units, some senior NCOs to form a training regiment for newly-joined tank commanders, who had no experience of battle – Stan Lockwood and Douglas Allen being two of these. We were to meet again years later. Now I was to enter a new and as yet unknown limbo of holding units but still, as the spirit of CLY was kind, a member of the regiment.

We travelled about by 3-tonner to begin with. As we drove through one ruined place, Ernie Hoggard said gloomily, "You know where this is?" As we looked about us from the back of the truck, he said, "Villers Bocage."

Later still, on our journeyings, we surveyed the devastation round the Falaise area. This was, of course, after the 'Break Out' from the invasion bridgehead. What grim sights met our eyes. Teams of men, dressed in anti-gas clothing and respirators and gum-boots, moved about among the wrecks of trucks and other vehicles, attending to decaying, bloated corpses in the hot, sunny weather. The figures of the soldiers in the protective clothing, with faces covered, added an unreal and sinister air to the grim task.

In what were by now the back areas of the bridgehead, great swathes of countryside had tracks winding through them which were intended for use by tanks moving up and down to the battle areas. I suppose that this was to save the road surfaces for wheeled vehicles. The tracks had our faithful friend, the 'flimsy' petrol can, as an aid to navigation. Each had a design cut in it, 'Star' or 'Moon', and could be lit up at night from inside. There was also a direction given, 'Up' or 'Down', so it was easy to follow a route to your destination.

Our duties now consisted of driving Cromwells to other units, fetching the tanks from vehicle parks further back down the chain, doing some maintenance on them ourselves and delivering them to regiments in the more forward areas.

The main drawback to the delivery business was the all-pervading dust. I well remember crossing a road where a military policeman was directing the traffic. It seemed a hazardous post, as we did not see him until we passed within arm's length of him in the clouds of dust.

Richard Dipple and I tried to be together in the delivery trade. He was driver and I was commander as we drove up and down in the Cromwells. On one trip, we halted, covered in dust, and a group of lads from a party working on a road came over to us with mugs of welcome, hot, sweet tea. Just the thing for thirsty throats and much appreciated.

One afternoon, we set off to Bayeux to collect a delivery of Cromwells. Instead of being with Richard, I was detailed to drive for Ernie Hoggard and all the Cromwells had been crewed. To my dismay, I was expected to drive a Sherman recovery vehicle. It had large bins inside the hull and was without a turret. It all seemed fairly straightforward except that things were in different places. The gear-lever was to the right, and the steering levers were in between the driver's legs.

Dusk was falling as we set off, first of all negotiating a Bailey Bridge. Ernie sat on the outside, perched on the co-driver's hatch. We were in convoy, of course, so it was just a matter of keeping up with the others: I had no difficulty with that and gradually got the feel of the Sherman. It was now getting quite dark and we halted to consult about our next move. Nearby was a field where some of the crews had spent the night on a previous run. They wanted to do this again, but the officer in charge was keen to push on.

We got onto the dusty 'Route Up' and it was now a matter of keeping close to the vehicle in front as we fumbled our way forward in the dust and the dark. We were led astray and found ourselves milling round in a large field, right off the track. We halted. There was no tank in front as the air cleared of dust. Some instinct made me switch on the headlights. Right in front of us was an enormous shell-hole. Had we got into this, we would have never got out without assistance and Ernie would have been catapulted off his perch on the front of the tank, with dire consequences.

We reversed and found our way back to the route. The rest of the convoy had vanished by now and we were quite disoriented by our experience. We started out on the route and then saw 'Down' instead of 'Up'. We turned round and prepared to go the other way. I was not sure how wide a turning circle I would need on a Sherman but hauled on the right lever. Not tight enough. I demolished a white picket fence in front of a farm house before I straightened out on the route again.

By now it was quite dark, and rather than try once more to find our way through dust and dark together, we decided to call it a night and lay down on the metal boxes to sleep. I took off my spectacles, to help me to sleep, and settled down for the remainder of the short night. We woke with the dawn and, though I had put my 'specs' within easy reach, they were nowhere to be found. Ginger Williams' words came back to me, about the inefficiency of soldiers who wore 'specs', but after groping about in various places, to anxious comments from Ernie, the 'specs' were found. I put them on and looked around. The first thing I saw was the head of a dead cow sticking out of a ditch, with other cattle in the field, also dead.

On we went, then, and found our unit. I must say Ernie was very good as he reported in, saying how well I had done as it was the first time I had driven a Sherman. Richard and the rest of the party were all asleep, having reached the unit in the early morning. Richard had removed his shirt, and the contrast between his face and neck, which were black with dust, and the rest of his body, was quite startling.

Travelling on the routes in daytime was easier, if just as dusty. Richard and I were following the convoy leader, a Welsh Guards subaltern, when we rammed his tank very firmly in the rear with our 75mm gun. I wondered if we had damaged the recoil, but all seemed to be well after inspection and the officer gave us the 'thumbs up' as we started on our way again, so his tank suffered no damage. I think that the same young man had cause to remember us, for we had got a bit fed-up with his fussy ways when he had been on our tank the day before. He wore cut-down riding boots and an unlikely neck-scarf, and anyway he was 'Guards Armoured' and was due for a leg-pull on that count alone. We drove, by courtesy of Richard, under a low tree. As on a previous occasion, low branches swept clear all loose objects on the top of tanks and the cry of, 'Oh! My map-case, my map-case!' was heard. 'Driver, halt!' He dismounted and came back clutching the map-case in reflective mood. I wonder if he knew what we were up to?

At the conclusion of one journey, I was guiding Richard into place in the tank park when an unusual tank roared up and parked beside us. It was something like a Cromwell but had on the hull a tall, flat-sided turret which carried a 17-pounder gun. Richard, who seemed to know about these things, told me it was a 'Challenger'! It had a door in the rear of the turret, through which peered the faces of three of the crew. I was of the opinion that this latest addition to the British armour collection was not able to challenge anything more deadly than your average garden shed!

Guard-duties came at the end of the day, when we had completed delivery or collection of tanks. We were to wear our despised steel helmets. I had painted a little fish on the side of mine, using the blue paint with which the squadron signs had been painted on the turret side of 4th CLY. There also appeared the name 'Tiddler', which Bill Williams called me when we first became acquainted. The orderly officer looked twice at this unofficial embellishment, but I was not ordered to remove it and so felt it added a little variety to the proceedings.

Now we were moved, we who were CLY, not further 'up the chain' and nearer the regiment, but sideways to a holding unit feeding Shermans to 4th Armoured Brigade.

We had heard tales of Sherman tanks, newly shipped out from the USA, being crammed with chocolate, gum and other goodies. The only thing we found once, in one of the tanks, was one of those crash helmets that American crews sometimes wore. Richard was the first to try it on, and we all did the same in turn, but decided we would not wear a thing like that – far too 'Hollywood'.

I had not come across the Browning machine-gun until now and so knew nothing about stripping one for cleaning. Once again it was Richard who came to my rescue. The Browning seemed to be more intricate than the Besa. "It has," said Richard, bending his fingers and waggling his wrist up and down, "parts which go like this." Whereas the Besa had to be removed altogether from the turret mounting in order to change the barrel or clear a serious stoppage, the Browning 'innards' and barrel could be removed from the mounting with little trouble. So, although my British loyalties were with the Besa, I had to admit that the American Browning was a more convenient tank machine-gun. To detach the barrel, one unscrewed it from the breech-block assembly; then to assemble it again, I remember, one screwed the barrel on again, observing the 'clicks' made by a simple spring device which engaged with teeth at the breech-block end of the barrel. "Screw up and then adjust two clicks back!" said Richard.

We were getting more sloppy in our general attitude and so, in this new unit, we were hauled over the coals, as a body, by the CO of the unit. He had his quarters on the top of a small hill, and we were summoned up there one day to hear him express his opinion of us. In short, we were a lazy shower and by our careless ways we were letting down the chaps who were at the front! As we toiled up the hill to answer his summons, I remember passing a Typhoon rocket head which lay, unexploded, in the grass. I was surprised how large it was.

Large also was the evidence before my gaze at another place we stayed in. There was the most enormous German tank I had seen so far. I think it was a self-propelled gun. The walls of steel towered above me with no way of getting in or out that I could see. The gun was absolutely enormous, too. When, later on, I told Ted Dunn about this find, he pleaded to hear no more as he was frightened enough by what he already knew of German armour, without further horrid revelations. In the orchard where this monster lay were three German soldiers' graves, with strangely elaborate markers at the head.

By this time, we were following the trail of our advancing army.

We camped in another spot beside a large farm house. Before the fireplace in a downstairs room was the body of a very dead German soldier. Some hygienic individual thought that cremation was the answer to this problem and so threw petrol over the corpse and lit it. Within a few minutes, flames were roaring through the room and then through the house itself. Shortly the whole house was ablaze and, peering in through a downstairs window, I was amazed to see the way in which the flames were running along the floorboards, just like liquid fire.

There was a call for some of us to move to be nearer the regiment, so we got our kit together onto a truck and moved off through the night. The light of the burning house was visible for miles, staying right behind us as we drove along what must have been a very straight road. Eventually, the spark, as it had now become, vanished in the blackness.

Stew had been our last meal before we moved, and in it lurked a 'bug', with devastating qualities of a gastronomic nature. I suspect that as no-one else had 'it', I was just unlucky. We reached our destination and were to sleep on the earth floor of a barn. It had come on to rain by now and seemed to be making up for the previous dry spell by coming down in buckets. I crept into my sleeping bag, the American one from the LST and tried to sleep. Alas, the promptings of the 'bug' made me stagger out in the rain into the farmyard at frequent intervals throughout the night.

Next morning I went sick and was taken to a field hospital, together with other people needing medical attention of a minor kind. I was given a pink pill and told not to eat anything. I crept about feeling very weak, but after a day or two the symptoms vanished. I had hung my sleeping bag out in the sunshine, which appeared after the night of rain, but when I eventually got back from sick parade someone had taken it. I wished him the joy of it!

I found myself on one of the regimental ammunition trucks, at last drawing a little nearer the tanks. I rode in the back, but as the weather was fine, the front of the canvas cover was rolled up and I was able to sit, with my arms on the cab roof, looking at the countryside as we motored along in convoy.

We entered a small village, with the street dipping down to a bridge over a tree-lined river. I called out to a Frenchman standing beside the road and asked him the name of the river we were crossing. "*C' est le Somme, M'sieu,*" he called back and, as if on cue, a distant gun thudded to underline his words.

In another village, as we drove up the street, the bedroom windows were crowded with people. I was on the same level as they and each person was calling 'Goodnight Tommy!' as we passed by. What an emotional time for these good people as they greeted their liberators after the years of occupation.

As the evening chill drew on, one of the lads in the cab told me that I could "Put this on." 'This' was a capacious DRs weather-proof coat. "But don't let anyone see you wearing it!" said my generous host. I was grateful for the warmth in the evening air.

Next day the convoy 'leaguered' in a field of stubble. We were a mix of vehicles: even a Sherman, I noticed, among the various means of transport. I left the parked trucks and wandered forward to a spot overlooking a little valley. As I looked about, I found a leaflet, obviously dropped by plane, telling German soldiers how to surrender. As I was studying this with interest, but unable to read it as I knew no German, a Frenchwoman ran down the track at the bottom of the valley. Her skirts were flying, revealing a pair of stout blue directoire knickers. She was shrieking something as she ran and, had I been able to hear and translate the words, I would have discovered that the large barn I could see on the opposite side of the valley was crammed with German soldiers. Oblivious, I strolled back to the convoy.

Before long, a group of 'Maquis', armed to the teeth, walked through the vehicles in the direction of the valley and barn. We gave them a couple of 36 grenades, explaining about the fuse: "*Un, deux, trois, quatre*, BOOM!" and they set off down the valley accompanied by one of our officers driving a Jeep.

Soon, a crowd of German soldiers, some wounded and carried on stretchers, began to climb the valley toward us and accompanied by their French escort, walked away into captivity.

The call came for me to join 'A' Squadron, and I was taken there on an ammunition truck.

I was to be gunner for Lieutenant Ted Dunn, No. 1 Troop Leader. Corporal Jock Campbell, the wireless operator, Tom Moore, the driver, and Cliff Clifford, the co-driver, made up the crew. The members of the crew were all '3rd' people and I wanted to look up any '4th' people who were around. I knew that Hugh Stanton had a brother who was at Villers. What had happened to him? I found Hugh and Ernie Riddall too. Apparently, Hugh's brother was a PoW, as were most of the regiment taken at Villers. The old Troop members were busy about their own affairs and so I went back to my new crew and settled in there.

Corporal Jock came from Perth and was the owner of a shop there in the High Street. His wife was managing the shop during his enforced absence. He was a rock-solid character, both in physique and personality, having played water-polo for Scotland. He told me how to foul an opponent at water-polo and, not being a swimmer, I was amazed that this could be done!

Tom Moore was a farmer from that most agricultural of counties, Nottinghamshire. He came from Southwell, which place he pronounced as it is written and not as is usual 'Suth'll'. He had a brother also serving in the regiment. Blue of eye and fair of hair, "A true 'Son of the Soil'," said my mother when she met him. I got a surprise when we set off in the tank, for a strange keening noise arose from the driving compartment. Tom was singing to himself as he drove along. I thought he was 'putting it on' but as the sound continued, I realised that this was Tom's normal rendition of popular songs. I had never heard anything like it and, in the confines of a tank, as music it left a lot to be desired.

Cliff had been a policeman in Slough and was older even than Jock, I think. He had a way of dealing with children who were making a nuisance of themselves in some manner or other and I thought it was a typical 'bobby's' way. He pointed his thumb at the offender, waggled it and said, "Hey, you!" and gestured in a 'Hop it!' kind of way. The kids always did 'Hop it', whether they were Belgian, Dutch or German.

Ted Dunn was a product of the Brigade of Guards, and this showed in posture and carriage. On our first afternoon together, a heavy shower of rain came on. The commander's hatch in a Sherman was wide, and rain tended to fall on the back of the gunner sitting below the front of the opening. This afternoon, Ted put a waterproof jacket over my shoulders to keep them dry. I hadn't expected this kindness and was grateful to him for this.

Commanders did not care to get wet when it rained, of course, and some had large black umbrellas which were raised at such times. One had the impression that some commanders were city gents in their civilian incarnation and so would not be parted from their umbrellas. From a purely practical point of view it made sense, for the umbrella was large enough to cover the hatch opening and so the occupants of the turret were able to keep dry.

One luxury peculiar to our tank was a supply of hot water for washing at the end of the day. The bottom half of the waterproofing exhaust chute had been left in place, and a Jerrican of water placed in this was heated by the exhaust gases during the course of the day. Bed-rolls were always warm and dry, as they rested on the engine covers. The benefit of this was mostly felt, of course, in the winter weather.

Meals were my undoing after a day or two. The bug struck again and it would not be possible to keep leaving the tank during operations, so I reported to the MO, who dosed me with the inevitable pills and sent me to ride on the ambulance in 'A' Echelon until my 'innards' had settled down again. When I got to the ambulance, the driver and the RAMC corporal were just tucking into juicy corned beef sandwiches, so bread and real tea and sugar must have been supplied to us by then. Why is it that other peoples' meals seem to be so delicious? I was really longing for a sandwich myself but to tuck in would be a big mistake, so I starved again for a day or two.

Seeing the Red Cross on the side of the ambulance, civilians came up to see if we could help them with their ailments. One girl, I recall, came along with her companions hoping for relief for a heavily bandaged sore throat. We had no drugs to help with this and anyway our French, much less our medical French, was non-existent.

We were fairly close to the front of the advance and so the French people were very excited as they listened to the news on a radio which was on one of the vehicles. Paris was being liberated at the time and there were eye-witness reports of the jubilation there.

By comparison, all the ambulance could muster in the way of entertainment was a wind-up gramophone, with one record of the depression years, in which a woman implored her listeners to 'Remember my forgotten man'. This did not draw the crowds!

Here in the street of the town where we had halted, the Town Crier announced plans for a parade to take place in the evening to mark their liberation. Then there came a reminder of the bitterness of the Occupation.

In the distance, I heard a sound like a flock of geese, but which was actually a human noise of hooting and calling. It was a flesh-crawling sound as a crowd of men, women and children walked down the road toward us. In front of the crowd, almost driven on by it, walked a solitary figure dressed in black, as so many women were in those days. How old she was, I do not know, her head had been shaved and, stony-faced, she walked along in front of the jeering mob. This display of the raw human emotion of anger has made me wary of mob rule ever since. I wondered at the time, though, if such a crowd, behaving in such a way, had howled for the life of Jesus?

The spur to my departure from this life of ease in the ambulance came one morning, when the doors opened (I was riding in the back) and a wounded German soldier was loaded in on a stretcher. The RAMC corporal also came in, and we set off. The German had been wounded in the hip, and the journey was quite painful for him. I imagine the bullet had lodged somewhere in the abdomen. He groaned as the ambulance moved on, being sick in an empty biscuit tin the corporal held for him.

The ambulance stopped and the MO got into the back to look at the patient. He drew the blanket away and rolled the German lad onto his side to examine the wound, ignoring the cries of pain, for this had to be done. Another ambulance reversed up to our doors and the German was transferred to this, I was pleased to see how carefully the stretcher was moved and how one of our CLY people made sure his small pack, with his bits and pieces, went with him. Another casualty hopped round the side of the ambulance, which was taking the German away, one of our own CLY men who had been hit in the calf. He appeared to be quite cheerful with his wound and joked with the medical people as he climbed aboard to be whisked away to hospital.

I asked the MO if I could return to the tanks, as the 'bug' appeared to have gone and I was feeling quite fit again. I didn't want to see any really gruesome sights in the ambulance, either, so it seemed a good time to return to my new companions.

This time, Jimmy Sale came to collect me in, or rather on, a scout car. I clung on the top as we sped along the road. The squadron had over-run a battery of 88mm anti-tank guns, the day before, and Jimmy naturally wanted to take some photographs. I think this was at or near Flixecourt. A halt was made at the deserted battery and photos were taken.

There were Belgian civilians around, hunting for any useful hits of stuff. One of them came up to Jimmy and asked if he could have a field telephone he had found. I expect the really desirable items, like the excellent binocular sighting gear, had already been 'liberated'.

I rejoined Ted and Co., and we continued to chivvy the enemy out of France.

We entered the village, where we could see a street before us. Cycling furiously along was a young Frenchman and by the way his head was turning, he was shouting the news of our arrival as he sped along.

We halted in the little village square, and I could hear the sound of the crowd of villagers and through my periscope could see them milling round. There was the sound of someone clambering onto the tank and a female voice exclaimed in surprise. She had caught sight of me and had not realised until that moment that there was a fifth member of the crew. Ted asked me the French for 'Where are the Boche?', so I asked Madame and also added, "Had they any '*cannons*' or '*tanques*'?" (which was the best I could do for tanks). That seemed to be an acceptable 'Franglais' word, for Madame knew what we meant and, to our relief, told us that there were neither tanks nor cannons with the German forces which had passed through the village.

I looked back along the street, which had been quite bare of decoration as we followed the young Frenchman. Now, it seemed only minutes later, bunting was strung from side to side of the street. The good villagers must have had it ready for our arrival.

We moved on, then halted at a cross-roads and got out of the tanks to speak to the people who had come out of a cluster of houses round about. As we talked to them, the sound of rifle shots could be heard across the fields. "What is that shooting?" asked 'Sunray' (the CO), over the air, to which the reply came from one of our other tank commanders on the spot, "It's a 'local', celebrating Liberation!"

Meanwhile, one of the French ladies had produced a camera and asked us to pose for a photograph. "*Vous avez beaucoup de photos, Madame*?" I asked. "*Oui M'sieu*," she said, "*Je m'amuse*." I was surprised to hear her use, without having to think about it, a construction we had learned at school!

Then she asked if we would like a cup of tea. "Ah yes! Thank you," and so several cups of tea were produced for us. Unfortunately, the water had not boiled and so the tea leaves were floating on top of the hot brew of water and milk. We drank, metaphorically holding our noses, and smacked our lips appreciatively at the drink, thanking Madame profusely. She had probably kept the tea through long years of occupation, waiting for the moment when she could offer a cup to the liberators as a sign of her appreciation.

The scene is now set in a large field of kale. We were advancing through it when suddenly a German soldier appeared, seemingly from right before our tracks, and scuttled off on hands and knees. Jack Geddes had told me that it was possible for someone to run on all fours. Alf Pitcher had shot past him like this when the 'Firefly' had been knocked out at Caen! I was amazed by this feat, which I now had seen with my own eyes. Cliff Clifford sped this enemy on his way by firing the bow machine-gun. Tracer flew all round the escaping figure and he vanished unharmed. I never fired a bow machine-gun. As it had no telescope, but only a periscope to see through when one fired, it was a matter of holding the trigger and spraying around with the gun.

We went on over the field. Ted told me to traverse right, and, through the telescope, I saw a line of trees on the edge of the field. Behind the trees, in the next field, were German trucks with figures milling around them, anxious to get on board and escape.

The 75mm high-explosive shell had a screw on the side of the nose-cone; this, if unscrewed, put a delaying action on the shell. It would then hit an object and explode seconds later. Ted told Jock to use this device, so that the shells I fired at the trucks beyond the trees would not explode when they hit the foliage but would delay and explode on the other side of them. I fired several shots through the trees and saw explosions among the trucks.

I got a rocket from Ted the next day, for I had neglected to clean the barrel of the gun after firing. To my horror, when he showed me, the barrel was spotted with rust and the residue of the explosive charge. Jock then helped me to push the cleaning rod up and down the barrel and found some rags with which to give it a final polish. He also read me a sharp lesson on the necessity for maintenance!

On the border between France and Belgium, we stopped for a few moments. A buxom Belgian lass was collecting souvenirs of the Liberation, and her well-filled sweater was festooned with badges and unit signs of half the British Army it seemed. The only thing I had to give her was a green lanyard we used to wear on our left shoulder, so she put that on as another memento of an historic day.

We were now passing through the old battlefields of 1914-18. There was a small chalk ridge before we dropped down onto the plain, which had villages and pit head-stocks set out before us. On the ridge were rusty wire pickets and three graves with French-style helmets on them, also rusty. 1914 or 1940?

We passed a house beside the road, and on the shabbily painted door of one of the outhouses appeared the word 'Cookhouse' in faded white lettering. That must have been 1940!

We passed a complete village street network. The buildings had been destroyed in the earlier war and only the footings remained; these were now all covered in grass and weeds. On entering another small village, I saw a grey, concrete pill-box, looking green and mossy with age, which was incorporated into the side of a house. A wooden sign, pointing up a road off our route, proclaimed 'Hulluch', a place well known to members of my father's regiment in 1915, as it is in the area of the battle of Loos. An aged Belgian gentleman asked me where our destination was. Mindful of security (and in complete ignorance of our destination anyway), I said "Berlin!" This seemed to be a good and satisfying answer. I was, in fact, destined to go to Berlin, but under slightly different circumstances.

We were experiencing the heady delights of Liberation ourselves. The population was very pleased to see us and as it was warm and sunny now (it had rained when we first entered the old battlefields – a suitable welcome, I thought), I rode on the back of the turret, as we motored along. An old lady ran down the garden path of her home, waving her arms and shouting "Boche kaput! Boche kaput!" It was the first time I heard that expressive word 'Kaput'. A line of young men stood in front of a monastic building waving to us across the fields. Maybe they had been given special permission to come out and see us pass, and I thought that maybe they would remember us in their prayers that day.

We passed people making their way to Mass and I thought about them hearing the words against a background of tanks roaring past.

A more distressing and maybe embarrassing sight was that of what was obviously a brothel, with the 'girls' working in the garden. They were all heavily, grotesquely, made up, and I remember looking at one of the girls, who was quite small and seemed to be very young. She caught my eye and nudged one of her companions. I wondered at the life she must lead and thought it very sad that one so young should be caught up in such degradation.

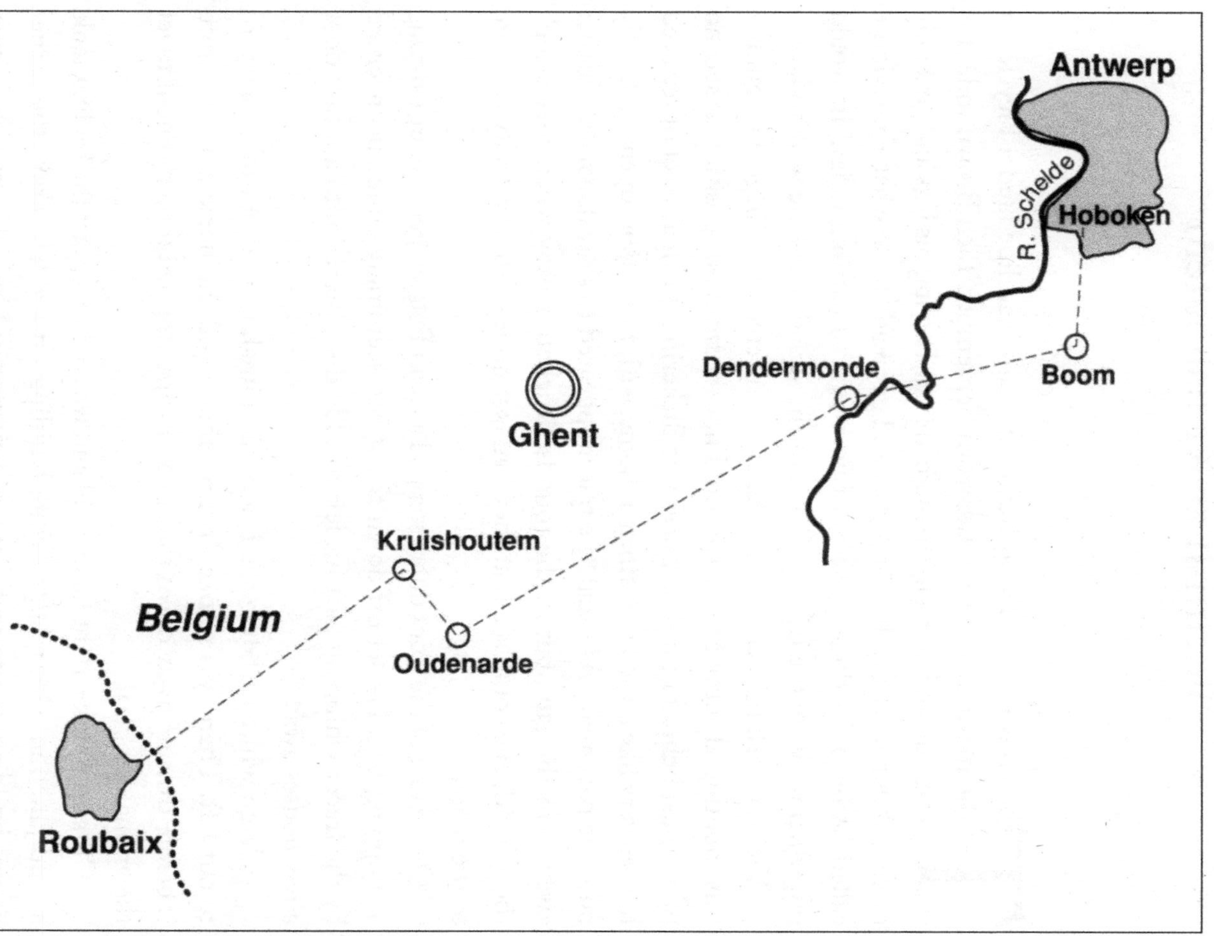

Map 2: Route from Roubaix to Hoboken.

Chapter 8

Skirmish at Kruishoutem

The crew on our Troop Sergeant's tank had liberated a bicycle on the morning of Wednesday 6th September. Tich Brown rode this cycle up and down in a ploughed field, bowing his legs and generally fooling about as we finished breakfast and got ready to do what Tom Moore called, "A bit of battling." "We must have a bit of battling today," he would say, when we were the leading Troop of the squadron, as we were today.

We were behind Sergeant Smith as we entered this village. His gunner was shooting at some enemy we could not see from our position as second in line, just behind him. The tracer was flickering down a street of terraced houses, very like a Victorian street at home, with front doors opening directly onto the pavement. As usual, the tracer appeared to slow down, the further away from the gun, but as the rounds ricocheted away when they struck the ground, one could see that they had lost none of their velocity en route to the target.

Out of one of the front doors stepped a small Belgian gentleman, carrying a shopping bag. He set off down the street, seemingly quite unconcerned by the tracer whipping past his left ear. He disappeared into another door a few houses away.

A large white cart-horse, a beautiful animal, trotted out of a farmyard to our left. There was smoke drifting about, and the horse emerged from it before trotting away down the street. Firing stopped for a moment to let the animal get clear.

The street took a right hand bend and we could see, past the leading tank, a road junction with a large, white building on the left. From the corner of this building, white material was being waved by field-grey-clad arms, indicating a willingness to surrender.

Sergeant Smith leaned out of the commander's hatch and beckoned the Germans to come out from the corner and surrender properly. Suddenly, he dropped down in the turret, and we thought that he had been shot. His tank began to reverse and so we pulled back too, to give room. The head of Tich, who was the operator, appeared above the rim of the hatch, guiding the tank backwards.

When the tank had reversed right round the corner, Sergeant Smith reappeared, to our relief, walking up and down outside the tank, shaking his head as if to clear it. As he had leaned out of the hatch, a German rifleman had shot at him. It was a near miss and the sergeant's headphones had been shot off.

Remounting again, the Sergeant took the tank round the corner once more and the sound of the 75mm gun could be heard. No more beckoning!

Sergeant Smith had been deafened by this incident and as was discovered later in the day, had suffered a fractured skull. Ted Dunn then took the lead, and so it was that we entered Kruishoutem, near Ghent.

On the maps that we had, the spelling of the town appeared as Chruysautem, which is the French version. So, the place instantly became known over the air as 'Chrysanthemum'. We turned left out of the town square and into Waregemsesteenweg (the way to Waregem).

There was a cafe there and, in front, a group of 11th Hussars, our recce regiment for 4th Armoured Brigade. They wore their brown beret with the cherry-red band round it, much as we wore a green band round our best berets. After a word with them, we went up the road to where there was a dead pony lying in between the shafts of a cart. We got some of the local population to move this out of our way and went up the road a bit more, the Troop Firefly, with Jack Geddes as gunner, in the lead. The road took a right-hand turn. The Firefly had just got to the corner when a column of German transport came flying down the road from the other direction. At once, Jack opened fire with his Browning, and the enemy column came to a sudden halt. As Jack was creating havoc and dealing out death and destruction, we drew up alongside him, on his left. Firing ceased. Some of the vehicles had caught fire and were burning merrily. We, on the left of the road, seemed to be right on top of the leading German vehicle, a staff car. After a moment or two, the door opened and a figure hurled itself into the ditch which ran along the side of the road. For the second time I saw

Cliff spray a fleeing figure with bullets and, for the second time, the figure vanished unharmed!

Ted asked me to shoot up the column and flush out any other people who might be hiding in the vehicles. This I began to do but, after a moment or two, the gun jammed. We reversed behind Jack so that the gun could be cleared of the stoppage. This Jock proceeded to do, with fierce, Scottish curses, as the gun was hot.

Ted told Sergeant Smith to take our place and this he did. I was watching him through my telescope and saw a plume of blue smoke rise from the front of his turret: at the same time there was the crack of the strike of an armour-piercing round and the tank rocked back on its tracks. Instantly the crew baled out. They ran down the ditch at the side of the road, and we reversed to give them cover. Unfortunately, Tich Brown had not got out with the rest. Under cover of the smoke from the burning vehicles, a tank had come up and, perhaps having a momentary glimpse of the Sherman, had fired the fatal shot.

As we reversed further down the road, I saw a column of flame shoot out of the commander's hatch of the stricken tank. After that, nothing.

Then an extraordinary sight. Sergeant Smith and Algy Manners (one of our Troop leaders) walked up the road to the tank on the corner. They were walking right into where the enemy were. I kept a keen eye on the edges of the road, and the trees where the enemy might be waiting. Undeterred, apparently, by the thought of any danger, they reached the tank. One of them climbed onto the hull and looked inside. It became obvious to us, when they walked back, that Tich was dead.

When Algy and Smudger Smith were safely back, we continued to reverse and I sprayed the ill-fated corner with machine-gun fire. As I watched the tracer, I saw a figure fall away from the side of one of the trees as if it was a large piece of wood being knocked from its side. It was a human figure, though. One of the German soldiers must have been watching us from round the bole of the tree.

We waited for the next move, and I fully expected the enemy tank to come round the corner. Would I be able to hit it? Suppose the shot bounced off! The enemy tank commander must have thought better of any move on his part, and we continued to reverse back into Kruishoutem unmolested.

Later on in the day, we discovered that Val Brent and Ernie Pinch had been killed further up the Waregem road as they were about to accept the surrender of some German prisoners. Val was later found dead beside his tank and Ernie in a field near the road. Also to die that day were nine Belgian civilians who were shot out of hand by the enemy, when they retook Kruishoutem again. The trouble was that we had no supporting Infantry near at hand and, without Infantry, tanks are at risk.

We were in Marlborough country now, near the town of Oudenarde, and the next afternoon we stopped in rough pasture, facing west, and busied ourselves with personal chores. A cooked meal was prepared and, before long, a line of washing flapped in the breeze. 'Drawers cellular' and other items were drying well after a good scrub. The line of washing stretched from the tank to a wire fence on our left.

A field of beet, with two Belgians hoeing beyond the fence, and to our front a farmhouse with a barn wall stretching along the side of a road which ran from left to right across our front.

During the course of the afternoon, a long column of German prisoners walked along the road in the direction of Oudenarde. Because the afternoon sun was behind the column, each man was a perfect silhouette. It was like the 'shadow show' before the Caen battle, but with men and not vehicles. The heads of each of the German prisoners were bowed in defeat as they walked along. The Infantry escorts were marching along at the 'High Port', heads up and with confidence in every step. A remarkable shadow-picture of victory and defeat, and a scene I have never forgotten.

Away down the road to our left, behind some woods, came the distant rattle of small-arms and heavier fire. We heard it but took no notice. It was someone else's fight. Then out of the woods along the road came a column of trucks, towing guns and led by an armoured car.

Ted put his binoculars up to his eyes and inspected the approaching column. "They're Jerries!" he announced in an agitated kind of way. Within seconds, it seemed, we were on the move, meal forgotten and clean washing on the ground as the line snapped when the tank moved forward.

I made two mistakes. The first was in not engaging the trucks towing the 88mm guns (for such they were) with the Browning. I went for the armoured car and fired an armour-piercing shot at that. What I had not realised was that the road ran at a diagonal and was nearer to us on the right than on the left. The shot hit the roof ridge of the barn directly above the armoured car as it drove past. Alright for line but not for elevation!

By the time we had reloaded, a matter of a few seconds only, the armoured car, trucks and guns had disappeared, and we gazed at an empty road. Goodness knows how they got away with it, for several other tanks had also fired at them.

Legend has it that the column surrendered to a quartermaster's truck which was delivering groceries to various of our units. 'Q' accepted their surrender graciously enough. He had, so the story goes, a Bren-gun but it was under a pile of groceries. Well, it's a good story and unlikely enough to be true.

We reversed to our former position and repaired the damage to our washing line. 'When in doubt, brew up!' was the motto, so we followed the time-honoured Sharpshooter custom.

The next morning, before it was light, we breakfasted in Oudenarde market place. The breakfast fires lit up the elaborate facade of the Town Hall, and I felt very much part of history and wondered whether 'Corporal John' Marlborough's troops had also eaten their breakfast in the market place, by the light of their fires.

Their battle at Oudenarde had been a bloody affair. Ours was more of a panic.

Chapter 9

City Interlude – Antwerp

Ahead lay the great city of Antwerp and we motored into one of the suburbs, Hoboken, which lay next to the River Scheldt. The citizens greeted us rapturously, for, although the city had been liberated a day or two before we arrived on the scene, we were the first members of the British Army the populace in that part had met 'in person'. We filled up with petrol, and I remember Tom using a collapsible oil-skin funnel to pour petrol into the petrol tank. Of course, some petrol dripped off the sides of the funnel, and excited owners of cigarette lighters pushed forward to this unexpected supply, crying "Benzine!" and holding their lighters under the drips of the precious liquid.

We were soon taken into the houses lining the street and fed with egg and chips. Everyone seemed to be able to produce chips! So it was that we made the acquaintance of Melanie and Gustave Gersem-Schepens and their small daughter. Gustave was a policeman. Opposite their house on the other side of the street was a bakery owned by M. Huybrechts. He could speak both French and Flemish, but his wife and daughter Nellie could only manage Flemish. This was my first glimpse of the problem of a nation with two languages and deep-seated antagonisms. The families made us most welcome and our rations, of course, supplemented many a household meal when we were staying in Hoboken.

Looking in the windows of houses and shops, we were surprised to see photographs of Queen Astrid everywhere but no photographs of King Leopold anywhere. To die tragically is to be assured of fame!

We left the street and rattled off in the tank to a point near the banks of the Scheldt, not far from one of the Vauban Forts, which ringed the city. I poked around in the tunnels and fortifications but could find no loot. Tom found a large mirror which accompanied us until it was broken. I thought it odd to carry a large, light-reflecting object on the back of the tank.

I climbed as far as I dared up a huge crane which stood on the dock side. We were to keep an eye on the south bank of the river, for that side had not been reached by our army as yet. I thought that the crane was a good vantage point from which to observe any goings-on on the other side of the river. Looking towards the mouth of the Scheldt, I saw a huge explosion, a great cloud of smoke and dust thrown into the air. I thought that it must be the German Army destroying an ammunition dump, perhaps. One of our fighters flew through the cloud as I watched, and I almost wondered if that had been the cause of the big bang.

Further up-river, on the south bank, was a small town; it may have been a place called Burcht – I don't know – but silence reigned there for a time. Then cheers began to be heard as our troops entered the place. Flags began to appear on buildings; bells rang and soon the place seemed to be in an uproar of celebration. I had been treated to a sound picture of the Liberation.

On our side of the river, the tanks were parked beside some allotments, and houses of modern design. There was also a small cafe, which had in it a large mechanical organ which took up a lot of floor space.

Our presence attracted the crowds, who were content to watch our everyday activities. Hearing sounds of wonder (Oooh! – Aahhh!) from a crowd round a nearby tank, we were amused to see a pancake fly up in the air above the heads of the spectators of English culinary art.

Our friends came to visit us. Melanie and Nellie climbed onto the tank while I took a photo of them, using Melanie's camera. Cliff wheedled some white bread out of an elderly Belgian couple who took us into their home and showed us pictures, painted by their son, who had been taken away as forced labour by the Germans.

A Belgian gentleman engaged us in conversation and, in answer to our enquiries about the marked absence of cats, explained that cat tasted like rabbit. "The cat," he said, "perspires through the skin and so the flesh is sweet." "Of course," we said. "On the other hand," he observed, "the dog perspires through the tongue and so the flesh is sour." We made remarks agreeing with what he said, for all the world as if such subtle distinctions about canine and feline delicacies were part of our experience too.

One of the things we discovered was that the Belgians, whilst knowing the chorus to *Tipperary*, also baffled us – or, at any rate, me – by also singing the verses. To my knowledge I had never heard these before. I traded off a lesson in singing *Sari Marais* ('Breng mai terug naar de oude Transvaal'), as taught by Nellie, for a lesson in which she learned the current popular song *Mairsi Dotes*, as taught by me.

When we got to Antwerp, I only met one person who spoke English, but when we returned on leave a month or two later, and the place was swarming with base troops, both British and American, many more people, especially Melanie, who had a very quick ear, could speak good English. When we were enjoying the hospitality of the Gersem-Schepens, Mme. Huybrechts thought she would proudly display her knowledge of English by quoting the one phrase she remembered that 'the English soldiers used in the first world war'. There was indrawn breath and tut-tutting from Melanie, and a shocked "Madame!" We talked hastily of something else and Madame was very quiet for the rest of her stay. When we returned to Antwerp some months later, Madame had a fine baby son and they named him John, which was rather a good name, I thought, for a little Belgian boy conceived, it seemed, in celebration of the Liberation!

Did we sleep beside the tanks or in billets? I have an idea that I had a bed at the Huybrechts', and such was the hospitality of the populace that I cannot imagine that they would let us sleep outdoors.

Jock and I decided that we would visit the Municipal Baths, so we set off with our soap and towels. Hard luck, for when we got there, we found that it was 'Mother and Children Day'. On the way there, a hearse, draped with the Belgian flag, passed by. The populace was already beginning to suffer casualties. A foretaste of the agony to come, as Antwerp shared with London the bombardment by V1 and V2 rockets during the coming winter.

A crowd came toward our tank, walking in silence: at the front, a tearful woman in a near state of collapse, supported by friends who were holding her arms. "She has just heard that her son has been killed," explained a passer-by. Oh, Mothers! – Mothers!

But to more cheerful moments. Ginger-haired Taff Evans, from North Wales which distinguished him from Taff Evans, our driver at the Caen battle, who was dark and a South Waleian, – tried to teach a Belgian girl how to say Llanfair p.g. in its entirety! 'C' Squadron, we heard, had a Belgian gentleman take his daughter round from tank to tank, asking if anyone would give her a child, to mark the Liberation. John Cotton, who told me about this episode, also said that he was very tempted to go absent in Antwerp and live with a charming Belgian girl for the rest of the war.

Jock tried to teach us all the 'Eightsome Reel' in the cafe with the mechanical organ. The music did not have that essential Highland quality, and when Jock leaped into the middle with wild Scottish cries, the thing came to an hilarious end.

There was panic one evening as we set off to deal with some emergency on the outskirts of the city. All came to nothing, however, and we halted in one of the squares. I volunteered to watch the tanks while everyone else repaired to one of several cafes which were round the square. A battery of artillery began to fire. Shrieks from the females in the populace as the sound reverberated from the buildings. The barrage continued, as singing could be heard in the distance, but drawing nearer. Down one of the roads leading into the square marched an infantry battalion. I did not recognise the song they were singing. Maybe it was a "Regimental Special', but it all sounded very '14-18' as they marched into the square and away down another road to the sound of the guns.

We returned to our place beside the allotments, but the time was drawing near for our final departure from Antwerp.

We learned that we were to support the 15th Scottish Division ("Real soldiers!" said Jock), and so away we went to engage the enemy on the Gheel bridgehead, across the Albert Canal. We must have seen a sign-post indicating 'Boom' as we motored along, for this inspired Tom to give us a recitation of some of 'How we brought the good news from Ghent to Aix', in which Boom is mentioned as a place through which 'We galloped all three'.

We trundled over a ploughed field in the late afternoon, the Infantry walking in files with us. We passed the corpse of a German who had been burned to death and was lying in a ditch. Ted Dunn asked me if I had seen him through my periscope, but I had not. When we came back that way, someone had thrown a blanket over the body. That made the shrouded form even more sinister. Whatever took place at Gheel, it seemed that we just motored along and then back to the start-line of the advance without firing a shot. Perhaps the enemy had decided to withdraw.

We did some canal watching around the Escaut Canal area for a day or two. Daytime was pleasant, the weather was good and the natives were friendly. There were one or two houses near where we were, and we sat at ease when off duty. Nights, however, were another matter. Watching beside the canal was a nerve-testing business. The shadows cast on the water could easily resolve themselves into a German assault-boat being paddled across by a crew of bloodthirsty Nazis. To add spice to the Canal watch, there was a story that a German army cap, quite dry, had been found beside one of the tanks one morning. The dryness of the cap indicating, to those of Sherlock Holmes minds, that it had fallen from the head of a German soldier in the early morning, after the dew!

Around the 17th September we were well and truly grounded, as all petrol was needed to support the Airborne troops engaged in operation 'Market Garden'. Photographs exist of aircraft and gliders flying near our leaguer, and members of the Regiment gazing skywards, watching. Aircraft came back from the dropping zone, flying low, some with glider-towing cables trailing behind them as they flew over. A Dakota appeared to be in trouble as it flew near us and headed our way, but the pilot turned away from us and brought the aircraft down behind a wood about a mile away. There was much air activity during the next few days, and we kept abreast of events by listening to the wireless. We were saddened, though, when Cliff came to tell us that what remained of the airborne troops were being withdrawn from Arnhem.

We found ourselves at Asch, which seemed to be near some colliery area. Parked in a field, with a road running by, we slept in our bivvys. Some went exploring and came back with items from a German supply dump.

I tasted black bread for the first time and found that I quite liked it. There was an item of anti-gas equipment in the form of a plastic sack to put right over the body. It had a transparent panel to look through but I thought our equipment far superior. With the German sack one had to crouch down and remain stationery, but our gas-cape and respirator allowed movement and the opportunity to fight on.

It was here that another squadron suffered three fatalities. As I understood it, a scout car drove over a mine. The driver had a broken ankle, and the other occupants carried him to the side of the road, where another mine exploded, killing three and wounding the operator, who nevertheless made

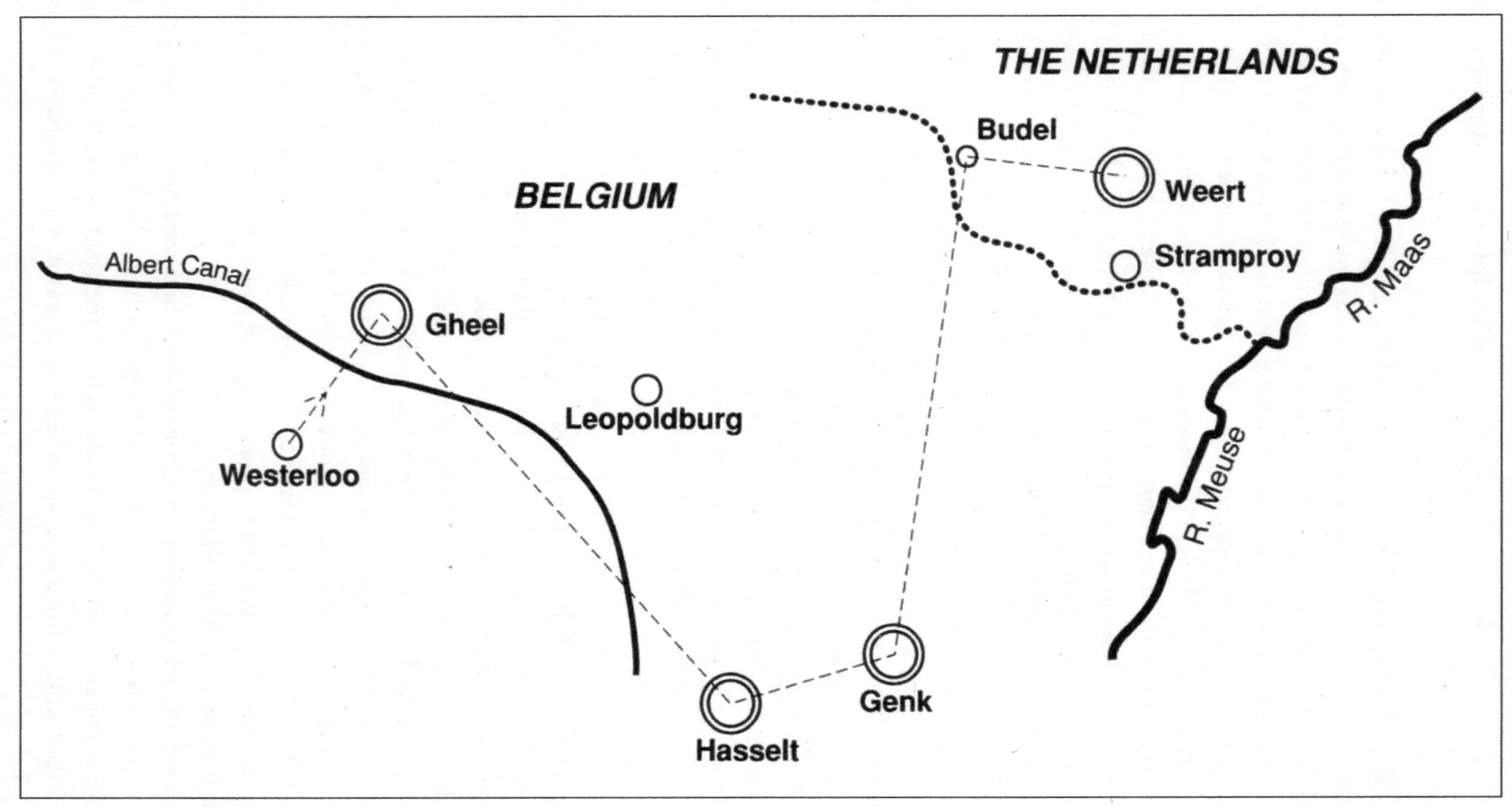

Map 3: Westerloo to Weert.

his way back to the scout car to radio for help. Because the scout car was not with other vehicles, it took some time for help to arrive.

Our Troop was detailed to dig three graves in the garden of a convent, right by the roadside. 'A' Squadron paraded at the roadside as the ambulance brought the bodies for burial. 'C' Squadron accompanied the ambulance, and the bodies were carried on stretchers to their graves.

The burial Troop (ours) waited discreetly behind bushes until the dead had been lowered into the graves and the burial service read by the Padre. When all was over, we moved forward to fill in the graves. I was interested to note how the dead had been prepared for burial. The bodies had been wrapped face-down in blankets, which were then pinned at the back. Another blanket was then used, on which the dead were laid face-up, and that blanket was then safety-pinned at the front. I assumed that this was to make it easier to lift the bodies out of the graves when the time came for reinternment in a War Cemetery.

When we had filled in the graves, some of the local young people came and placed on the graves, wreaths of flowers, decorated with ribbons in the Belgian national colours.

Chapter 10

Into the Netherlands

A few days later we found ourselves crossing the border into the Netherlands. The first Dutch house I saw through my periscope had what we now call 'picture' windows. It looked light and airy and so modern. Just what I imagined a Dutch house to be like. So, we found ourselves at Weert. In Weert, our accommodation was in an empty shop on Roermondesweg. The proprietor of the shop was not in evidence and had probably been taken away for forced labour by the 'Moff', as the Dutch people called the Germans. His wife and small daughter still lived in the rooms at the rear of the shop and upstairs.

After we had appeared on the scene, two young women came to look at the tanks and they talked to us. They were outstanding in appearance, as they were both attractive blondes, but also because they wore red trouser-suits. An unusual outfit, contrasting with the war-worn drabness of the general population of women and girls. Both girls spoke good English. They vanished from the scene, and I believe our Troop Leader, by now Mike Smethurst, took one of them in his Jeep for interrogation. It was no surprise to us when the rumour began to circulate that they were spies!

We made several sallies from Weert in infantry support roles, working with our own Infantry, The King's Royal Rifle Corps.

At about this time, thin sheets of steel were welded on brackets at the front of the tanks. This device was to baffle the explosion of the German equivalent of the 'Bazooka'. Called 'Panzerfaust', the weapon came packed in a cardboard box, which had on the top an illustration of a giant fist crushing a tank. The idea was that the round should hit the sheet metal and, having penetrated that, would explode before striking the hull of the tank.

We were called to worry some enemy troops on the other side of one of the canals, so we drove up to lie alongside one of the farms in the area. Then Mike sent three of the Troop tanks back out of sight and sound. He

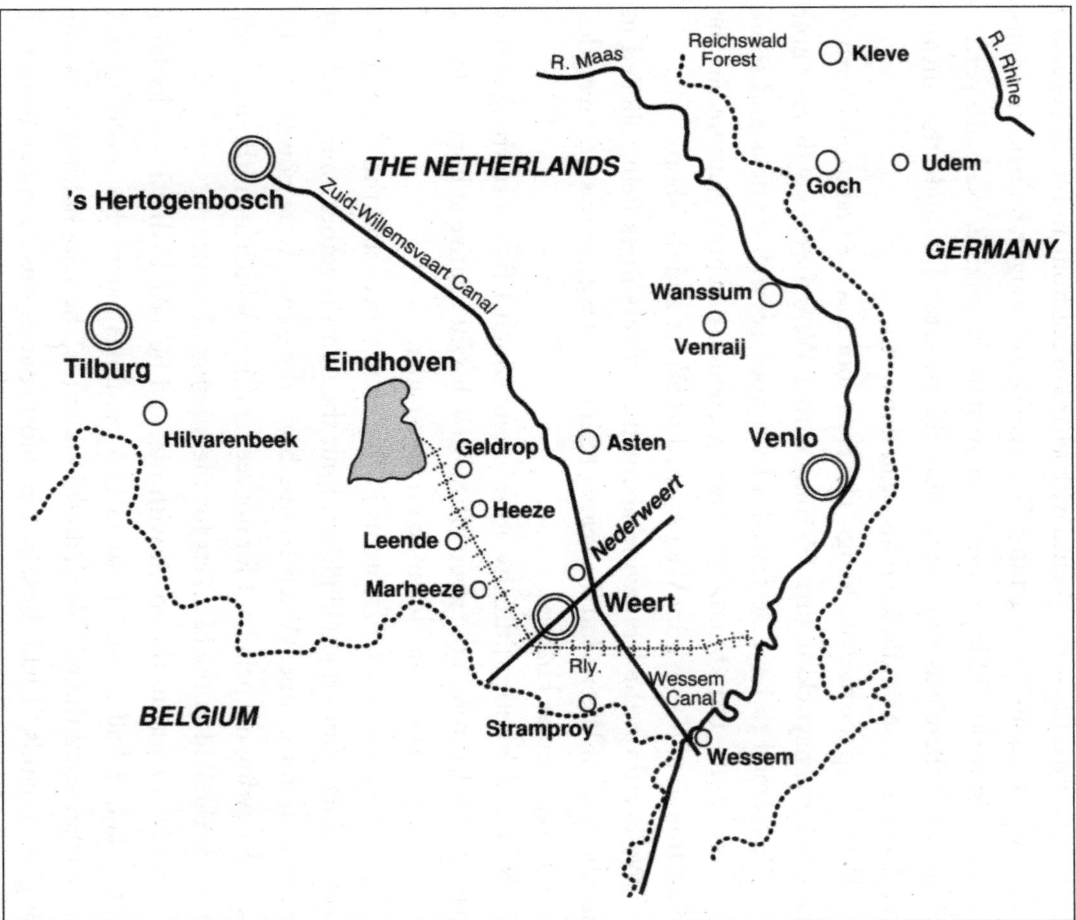

Map 4: Operational Area, autumn and winter 1944–45.

reasoned, "To a man in a slit-trench, tanks come, tanks go, and then he sticks his head out to look!" We waited for a head to appear out of a slit-trench somewhere. No head appeared!

We surveyed the scene. A farm with a barn to our front and several heaps of hay, drying on tent-like structures. Good cover, we thought, for machine-guns.

To my surprise, Mike ordered Tom to start the engine. We had a perfect view and so there was no need to move the tank, but I thought that anyone hearing the noise would keep his head down still.

We shot up the farm buildings. The barn door was the first to go, blown to bits, then the hayricks in turn. Nothing stirred. Were the enemy there or not?

We seemed to have destroyed a barn door, several hayricks and some windows in the farm buildings next to us, which had been shattered by the blast from our 75mm gun. We returned to Weert and the shop.

We heard on the 'grapevine' about the officers mess being shelled in another part of Weert, and the death of Sergeant Tovey, as was later recorded in the Regimental History.

Now a 'domestic' difficulty arose – one which I find disturbing still. I had received, through the good offices of a distant relative at home, a forces comforts parcel from a Nottingham newspaper.

There were many useful items in the small parcel, and they included a pair of finely knitted khaki gloves. I put the items together on my bed and went away for a time. When I came back, the gloves were nowhere to be seen. Knowing my penchant for not seeing things which are right under my nose, I searched in the blankets for the missing gloves.

An NCO was in the room with me, and he asked what I was looking for. I said, "I had a pair of gloves in a comforts parcel this morning and now I can't find them." "Well, don't look at me," he said, holding up a pair of gloved hands, "I had these in a comforts parcel this morning as well." I continued looking for a moment of two, sure that it was my gloves he had on. What could I prove? My name was not in them. No-one, as far as I was aware, had seen the contents of the parcel. His word against mine. Would he really have risked demotion and disgrace if he was not sure of his ability to bluff his way out of it?

Forget the gloves, then, and carry on with the war!

Out again to take part in an affair with our friends the KRR. We were to motor out to a position near a demolished railway bridge. German infantry patrols were supposed to use this bridge to cross to our side of the canal, which it spanned, at night. We got ourselves into a fir plantation from where we could shell the bridge and noted our position. This was in the afternoon, so it was easy to mark exactly where we were. The idea was that we should register shots on the bridge, note traverse and elevation and, placing ourselves in the same spot at night, using the same traverse and elevation, hit the bridge when the KRR patrol signalled that the Germans were crossing. We would be able to catch the patrol in mid-canal if not up the creek!

Then to register on the bridge. I let fly and hit the structure. "Fire again!" said Mike, so I did. "And again!" And so, we fired several shots at the bridge super-structure – Jock loading and all the while cursing at the "Waste of taxpayers' money!" (I could hear him quite clearly even though I was wearing headphones). I think Mike was carried away by our ability to make things go 'Bang!'

A withdrawal, and night fell. We drove up to our allotted place and Mike conferred with the KRR officer about the plan.

Poor Jack Geddes had the unenviable task of trudging out with the bow gun and a tripod to take up a position in a slit-trench with the infantry. Unhappily, I was unable to find the clamp which held the Browning in place on the tripod which we carried on the back of the tank. I had been unable to beg one from any of the other gunners, so Jack had to make do with a piece of stout string. Goodness knows what would have happened if he had been required to fire the gun.

But other ears had heard our arrival and, no doubt warned by our shelling of the bridge in the afternoon, the wily enemy was to foil our plan.

It was not long before shells began to fall in the wood. Fired at random, but uncomfortable, none-the-less, especially for the Infantry. Shells bursting in the trees were decidedly unhealthy. The infantry decided to beat it. No-one told Jack, and the first he knew of the withdrawal was when he saw fleeing figures rushing away to the rear. He lost no time in rejoining us, complete with string, Browning, tripod and all, and we too joined our infantry comrades.

Another 'woody' experience was mine as I stood on sentry one dark night, outside a shop which was our billet in Weert. The road stretched away before me in the gloom. Nothing stirred. Surely, though, I heard a footfall? And then another! Then several together! Then I thought that I heard the sound of a rifle banging against a tree-trunk. I hurried into the shop to wake Mike. He emerged wearing boots (unlaced), a shirt, startlingly white drawers (cellular) and carrying a naval Luger of deadly proportions. "Right! Where are these (blank) Jerries?" he asked.

"Listen!" I said.

We heard the sound of ripe acorns dropping from the trees onto the pavé. I was glad to come off guard and leave the listening to someone else.

On some other occasion we had fired several belts of Browning ammunition. A bag held under the gun, in which spent cartridge cases were caught, became full and it was hauled out of the turret to be emptied.

Because of our air superiority, the Germans had bored deep, wide holes in the verges at the side of the road. They were more than six feet deep and were wide enough to accommodate three or four men. Beside each hole was a stick about four feet high, with a wisp of straw tied to the top. These markers enabled one to see where the holes were and dive in quickly if need be.

Into one of these holes, which was near the shop, the empty cartridges were poured. Standing by, watching us, was a young Dutchman, Jo van Aken: he observed that his country would need metal and it would be useful to know where such caches were. Jo was a friendly character who lived in a house set in extensive grounds, next to the shop. He once asked us if we had tried to call on him one night. "Was that you, knocking, knocking?" he asked. We said that it was not us and he ought not to answer the door, as it might be a stray German patrol wandering about. He said that the girls quite liked English soldiers but, and with a shudder, "The moustaches they do not like!" This with a sideways glance at Jack, who sported a neat black decoration on his upper lip.

Chapter 11

Canals at Nederweert

Nederweert, two or three kilometres from Weert, was a place which seemed to be strategically important, as there was a canal junction at the place. We stayed there for several days, watching the canals and surrounding countryside for enemy activity.

In the centre of the canal junction was a small island, occupied by enemy troops. This island had been fortified by the Dutch and on one side of the island, which was roughly triangular, was a steel plate, presumably concealing a gun loophole. One of the canals, the Wessem-Nederweert had a swinging road bridge and a footbridge, and the loophole faced up this canal. The swinging bridge was kept swung open to prevent vehicles crossing. The footbridge, however, was open to pedestrians. One Troop guarded this spot, and a surprised Trooper had a coin pressed into his hand by an old lady who wanted to cross the footbridge. Perhaps there was a toll to pay, and in the absence of the toll-keeper, the lady did the next best thing. As she was crossing over to the German side, we asked the Trooper if he had glanced down to see if boots were visible beneath her long skirts.

Our Troop was just across from the island, at the junction of the canals. We were concealed by high, sandy banks into which slit-trenches had been dug for observation purposes. Our arrival had aroused interest on the island, and one of a party which was inspecting the area had been shot by someone firing from there. I believe it was a leg wound, and Jimmy Sale had put his coat on the wounded man as he was taken away on a stretcher. I had the task of returning this coat to Jimmy later on, during our stay at Nederweert.

There were clusters of houses near the canals, away from the village, and there was a row of houses running at the back of our position, with a road in between. These houses and many of the others were still occupied by civilians.

We took it in turns in one of the slit-trenches, keeping an eye on the island. We had binoculars with us and one afternoon I saw a German soldier, lying full length, observing the tanks which were up the canal, at the footbridge. He was completely exposed to view, and Jack Geddes, who was with me, saw him too. Whether we had a rifle with us, I don't know, but a rifle was certainly on the scene, and I have an idea that we asked for one to be sent to us. I decided that I would shoot at the enemy, and I found myself tying a piece of sacking round my steel helmet (I must have gone back to the tank for that!) to break up the outline. There were some cardboard boxes perched on the edge of the slit-trench, which also gave visual cover. I crawled out of the trench and took up a firing position. When I operated the bolt to shove a round 'up the spout' I noticed to my dismay that the rifle had been loaded with tracer rounds! To an acute observer, this would show where the shot came from.

I got myself into the best position to shoot, sliding the rifle on its side over the bank. I looked through the backsight. The No. 4 rifle had a flip backsight, a battle sight and one for more accurate shooting. Which was which? I could not remember! The rifle was zeroed to fire with bayonet fixed and there was no bayonet on this rifle. Added to this, the head of the soldier had shrunk from pumpkin size, as when seen through the binoculars, and was now very small when observed with the naked eye.

Jack was still looking through the binoculars at our intended victim. I told him that I could not shoot; in addition to all the other factors, it seemed too much like cold-blooded murder of an unsuspecting victim. How happily I had blazed away with Browning and 75mm on the tank, but this was much more personal, and I could not bring myself to shoot at him.

Later on, we heard how a KRR sniper had come into the houses beside the footbridge and had been shown up into a bedroom. The house owner, in his eagerness to oblige, had pulled aside the curtains to let the sniper see how good a view there was. "Whose side is he on?" asked the expert. Another 'hide' was rigged up, with empty sand-bags arranged across a number of strings running across the room. From here, the man had a good view into the trenches on the island and several of the enemy fell victim to his fire – one being shot as he crawled back to retrieve a helmet he had stuck up as a decoy!

We had another trench with a view down one of the other canals, and I was watching there on my own. I saw a figure in field-grey run down the

Plate 1: The author, John Fisher, in uniform.

Plate 2: Recruits in the Primary Training Wing, on Amiens Square, Bovington. The author is fifth from the left, next to the back row. John Cotton is third from the left, second row from the front.

Plate 3: On the Gheel Bridgehead. 'A' Squadron and infantry of 15th Scottish Division, 12th September 1944. (*Reproduced by courtesy of the Director, National Army Museum, London*)

Plate 4: Crossing Nijmegen Bridge. 'Olly' Woods, leader of 'A' Squadron, returning from 'The Island', early October 1944. (*Reproduced by courtesy of the Director, National Army Museum, London*)

Plate 5: On the way to Tilburg. With assault troops of Princess Irene's Brigade 'up'. (*Reproduced by courtesy of the Director, National Army Museum, London*)

Plate 6: Ruins at Tilberg, after the battle. We approached from the other side of the buildings. The 'stream' (Rover Ley) is beyond them. (*Reproduced by courtesy of the Director, National Army Museum, London*)

Plate 7: At Hilvarenbeek, after Tilburg. No.1 Troop Leader, Mike Smethurst, waiting to go to the rear. 15 Scottish 'Kangaroo' personnel carriers move up past waiting Churchill tanks. (*Reproduced by courtesy of the Director, National Army Museum, London*)

Plate 8: On Parade in Stramproy. 'A' Squadron, early November 1944. (*Reproduced by courtesy of the Director, National Army Museum, London*)

Plate 9: Trouble at the Wessem Canal crossing. Tanks came to grief whilst negotiating a hairpin bend. (*Reproduced by courtesy of the Director, National Army Museum, London*)

Plate 10: Wessem Canal assault. No.1 troop Leader's tank slips into a tunnel under the bank and the left-hand track comes off the driving sprocket. The crew wait for the fitters; the author is standing on the right. (*Reproduced by courtesy of the Director, National Army Museum, London*)

Plate 11: Returning from Wessem. Alan Archer and crew in Asten, 9th January 1945. (*Reproduced by courtesy of the Director, National Army Museum, London*)

Plate 12: In the Netherlands, autumn 1944. No.1 Troop, 'A' Squadron, 3rd/4th County of London Yeomanry. The author is at the rear, fourth from the right. (*Reproduced by courtesy of the Director, National Army Museum, London*)

Plate 13: The White House, Elmshorn, May/June 1944. The regimental headquarters for the civilian administration of the Elmshorn district. (*Reproduced by courtesy of the Director, National Army Museum, London*)

Plate 14: The billet at Elmshorn. The author on the steps outside the large house that was divided into flats

Plate 15: Clerk's Course, 'Quill'. The author is third from the right, middle row.

garden of one of the houses across the canal junction. It was such a fleeting glimpse that I wondered if I had seen the man at all. Nevertheless, I reported the sighting and Mike said to me, "As you saw him, you'd better report on the shooting," for he was going to ask for a 'stonk' to be put down on the area. I crept back to my vantage-point, very conscious of my adventure with the enemy soldier and wondering which of them had got his sights fixed on me.

Our guns fired and shells thundered down on the gardens of the houses, but the explosions were very close, and I kept my head down until the banging had stopped and the splinters had ceased whirring through the air. Then I put my head up over the parapet. All was quiet once more and only the drifting dust remained to mark the fall of the shells. This was no good to the gunners. I could not report where the shells had fallen as I had not seen them explode. Sergeant White had to replace me, and he was able to report on the fall of the shots when the artillery obliged with another salvo.

We were engaged on various household tasks one morning when there was a loud 'crack!' and Hugh Stanton's tank, which was parked behind us but on the other side of the road, began to 'brew'. Fortunately, no-one was inside. We could only watch as it steadily burned away to the sound of exploding ammunition, accompanied by clouds of black smoke.

Some enterprising marksman had taken a shot at the tank, which we had assumed was concealed behind the high, sandy bank. It was a good bit of shooting from well inside enemy territory.

An Auster aircraft came over to try and spot enemy positions from the air, but as the pilot flew up and down over us, there was a rattle of machine-gun fire from the island, and the aircraft took such violent evasive action that I thought it had been hit. However, I may have been wrong, as he simply hedge-hopped across the fields out of harm's way.

Our Troop pulled back at night, leaving others on guard. We lent them half-a-dozen 36 grenades in case they had to repel boarders in the hours of darkness. When we resumed our day-time position, I went back to the village of Nederweert to collect our grenades.

Before I went, I was given Jimmy Sale's coat, which he had put over the wounded man on the stretcher, and this had now been returned to us. The American Army were to take over from us, and Jimmy was showing one of their officers round the place. They were grouped in the door of a house when I saw Jimmy, so in the presence of our Allies, I walked up and gave a smart salute when I handed the coat to him.

Then to collect the grenades. I stowed them in my battledress blouse for safe keeping! When I had done so, Jimmy and the Americans came bowling down the road which ran through the village, in a scout car. Enemy eyes were watching and mortar bombs rained down on the village street when the scout car should have been passing through. The timing was a bit in advance, however, and the scout car had not reached us, but those of us standing in the main street hit the deck as the bombs rained down. Little damage was done, a few tiles off a roof, and no casualties.

Out of the dust of bricks and tiles came the scout car and a group of Dutch people and some of our lads who were in the house which had been hit. The scout car went on its way. I found the noise and excitement triggered some amusement in me and I roared with laughter at all the kerfuffle and the futility of it all – much to the bewilderment of Johnny Douch, who was standing next to me. The grenades were safe, so I strolled back to our tanks with them and took them out of my blouse like a conjuror producing eggs from a hat and wondered aloud whether any German had me in his sights as I walked back along the track. "I always weave to and fro," said Hugh, "that fools 'em."

In the evening, I scrounged a lift back to Nederweert on the water wagon, clinging to the cab and standing on the running board as the cab had two in it already. As I clung to the hood of the truck, I heard bullets snapping overhead as someone shot at the sound of the truck as it moved away from them. It was dusk, so I doubted if the Germans could see the truck from the island. Nevertheless, I stuck my head inside the canvas hood as if it were bullet-proof.

Chapter 12

On 'The Island'

Our next spell was on another island, the stretch of country between the Waal and the Lower Rhine.

We crossed over Nijmegen Bridge, the girders on the sides having hessian strips erected against them, to prevent German eyes seeing troop movement over it.

When we had established ourselves in our particular area, we found that we were in an orchard of cooking apples, near a farmhouse. I think that the orchard had been used before by tanks, for there were pits dug, about three feet deep, over which we placed our vehicles. These pits made excellent sleeping places. No-one would sleep under a tank normally, for it could sink overnight and crush the sleepers, but in the pits, we were quite safe.

The farmhouse was complete with inhabitants and so we used to congregate in the cellar with the family – adults and children – conversing in 'Anglo Dutch' and having a sociable time together. The daughter of the house was what might be called a 'strapping wench' and one or two of the lads had tried to become more closely acquainted with her. I don't think any of them managed so much as a cuddle in the candle-lit cellar.

Percy Pether had acquired a zither and played on it, among other tunes, an old Dutch melody, a hymn. This tune turned up again in the 1970s, when it was played as a voluntary at the end of a Remembrance Day Service in one of our Somerset village churches. I explained to the organist where I had heard it before, and she played the tune after every Remembrance Day Service from that day on.

Warfare took more than one form. One of these was the Battle of the Apples. There were many large 'cookers' lying all over the ground in the orchard. It only needed one of us to throw an apple at someone else and, in a few moments, apples were flying everywhere. Trooper Rose, who was tending a brew of tea, kept pleading with the throwers to "Mind my brew!",

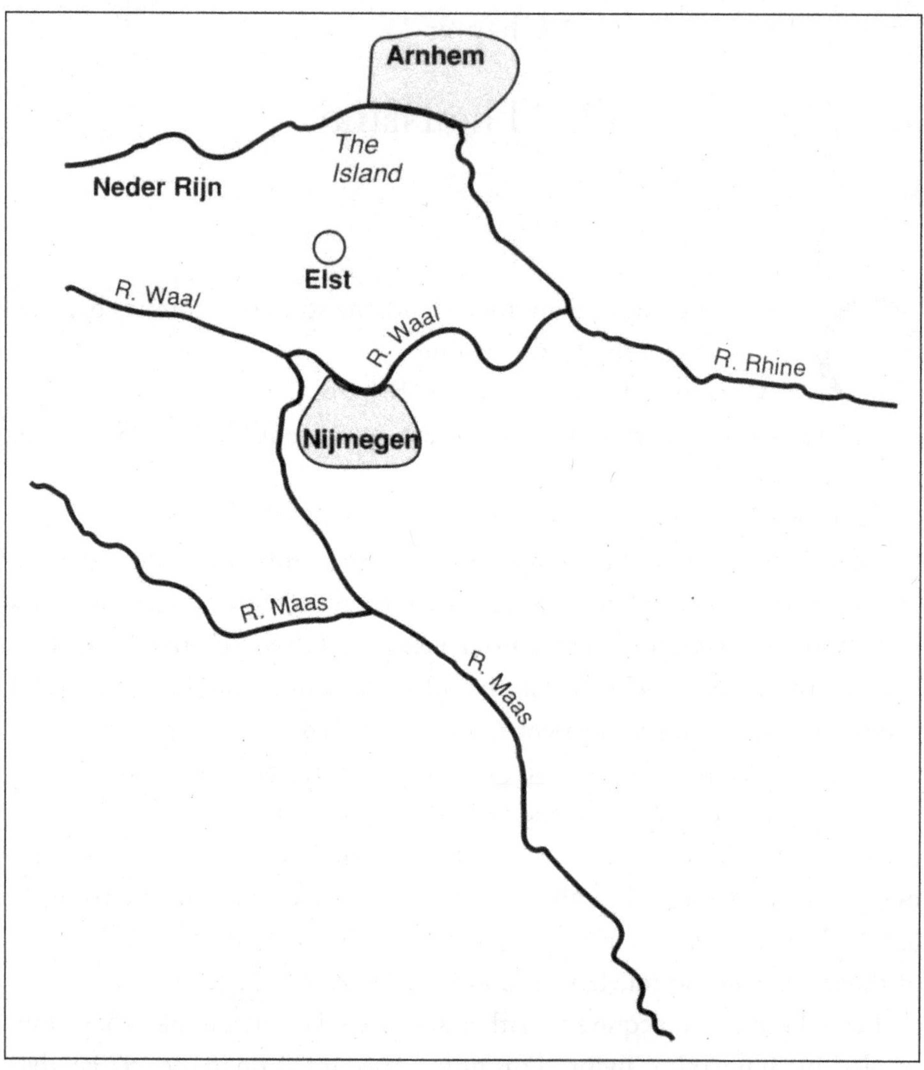

Map 5: The Island.

gesturing with a spoon to point out the billy-can balanced on his wood fire. Certainly, it looked to be in peril if a hard, violently thrown apple hit it. I stopped one of these missiles and retired hurt, seeking refuge in our own pit under the tank.

When the real bombardment began it was night. The shells began exploding in the orchard and we leapt out of our pits and sat shivering in our shirt tails and drawers cellular, inside the tanks, waiting for the 'stonk' to end. The story goes that the officers, who were in the farmhouse, listened in tense silence to the shells falling until Major Woods said that nature was calling for relief. Mike Smethurst later said, "Then several people hurt themselves trying to get out of the door at once."

Morning revealed the extent of the damage. There were a few branches down from the trees but the blast from one near miss had torn into a bed – empty, as the occupant was in his tank. His trousers, kept in between the blankets to maintain the creases, had been reduced to their component parts, as the blast had ripped all the seams apart.

There were American troops about, asking if anyone had a Luger to exchange for American gear. One of the lads negotiated for what one of the Americans described as "One of them aviator's jackets" – a leather one with sheepskin lining, that would be, but I wondered if I was hearing a description of the Wright brothers.

Whether as a result of this transaction or not, a trigger-happy (or maybe just happy) American wandered among the tanks firing his newly acquired Luger into the ground as he walked along.

We took a dim view of this and kept well clear of him.

We travelled back across the Nijmegen Bridge again as our stint on The Island was over. We halted just after we had crossed the bridge again and on a bright, sunny morning, dismounted.

Tom Moore saw a young lady of his acquaintance who was cycling past. She had come into Nijmegen from one of the towns where we had been billeted, perhaps Weert. On her bike, she had a long parcel, wrapped in newspaper. Tom, ever on the scrounge, thought 'Rhubarb!', and so engaged her in conversation, persuading her to unwrap the parcel.

He came back grinning. "I thought it was rhubarb," he said, "but it was a pair of corsets!"

Chapter 13

Baffled at Tilburg

After our stay on The Island, we were engaged in action in the area of Tilburg, where we were supported by the Dutch 'Princess Irene Brigade'. This brigade was made up of Dutchman who were fighting their way home, having escaped to the UK at some stage of the war, or who had come from the Dutch East Indies, for some were of a swarthy complexion and had an oriental cast of features.

I now know that the 'Brigade' was not a brigade at all, but only a strong battalion, and political considerations made it important that their casualties were not too heavy (this from the Regimental History).

Of course, we did not know this at the time and as the day went on, we would have given anything to work with our own 'Rifles'.

We set off to mount our attack on Tilburg, the infantry riding on the back of our tanks. We reached the start line, the infantry dismounted and the attack began. All seemed to go well at first, with many German troops running past us, hands in the air, hotly pursued by almost too many Dutchman, I thought.

We advanced up the road towards a bridge over a wide stream, which ran across our front. The road stood above the surrounding fields and there was a ditch at each side of the road. On the left, a farm. Over the stream there was a factory, which could be a source of trouble, as it overlooked the bridge. There were three chimneys rising from the factory buildings. We soon discovered that the bridge had been blown up, so there was no way for the tanks to cross without help in the form of a mechanised bridge of some kind.

We were the leading Troop that day, so we sat and waited for developments, keeping an eye to our front. In front of us, partially blocking the road, were two Honey tanks of our Regimental Reconnaissance Troop. They had been knocked out, one by AP shot and one by an HE shell, and were abandoned. Two figures, one certainly Lofty Long, and the other, I think, Jim Poole, walked up to the Honeys and returned, carrying boxes of rations from the tanks on their shoulders. Never miss an opportunity to colour a few extras in the way of rations!

Next, Hugh Stanton drove past us. He had acquired another tank by now and this had on the front a device like giant prongs, originally made for dealing with banks of earth and hedges in the Normandy bocage. With his device, he pushed both the Honeys into the ditch on the left of the road, leaving it clear for us to advance.

What had knocked out the Honeys? As we watched, there was a flash and a bang as a gun fired from a copse in front of the factory. It was very strange, as the flame from the gun indicated that it was firing, not at us, but at a target to our left.

"Did you see that gun?" asked Mike.

"I saw the flash!" I said. So, I fired at where the gun or tank would be, according to the muzzle flash. We heard no more from that quarter and so we continued to sit, unmolested, on the road.

Someone drove up in a scout car; I think it was the adjutant. He sat on the hatch cover and seemed to be inspecting the gap and the remains of the bridge for some time, seemingly quite unconcerned about his exposed perch on top of the scout car.

We shuffled up and down the road a bit and then a Scissors bridge came along and parked in a field to our left. This began to look serious. If the Scissors bridge was successfully laid, then we would be first across. We watched as the bridge began to unfold, but it got stuck, half open. There was some discussion between Olly Woods and the driver of the bridge. Olly threatened to report the driver to his CO for failing to maintain his bridge.

Somebody suggested over the air that the rubble from the blown bridge could be bulldozed into the gap, but this idea was vetoed for the strange reason, to me at any rate, that the rubble would block the stream, which would then flood the area. I thought '*Après nous, le déluge*', as we would be well out of the way when the floods came. Anyway, if we crossed the stream, it would not be long before the Engineers would unblock it.

We became reconciled to the idea of just providing supporting fire for the infantry. This we proceeded to do but the 'feet' did not want to leave the shelter of the ditch on the right hand side of the road. Their company CO, a major, was wounded, and brought down to us on a stretcher. He was put on the back of our tank and Mike asked me to get him a drink of water. I did this, walking round to the front of the tank to where the Jerrican of water was kept, turning my back on the enemy and showing these Dutchmen that I was not going to cower in a ditch.

Drink administered, we reversed with our casualty, and he was taken to an ambulance. Mike had given me his greatcoat to put on the wounded man and, unfortunately, I had not removed it when he was transferred. I was in trouble for this, the more so because I was unable to retrieve the greatcoat as it had gone further back down the line with the officer. Back up to the 'sharp end' again, where we proceeded to knock down the factory chimneys. Our supporting artillery was shooting too and soon the chimneys were no more.

We tried to get the infantry moving forward and asked for more artillery support. One 'stonk' landed among us and Mike said over the air "That was us!" The infantry were all in the ditch alongside our tanks. "That'll wake the buggers up!" said Olly in reply.

It was obvious that we were going to get no further in our effort to cross the stream, so we pulled back and prepared to spend the night with the infantry around. Some of these Dutch lads had been sleeping in a barn the night before our assault and had woken up to hear two German soldiers arguing in another part of the barn about the desirability of surrender. They were given no choice.

On the morning after our failed attempt, infantry began to file past us and there were some in carriers too. A Churchill 'Funny', with a huge bridge on the front, sticking up in the air like a crane, moved past to join the fresh troops. Tilburg would surely fall now.

We undertook a night march to our next location. I sat in the co-driver's seat and fed Tom cigarettes as he drove along, but it came on to rain, so cigarettes became soggy as soon as lit. So, we motored on, following the single light of the tank in front. We passed through Nederweert, seeing again Hugh's brewed-up Sherman by the roadside.

Stramproy, which is a village right on the border with Belgium, was our patch for ten days. We drew up at a farmhouse belonging to the Teuwen family. There were three sisters and a young brother, and they all wanted to look inside the tank. Gertrude, the eldest girl, spoke French, as did the father. Gertrude asked me where we had come from and I said, of course, Tilburg. I got a rocket from Mike. "That's what Jerry wants to know," he said.

We planned to stay at the farm for one night at least but stayed for several. We slept on the floor in the front room, and the women of the family tip-toed through our sleeping forms as they made their way to Mass in the mornings.

I think that this was the first time we had seen life in a Dutch village and I was impressed by the devotion shown to the Sacrament as it was carried to the sick. The parish priest, carrying the consecrated elements, was preceded by a crucifer and an acolyte ringing a small bell. The villagers genuflected as the procession moved past them. I was interested to note that one knee, though seeming to touch the ground, did not actually do so, but hovered two inches above the muddy street. What were we to do? We resolved the problem by coming to attention as the little procession went past. This met with approval, I understand, as the German soldiers had always jeered in derision.

We moved from the Teuwen farm to the empty bedroom of the house of the parish priest. I believe that there was a back stairs which we used, for I never remember seeing the good Father in the house.

I used to walk down to the Teuwen farm, for I was sure of a welcome in the family. We used to gather round the table in the evening – Menheer Teuwen and I smoking and all the family joining in conversation in Dutch-French and some English words. The girls had been to a French convent school in the village. Gertrude, therefore, knew more French than my poor schoolboy stuff, but we could make ourselves understood. As I walked down to the farm, I had to pass a gigantic windmill. I was not happy going near this structure, never being comfortable with heights either up or down. I went down one evening, taking with me a Berretta pistol, which belonged to Jock. He had gone home on compassionate leave, so I borrowed it for the evening. There was no need to carry any weapon at all, of course, but I wanted to impress, I suppose.

When I put it on the table, reassuring the family that it was not loaded, Harry, the son, said something in Dutch to Gertrude. "Harry wants to know if that is from a German you have killed," she said in French. Rather shamefacedly, I had to admit that it belonged to Jock.

There was a radio, so we listened to broadcasts in Dutch and English, too. One night the tune of 'For he's a jolly good fellow' came on the air and so I sang the English words to the family. Menheer Teuwen responded with 'Marbrouck s'en va't en guerre', and I felt as if I was one of 'Corporal John' Marlborough's Troopers and had a bay charger champing at the bit outside the front door.

When the evenings drew to a close, the members of the family went to bed in order, beginning with the youngest, Harry, then the youngest daughter. She must have been about twelve. That was my cue to make myself scarce and the middle daughter always saw me to the door, never Gertrude. I think that the parents were wary of me trying to make a secret assignation with her. As I walked past the end of the farmhouse on the way back to the billet, the youngest daughter, who had not really gone to bed, sat by her window to wish me "Goodnight" as I walked away past the windmill on my way 'home'.

This kind family knew that soldiers bought 'Klompjes' (clogs) as souvenirs and so Gertrude presented me with a painted 'Klompje' one day. It was painted yellow and had, by the look of it, once been a money-box.

Being on guard one night, I observed to the north what I at first thought were tracer shells going up into the air. There were two glowing lights and as they kept climbing, even through cloud, I realised that they were V2 rockets being sent up from the north of Holland on their way to London or Antwerp.

Other activity, this time on the ground, included the sight of an American unit passing through the village. Each machine-gun mounted on the vehicles had a condom on the end of the barrel. A practical solution to keeping rain out of the weapons.

Another visitor was a Crocodile 'Funny', a flame-throwing Churchill from a unit of 79th Armoured Division. We all turned out with many of the villagers, to watch a demonstration of this fearsome weapon. Here I met a Welsh member of my original Troop at the training regiment, another Taff Evans.

Then more 'Funny' stuff appeared in the shape of 'Buffalo' amphibians. An assault was to be mounted over the Nederweert-Wessem Canal by the 160th Infantry Brigade of the 53rd (Lowland) Division.

I said to Gertrude that I would be calling round that evening, knowing that we would be gone and I would not be around, so feeling awkward but conscious of 'security'.

We made ready to move off, in the afternoon. Other squadrons were moving off before us on the route, and I had to double up to Jimmy Sale and report over the air when they had passed a certain point. Then we set off. The other tanks had churned the route across fields into deep mud, so we scraped along, wondering if we would 'belly', and our tracks would no longer grip.

All was well, and as night fell, we found ourselves near self-propelled artillery, which began to fire as the attack began. The flanks of the attack were marked by Bofors firing tracer into the air, and I believe 'Monty's Moonlight' (low searchlight beams) were also employed as the infantry crossed the canal.

A new lad, Don Banks, had joined us. He had come from 79th Armoured and was married to the daughter of the Postmaster of Penrith. We sat on the turret of the tank – the others had sensibly retired for the night – and listened to sounds of the assault. I, a seasoned warrior of at least six months, pointed out the distinctive crackle of Spandau machine-gun fire to him!

Next day we crossed the canal by Bailey Bridge and set out along the canal bank. On the trees which were planted on the bank, wires had been strung at tank turret height. They were attached to grenades which were in the trees, at the right height for the heads of tank commanders. Fortunately, they had all been disconnected, for the attack was now several hours old. As we went along the bank we ran into trouble, for there was a tunnel, one of several, which had been dug through the bank from the 'land' side to the 'canal' side. This tunnel collapsed under the weight of our tank and, as Tom tried to reverse out, a track came off the driving sprocket on the front.

Mike Smethurst transferred to the tank of the Troop corporal, 'Shorty' Higham, and Shorty came to us. We sat and waited for the fitters to come to our aid. The name of the fitter sergeant was Webb, so we always asked for 'Spider's Boys' over the air. They would break the track, tow the tank out backwards and join the track up again when it was on level ground once more. I believe they did this by late afternoon, but by then our services were no longer needed in a fighting capacity.

An amusing footnote from Antwerp: Melanie found 'Shorty' hard to pronounce, so she asked him what his real name was. "Harold," he said, but she found this even more impossible, so had to stick to Shorty.

We were billeted in villages round the countryside during the next few weeks.

Once, I remember being in a house where the son was on holiday from the seminary where he was training to be a priest. Father and mother and a daughter were the other members of the family. The son spoke good English, so we had an interesting time yarning round the stove in the winter evenings. The electricity was supplied from a power-house still in the hands of the Germans. Every evening, for twenty minutes, there was a power-cut. The seminarian declared that this was 'a time for the young people to have a cuddle in the dark', which I thought was very broadminded for someone training for the priesthood. For some reason, I was billeted in the house on my own, which I thought unusual.

Chapter 14

Leende – And a Scare at Night

The beginning of December found us at Leende, then a small village on the outskirts of Eindhoven. We were billeted in a farmhouse where there was a large family. We slept in a loft of some kind, where I think there was hay. Once, we held a parade for inspection, and I recall that the young boy of the family was amused by the way in which I stood to attention. He was fond of repeating "Protestant good, Catholic bad!" and looking at me for approval, but I was having none of this sycophancy. He was only a ten-year old, after all, but it made me sad that he should think that he could please me by appearing to reject his Faith.

Here we made a brief acquaintance of the ME 262, the German jet fighter. One swept over the village one afternoon and fired its cannon as it passed. I was interested to see that the puffs of smoke from the cannon hung in the air, quite separate from each other for a second, before they were swept away by the slip-stream.

One of the lads put up a 'black' with the wife of the house where they were billeted. He brought into the front room, which had been allocated as living quarters, the petrol stove from the tank in order to make tea. The good lady of the house protested – his assurances that it would be "Alright, Ma!" fell on deaf ears. The bottom of the sash window was open, and net curtains were blown by the draught. The stove having been lit and the tea made; a black strip was observed at the bottom of the curtains. 'Ma' was very indignant, saying, "I told you so!" in Dutch. A bar of soap was produced, and this went some way towards calming the atmosphere.

The day came for our inspection by Michael Carver, the Brigadier. We and the tanks were duly inspected, with one surprise bonus for me. Above the gun, in a small rack, was kept a record book in which the number of rounds fired by the 75mm, and belts of ammunition by the Browning, were noted. Some fit of organisation had seized me, and I had duly entered all the details in the book. Apparently, I was the only gunner in the squadron, if not in the regiment, to do this and I got a pat on the back from Mike for my little effort.

The guard room was in one of the houses in the main street. Unhappily, the family there had an aged aunt or grandmother who had her house destroyed by gunfire. She could be heard, muttering in her derangement, in a room which opened off the guard room.

In a film I had seen some years before, called *The Old Dark House*, featuring Karloff and Charles Laughton, the most spine-chilling scene occurred. There was a shot of the bannisters on the stairs, and a claw-like hand appeared resting on them. The sight was accompanied by a hair-raising cackle of manic laughter. As I sat in the guard room, the door of the room where the deranged relative slept slowly swung open. I was fully expecting a claw-like hand to appear round the edge of the door and a cackle to ring through the house. I expect a sleeper in the other room had turned over and a floorboard had moved, so making the door open. But I sweated for a minute or two!

We were in a hamlet, outside an isolated farm house where we had spent the night, when we came to move in the morning, we discovered that we had been afflicted by one of those mysterious things, a hydrostatic lock. This was a condition to which radial engines were prone, and our engine was, well, locked. The rest of the squadron charged off to do battle, and we were left high and dry to await the fitters, for we could not release the engine without their aid.

Night came and we were still waiting, for other events had taken place. The squadron had come under shellfire and Topper Brown had been wounded in the thigh, sustaining a broken femur. He told me later that, as he was wearing a 'zoot suit', Jimmy Sale had told the people who attended to 'Topper' not to cut the suit. This made Topper very cross, he told me. It reminded me of the Duke of Marlborough, John Churchill, who forbade his servant to cut off the ducal gaiters when they got soaked.

Topper was sent to a hospital in Nottingham and so my father was able to visit him. I saw him there when I went on leave in early 1945. I took a friend who was in the Navy with me and Topper flung aside the blankets to reveal a plastered leg. There were pins projecting out of the plaster where the broken bones had been joined up again. I looked with interest and then turned to my naval companion, who had gone a pale shade of green!

To return to the hydrostatic lock. We spent the night at the little farmhouse, each of us taking a turn at 'sentry', mostly sitting in the kitchen but taking a stroll outside now and again to see if all was well. The two men of the farm sat with us, despite our endeavours to get them to go to bed. Perhaps they didn't trust us or thought maybe we had been left behind to deal with any German attack. Though I suspect that we had told them that the tank was 'kaput'.

The fitters came in the morning, and we rejoined the squadron again.

As Christmas drew near, we moved to Asten and were billeted in the home of the van de Zanden family. There were three sisters and two brothers, none of whom had ever married, their parents dying young. Marie was the eldest, then came Piet, Grada, Yet and Wim, who was the youngest and was slightly disabled. When there was fighting round Asten, they were forced to leave their modern house and become refugees for a little while, but now they were back home again and welcomed us in a very hospitable way.

In his book *I was a Strangermil*, John Hackett writes of the Dutch family which sheltered him after Arnhem. The same air of quiet devotion and faith prevailed in the van de Zanden household. We gathered round the dining-room table at night and, with the curtains drawn and the stove burning, enjoyed the quiet company of the family. They were reticent about the difficult years of the Occupation, though I recall a story of a young man who had some RAF aircrew in his baker's van. He caused it to break down as they drew near a German road-block and he enlisted some members of the Wehrmacht, who helped him push the van until it started again and he drove away.

The Burgemeester, named Wijnen, and the Burgemeester of the next district, Someren, whose name was Smulders, had been taken away and summarily shot on the bank of the Wessem Canal in August. The spot was, of course, on the border between the two districts. Later on, the street where the van de Zandens lived was renamed from Molenstraat (Mill Street) to Burgem, Wijnenstraat.

We slept on the bare boards of the front bedroom and were warm and dry during the coldest weeks. On guard one night, when it had snowed, I found the corpse of a little dog which had frozen to death. It was as stiff as a board because of the frost.

We were sent to play football on the village pitch, but it was like a skating rink where snow had melted and then frozen again. We trailed a little way into the woods and fired a Bren-gun and threw a couple of 36 grenades just to remind ourselves that there was a war on. There was plenty of air activity to remind us of that and, in the hours of daylight, the Fortresses of the US Air Force flew overhead, trailing clouds of vapour in the icy air. At night, too, we heard bombers flying over and, once, my companion on guard saw a parachute come down a little distance away. Though it was bright moonlight, I could not see it and there was no sound of aircraft engines. Within a few minutes a Jeep drew up, and the occupants asked us where the parachutist had landed, so it was not imagination on the part of my companion. I had not been looking in the right direction.

Other notable air activity before Christmas took the form of a V1 which clattered over the village one night when I was on guard. A Dutch farmer was standing with me. "A Londres!" I said, thinking of the people at home, sheltering in the Underground. "*Oui!*" he agreed, "*Mais il ne mange pas!*" I could not take comfort from the fact that a flying bomb wouldn't eat, but I had not spent years under Occupation. Maybe it was a stray which had gone off course, and perhaps it was directed at Antwerp anyway.

We had gone to Antwerp on a short leave (although we were not supposed to do so, because of the V1s and V2s).

To Antwerp, then, and the renewal of our friendships there. I stayed with the Huybrechts family and noted how jumpy everyone had become because of the rockets. A V2 rocket had fallen on a corner of the street, killing a friend of Melanie. The friend's small daughter was staying with Melanie for the day and, when Melanie said that her friend was 'kaput', the small child danced round the table chanting, "Kaput, kaput!"

We went to the cinema and saw *Alexander's Ragtime Band.* This was a film which seemed to haunt us, and we saw it several times, courtesy of the Army Film Unit, in various locations, both in the Low Countries and in Germany.

Several of the lads went into town with the lady of the house where they were staying. When they reached the shopping area, the good lady directed the boys to the 'Red Light' district and said that she would meet them later on. She was surprised and pleased when they said that they preferred to come shopping with her. A bit of home life was what they craved, not dubious pleasures.

Back to the regiment, then, thankful to be safely out of the way of rockets and V1s, which were taking a toll of dead and injured in the city.

Christmas drew near. A group was sent into the countryside to get holly for the large room in a cafe on the corner of Molenstraat, which we used as a dining room. They managed to get holly with no berries on it. I was asked to make some berries and remedy this deficiency. "Here is some wire," said one of the sergeants, "some soap, a knife and red paint. You scrape some soap off the cake with the knife, knead it into a ball, thread it on the wire and paint it red."

I could hardly believe my ears.

I scraped, rolled and painted very reluctantly, making about four berries in the course of an hour. Here were the nations of the world locked in mortal combat and here was I making soap berries. The holly appeared, berryless, on the walls of our dining room.

Various treats were laid on for the population at Christmas. There was a concert, and we were told that the roll of drums which began the evening's entertainment heralded, not the British or Dutch national anthems, but the Egyptian one. That got things off to a good start.

There was a procession through the streets in which Olly, heralded from the Town Hall steps by a trumpeter, played St. Nicholas, riding on a horse belonging to the local baker. Leading the horse was Clifford Pace, suitably made up as Black Piet, the Recorder who decreed whether or not children had a gift, according to their behaviour during the year. There was a party for the children. There were sweets and other goodies to eat, and I heard how popular the Colonel, Bill Rankin, was with the children.

I had resolved to go to the Communion Service on Christmas morning and so put on my best battledress. Unfortunately, Jock appeared (now back from leave) and said he had been up to the tank. There was ice all round the outside of the turret and I must come and chip it away so that the turret could traverse. I made my way up to the tank park. Sure enough, there was ice at the base of the turret. The snow had melted and then frozen again. I set to and chipped away, thinking that Christmas Day services were difficult to attend in the army. After a little while, Tom came to start the engine and move the tank up and down a bit to make sure all was well with the machinery. As he moved the vehicle, with me on the back, I noticed that the turret moved anyway. The ice had just stuck to the turret and did not hinder movement. By that time, it was too late for me to go.

Shortly after Christmas we held a dance. Some of the village girls came and those who could dance did so. I was not a dancer, so I had a beer or two and chatted to the others. Ted Dunn and Mike Smethurst were there for a time and Ted told me that the KRR Infantry had found about thirty dead German soldiers at the place where I had shot through the trees as they tried to escape on trucks. He and Mike declared that was a "Good show" on my part. I wondered!

The party got noisier as the beer flowed. Two policemen appeared and spoke to the girls about the time and said that they ought to be leaving. Jock was indignant and wanted to protest in a physical way, but we persuaded him verbally to curb his enthusiasm.

'Cliff' Clifford and I found ourselves escorting comrades back to the billets. Nick, I remember, was in a bad way and we had to practically carry him, stopping at intervals for him to ease his laden stomach. I am never at my best when others are being sick, but we managed with him. We got Bill Williams home and Cliff and he had an argument. I was amazed when Cliff just chucked him under the chin. Bill's teeth clicked as his jaw shut and he collapsed on the bed, out like a light. A figure (Tommy, one of the drivers) detached itself from the wall of a house and rolled into the road like a hedgehog. He had desperately wanted to come outside, so we propped him against a wall and left him to it. Goodness knows what the locals made of all this debauchery.

Boxing Day was quite exciting, as the Luftwaffe decided to liven things up. Raids were carried out on Brussels airfield and other places. Focke-Wulf and Messerschmidt aircraft seemed to be everywhere, roaring over the houses.

The fitters had a large-calibre Browning on their half-track and opened fire with this, chopping a telephone wire in half and giving a Dutch housewife hysterics as she fled indoors from the noise: otherwise, no damage to friend or foe!

Home leave time came and lots were drawn. I was in the first party but was asked to exchange with SSM Rhodes who wanted to go home for pressing personal reasons. I willingly exchanged places with him and so was to go on leave in early February.

In between times, there was a 'bit of battling' at Wanssum, on the banks of the Maas, where the Germans had established a toe-hold on our side of the river.

Chapter 15

Winter Landscape – Wanssum

We were taking turns on duty, day and day about, with the Royal Scots Greys and it was our turn when the call to action came. We had to help the infantry to dislodge the enemy and send him back to his side of the river Maas again. Several attempts had been made to do this, but the small bridgehead was covered by good defensive fire from their side of the river, and the attempts had failed for this reason.

Now we were to support the 1st Battalion Suffolk Regiment, 3rd Infantry Division, in another attempt. Not only were our tanks to support the attack but 'Kangaroos', armoured personnel carriers adapted from 'Ram' Canadian tanks and looking like Shermans without turrets, were to bring the infantry to the attack. With our support, they were to dismount, then clear and occupy the wood where the Germans were established.

It was bitterly cold, snowy weather by now. The call to action came and I had to rush round to RHQ where one of our drivers, George Ellis, was on guard, and grab him.

We drove off and established ourselves in a barn near Venraij for the night. Alf Pitcher was on guard here and he had come without his 'zoot suit' (the name we gave to the tank suits which were issued to us in the autumn). I had my suit and Alf asked if he could borrow it. The suit had two zips which ran from ankle to neck on each side, down the two legs. The idea was that they could be zipped up to make a sleeping-bag in cold weather! One of my zips had come to pieces and I had put it together by hand, climbing into the made-up zip part and then zipping the other side normally. "Whatever you do," I said to Alf, "don't unzip this side!!" Naturally, Alf forgot my instructions and so my suit was unwearable in the morning, as there was not time to do it up again by hand. I wore my greatcoat instead!

We set off in the morning darkness. It was my job to see to the bed-rolls on the back of the tank when we got ready to move. There was a tarpaulin on the back of the tank, on the engine cover, and the bed-rolls were laid on this. The tarpaulin was then folded over the bed-rolls, to make a waterproof parcel. The whole thing was tied down by an empty ammunition belt from the Browning. This was strong and ideal for the job.

This morning, I had got the bed-rolls in place and was just about to tie them down, when we moved off, so I was fighting with the belt as we moved along. When it was securely tied, I squeezed past Mike, who was standing in his hatch, and got into the gunner's seat.

We moved forward with the 'Kangaroos' to attack the enemy in the woods. As the dawn broke, I commented on the tank being camouflaged by snow, but Mike said that it had melted and so we stood out, black against the white landscape. Mike told me to fire the machine-gun. I sent a stream of tracer into the whiteness of the sky, hoping that Mike would direct my aim. All I could see was whiteness.

"There's infantry there!" shouted Mike down the microphone. I elevated the guns and saw a file of infantrymen plodding through the snow. I had been firing just short of them. Snow and sky were indistinguishable, but more elevation brought into sight a wood, black against the winter background.

We shot with high explosive. Frozen earth, bits of wood and other debris flew up in the air with each shot. The 'Kangaroos' went in, the infantry advanced and cleared the wood. A lot of the Germans had retired over the Maas when the tanks appeared.

There were casualties, some caused by mines; we had two tanks disabled, but worse was to follow as the enemy retaliated with shellfire. One of the shells burst inside the turret of one of our tanks, killing the three who were inside. The driver and co-driver baled out. An unhappy end to the engagement. I watched through my periscope and saw smoke pouring through the open hatches of the stricken tank.

The squadron assembled behind farm buildings, for refuelling and the replenishment of expended ammunition. From where we were we could see figures toiling round the tank that had been hit. It had been driven to a spot near a small Bailey bridge, and the dead were being buried there. A thin snow began to whirl, driven by a biting wind. As I watched the distant figures, the music of 'The Ride of the Valkyries' came to mind and I thought how appropriate such music was, in the circumstances.

The journey back to Asten was not without incident.

We crept along at first but soon the pace quickened, as we rattled along over the roads packed with a topping of hard frozen snow. I had elected to sit on the back of the tank, as I usually did when we were moving from place to place. From that vantage-point, I saw an amazing sight as the tanks roared along. As each tank slid down the camber of the road, it hit the frozen verge and shot back to the centre of the road again. Looking along the line of tanks, one had the impression of a long, steel snake wriggling along as the tanks bounced back and forth on their journey.

I could see that the next slide down would happen when we were crossing a Bailey bridge, and I moved across the back of the tank, away from the stream, ready to jump for it if we went over the barrier; but Tom, cool as ever, kept his foot steadily on the accelerator and the hazard was safely passed.

I was surprised by the emotional welcome I got from Piet van de Zanden when we got home. "You were lucky, John!" he kept saying as he shook my hand. I suppose I seemed very young to him.

We stood in the tank park one morning, working on the vehicles. It was very misty, but the sun was glowing above the mist and turning the air into a shining golden cloud.

Suddenly, out of this cloud there came a bride and her father, slowly walking to her wedding. He wore formal attire of black coat and top hat; she in radiant white, carrying a small bouquet.

They paced slowly along in complete silence and vanished into the golden vapour again like wraiths. Their solemn dignity impressed all of us, I think, for no-one spoke as they passed before us.

We left Asten behind us, with many regrets, and moved back to the Leende area. This time I was billeted in an upstairs room of one of the houses, on what had been the guard room side of the street.

With us was a lad, in Signals, who had one of the infantry wireless sets, a number 18, I think it was. We could listen to the popular numbers of the day on this wireless and our Signals friend very often went to sleep with headphones clamped on his ears and the set switched on.

Shortly before the date of my leave came along, I was put on a gunnery course. I was sent to another village and billeted in a small cottage – almost a hovel. The lady of the house was very large, and she had a face like something out of the more grotesque paintings of Breughel. She appeared to be speechless at my presence. The ground floor room where I was to sleep had a large gap under the door, an outside one, where the step had been worn away over the years.

Fortunately, I reported to the officer in charge of the gunnery course, who was dismayed by my intending to go on leave.

"Is anybody else doing anything silly?" he asked. I think that there had been confusion over my swapping dates with SSM Rhodes.

Back to Leende then and leave. As we stood on parade, waiting to go on the truck to the train, a Jeep roared up with a huge reel light on the mudguard, which had been taken from a tank transporter. Behind the Jeep was a staff car containing Montgomery.

Off, then, by truck and train, and eventually our carriage waited outside Calais station. We heard the wind bowling through the gaps at the sides of the carriage windows. As we prepared to embark, we made purchases of gifts for the folks at home. I bought, among other things, a large, white toy rabbit for a new girl cousin. So, on board. The ship's Captain addressed us over the loudhailer. "As you will probably see, there are loose mines drifting in the Channel, but we will get you across safely." We were then issued with life-belts, as on D-Day, made of balloon fabric. We left harbour, and the strong wind blowing up-Channel held the ship firmly tilted to port all the time, sometimes very much so, all the way across. I pass over the misery of sea-sickness!

On the train from St Pancras to Nottingham, I fell into conversation with a Canadian who had been at Caen, so it was interesting to hear his side of things.

It may have been my imagination, but I felt I could smell Nottingham as the train drew into the station. There were car drivers who got an extra petrol allowance for running a taxi service for service men and women coming home on leave. We all crammed into a car, and I was fortunate enough to have an attractive WAAF sitting on my knee. Then some idiot came and said he was going my way and so I had to untangle myself from her and go with him to my home town, Stapleford.

There was an emotional greeting from my parents and after a restful night, leave began.

I made a journey to my old school. Goodness! Was it only two and a half years ago that I left? Some of my form-mates were now in the Upper Sixth on their way to university. I was to find out later that they were embarrassed about still being civilians.

War had touched the school, though. Masters had been 'called up' and two had died, one in the army, and the other, the Art Master, a hero of mine, in the RAF in the Middle East, flying Wellingtons on convoy patrol. The school secretary, a beautiful young woman, with lovely dark red hair, had joined the WAAF and had been killed in an air crash in Italy.

An 'Old Boy' of Italian extraction had been shot when he had been captured during a parachute operation to blow up a viaduct in Italy.

In Nottingham, I saw another form-mate, Alan, who was in aircrew, Bomber Command. I was shocked by his appearance. His face was like that of a wizened monkey, and his eyes were round and staring like those in photographs of First World War soldiers who had endured too much horror in the trenches.

I went to tea with relatives and friends. One friend, who had just married, turned off the wireless when the news came on. "You don't want to listen to that," he said. But I did. Suppose an offensive had begun and we were in it?

The BBC broadcast bulletins for those on leave from the Continent and gave out the news of delays in sailings which had to be made because of bad weather. We had a leave number and listened to see if this was on the 'Delayed' list. My leave number was delayed three times, meaning I got three extra days leave because no ships were able to sail.

When I returned to 'A' Squadron, Harry Gill was orderly sergeant, and he threatened to put me on a charge for being late back. I managed to persuade him that my late return was all official!

I learned that our Signals friend had an accident while I had been away. He had tried to climb a tree in a Jeep and was now in hospital. A friend, who had been to see him, reported that he was 'on a catheter' which he found most useful if young women came to see him, as he did not then have the embarrassment of asking for a bottle. He must have been shipped to the UK.

We went to see a live show in Eindhoven, which was put on for us by a Belgian concert party. There was the inevitable Can-Can, a young man mimed the sculpting of the Venus de Milo. Much scope for rudery here as he had to consult a young lady member of the cast for anatomical details. There was an Apache dance when another female member of the cast pretended to have a row with a Sharpshooter who had been invited to sit at her table and flew into the arms of her vigorous dancing partner.

The concert over, we returned to Leende, giving a lift to two American soldiers. We sang our usual songs and then asked the Americans if they knew any they could sing to us. They said, "No!" quite meekly. I think that they were a bit daunted by our repertoire.

Chapter 16

Return to Tilburg

The weather was getting milder by now and the snow had gone by the time we returned to Tilburg, now a stage on the way to the Rhine and not as a place to be fought into.

Here we stayed for several days, sleeping in 'civvy' billets. There were several incidents here, mostly of a humorous nature. Lofty Long was chasing another member of the Troop, who fled into his billet. Lofty, chasing him, tripped on the step from the pavement to the garden path and flew, quite horizontally, head-first towards the corner of the house. Head and brickwork met with a thud which I heard, though I was standing yards away. Lofty crashed to the path, picked himself up, shook his head and resumed the chase.

There were V1s which flew over at night, I presumed on the way to Antwerp. One lad told a remarkable story about how, when a V1 clattered overhead, he had flung himself down on top of the young lady he was escorting from one of our dances.

Some people went to look at the scene of the autumn battle near the factory and were sworn to secrecy about how we had been responsible for the demolition of the chimneys. No word of our complicity must reach the ears of the good burghers of Tilburg.

There was a drill parade – a most unusual event – and added spice was given when a Dutch housewife began to shout abuse at the NCO taking the parade. We agreed with her sentiments, though expressed in Dutch!

Here we put extension plates (spuds) on the tracks to widen them and thus give more purchase on muddy ground. There are photographs of tanks coming back from Wanssum, equipped with these. The track had to be broken and then joined up again, each link on the outside of the track now being replaced by a 'spudded' one.

Richard Dipple distinguished himself by driving a tank so close to a newly 'spudded' one that he shaved the side and knocked off all the new 'spuds'.

We drove away from Tilburg in fine style, turning at the end of the street, the tracks digging into the pavé of the road, each tank digging in deeper and flinging the pavé blocks all over the place.

We crossed into Germany! News came that Colonel Rankin had been wounded and our new CO was Major Skelton. He was a Sharpshooter but had been with the Northants Yeomanry when Fireflies in the squadron which he was commanding fired at a group of three Tigers in Normandy. In one of them, Michael Wittmann met his death: he had been responsible for the Villers debacle.

I was beside the tank, brewing a cup of tea on our first day in Germany, when I caught sight of a movement out of the corner of my eye. As I turned to look, a huge column of earth and smoke rose quickly into the air, followed a second later by that curious flat bang of a mine exploding. A Jeep could be seen amidst the cloud of smoke and dust. The driver staggered out of the wreck, hands over his ears. Bill Cotton was a passenger in the Jeep, and his feet were badly injured by the explosion.

I remember little of the Reichswald Forest fighting, though I do remember a creepy feeling, standing in the woods and hearing not a sound. There were branches lying about, chopped off by shell splinters or machine-gun fire.

We were wary of 'Bazooka men' in this close country, so the sides of tracks and woodland rides were sprayed with Browning fire as we drove down them. The trouble was, that as the barrel overheated and expanded, the trace described fantastic corkscrew flights in the air. We then had to let the gun cool down a bit before we fired again.

So, we drove at night, passing through Cleve. I was on the back of the tank, and I remember seeing the ruined buildings silhouetted against the fitful moonlit sky.

Next day saw us in Udem. We were parked under the church tower as we waited for orders. Mike Smethurst was still the commander and Jock Campbell the operator. Myself as gunner, of course, but we had Tug Wilson as our driver now and also had a co-driver, Alan Hughes.

While we waited, the German artillery began to range on the tower. As shells began to bang about, Mike moved to the operator's side of the turret. The wide, standard hatch for the commander had been replaced by a smaller, British-designed hatch. It had a number of periscopes fitted, giving all-round vision when closed down. Smaller it may have been, but a chunk of brick flew through the open hatch and scored a line down my leather jerkin. I must have exclaimed, for Mike asked if I was alright. I told him, "Yes," but we decided to move on a bit, away from the tower. It was fortunate that he was not on his usual side of the turret when the piece of brick flew down.

In the film *The True Glory*, about the liberation of Europe, there was a shot of a small, dead German girl lying on a heap of rubble. I saw this child through my periscope at Udem. She was blonde and had on a blue dress.

As we began to climb the gentle sloping road out of the town, we passed a knocked-out Sherman which had large numbers painted on the side of the turret. Not one of ours, therefore. We drove past this popping, banging bonfire as it brewed away to itself.

German prisoners were coming down the road, dressed, it seemed, in tattered greatcoats and flapping rags. An infantry CSM was helping them on their way with a well-aimed kick on the rear.

We paused to take on board our Infantry support, a Battalion of the Hereford Regiment, and began to climb out of the shallow valley where there were a few ruined houses.

We churned across a huge, ploughed field toward the crest of the rising ground. As we reached the top of the sloping field, some of the infantry and tanks were skylined, and heavy guns began to fire from the other side of the Rhine. As they exploded, the shells from these guns made large craters in the soft earth.

The infantry began to leave the tanks and to dig in. We pushed on a bit but began to come under fire from tanks or anti-tanks guns firing from the valley before us. They had an excellent view of us on the skyline and before long three or four of our tanks were brewing. I saw Tom Wellbourne's crew scuttling to the rear, leaving an inert figure beside their tank. Behind us, another tank had the driver hit as the shot penetrated the driving compartment. As the crew tried to get him out, so another shot in practically the same place hit him again and pulled him from their grasp into the tank. It instantly caught fire and they had to leave it and run, for there were machine-guns firing from farm buildings in front.

We moved forward and received a resounding smack on the front of the co-driver's side of the hull. A large piece of armour flaked off the inside of the hull, crushing one side of an enamel mug kept there by Alan. No damage apart from that.

'Tug' put the tank into reverse and began to move back. The others, seeing us hit, put down smoke round us to help if we wanted to bale out. Unfortunately, we could not see where we were going, because of the smoke, and so reversed into one of these enormous shell craters, where we stuck, unable to move forward or back.

The tank was canted over toward the left and, in fact, the top of the turret on that side was level with the ground around the crater.

As I looked out at the scene through my periscope, I saw 'Bunty', another Troop Leader, manoeuvring into position to try and tow us out. As I watched, I saw machine-gun tracer flash past his head.

Mike called him up and told him not to try and pull us out, for he would put himself in danger, towing us to the place where we had been hit.

Mike, Alan and Tug got out of the tank to assess the possibilities, but we were well and truly stuck. Mike called out something to me – it was about removing the firing-pin from the 75mm, and the breech blocks from the Brownings, but I could not hear him above the noise of the battle. It was evident, however, that we must leave the tank.

Jock was the first of the two of us do so. He got his Berretta from the top of the wireless levered himself up and tried to get out of the hatch, but it was small and the tank was on a slope. I watched as he had two goes at getting out, legs kicking, then he was out and it was my turn. The door of the hatch was locked in an upright position. I put my Sten gun on the top of the turret and opened the hatch door so that it lay flat on the tank turret roof. I had not realised that I had trapped the Sten sling in the catch holding the door open. I got out and tried to dislodge the sling from the catch. Then I heard shots snapping past my head. I remembered seeing the tracer shoot past the head of Bunty a few moments ago and decided it was also time for me to go – Sten-less.

I slid down the roof of the turret and took shelter with the others in the shell hole on the lee side of the hull. I then discovered that Mike expected me to have disarmed the guns and bring with me the vital parts, but he told me not to try to return to get them. Tug had left his Smith and Wesson beside his hatch, too. That would have to stay.

We debated our options and decided to make a run for it. A small hayrick to our front would be our first objective, or 'bound'. As we talked about this, I exerted my one bit of leadership and said, "We could be there while we're thinking about it," and set off, the others pounding along with me. A startled infantryman yelled, "What's up?" as he saw us making for the rear at speed, but appropriate hand signals and a shout of "It's OK!" reassured him.

On, then, from the hayrick and more galloping to the rear. We seemed to be pursued by mortar shells and, glancing back, we saw our first 'bound' vanish in smoke and flames.

We found ourselves in a dip, where a track came down from the high ground. Several others were there, including the survivors of the two tanks that had lost crew members. Tom Wellbourne had been hit in the wrist and the sergeant of the crew which had lost the driver was reliving the moment when he had been pulled out of their grasp by the second shot.

Coming down from the hill were casualties from the infantry. Their CO walked past, supporting an infantryman. "It's my batman," he said, "he's been wounded! I'm taking him to the rear." I was very surprised by the fact that a CO should leave his battalion at such a time and explain to other ranks what he was doing, and why!

We decided that we, too, ought to make our way to the rear. Jock was keen on making his way back to the tank, as evening was drawing on. I walked up the track again and looked over the battlefield and saw that other tanks were on fire. If that were so, it would seem that our tank could be one of them. In fact, I was mistaken about this. The tank was partially in a hole and back from the ridge, so it could not be seen from the valley from where the hostile fire was coming. That night, however, there were bazooka teams out on the prowl and, had activity been seen round our tank, we might have fallen victim to one of these – as did another of our tanks during the night.

We turned to go down the road into Udem. Among the wrecked houses on the right of the road were two figures in field grey. They had rifles with them but seemed to be intent on looking for somewhere to sleep, so we walked on and left them to it. We met our own infantry waiting to move up. "Where's your tank?" they quipped. We made remarks about expensive garaging fees "higher up" and went on our way.

We came to a barn and saw infantrymen gathered round. The smell of cooking wafted toward us, and we heard the roar of cooking stoves. Someone invited us to join in and found us mess-tins and forks or spoons. We joined the queue and ate delicious stew. We went on our way again as dusk began to fall and found a field by the roadside. Was this an agreed rendezvous or had we fallen on this place by chance? I was too tired to articulate the question but stretched out on the grass and went to sleep.

I was awakened to find that a three-tonner had come for us, so we clambered aboard and were taken back to our supply trucks.

Joe Holway, the RSM, was there and took charge of us, indicating that the cook sergeant, Jim Cooper, had something for us to eat and, of course, a mug of tea. Thick, juicy, meticulously cut bully-beef sandwiches, and the tea was hot and sweet. How welcome it was. It was now quite dark, so Joe showed us to our beds in some nearby houses. The houses had been cleared of all furniture except the beds. This seemed to be common practice in the forward areas.

We were given blankets and Joe said, "Get up when you want, lads." We slept the night through and then had a little lie-in as instructed by our compassionate RSM.

The chaplain came – not Hubert Crane, for he had left us by now, but an eccentric Welshman. He gave us cigarettes, notepaper and envelopes so that we could write home.

During the next few days, we seemed to find ourselves assembling as a tankless regiment. So many had been knocked out. We were all together in an orchard, having a mid-morning mug of tea, I remember, and I bent down to pick up my mug from the top of a box. As I did this, there was a loud explosion near at hand. I stood up and everyone had vanished! There was a mess-tin on the grass, and a driving gauntlet, but no sign of anyone at all. I had no idea that human beings could move so quickly! They all crept back and continued their break. An RE sergeant drove up in a Jeep; he excitedly told us to get fire extinguishers and help put out the fire which the shell had started. He roared off in the Jeep; we looked round for fire extinguishers but couldn't see any. I presume the fire was eventually extinguished, for we heard no more.

The regiment had still been in action while the crews from the knocked-out tanks had been assembling. When they came out of action, we joined them in the valley from where the enemy tanks had fired on us on our first day. Don Banks was around one of the 'A' Squadron tanks when I saw him. His chin was covered by an interesting growth of three or four days. "What's this?" I asked. "No water!" he replied. Times were hard!

We learned, when we rejoined the regiment, that the CO, Major Gray Skelton, had been killed in the fighting.

When in France, this officer had been on detachment to the 1st Northants Yeomanry and had been CO of 'A' Squadron in that regiment. On 8th August the regiment engaged enemy tanks near the village of St Aignan de Cramesnil and in the fierce fighting three Tiger tanks were engaged by a Firefly of 3 Troop. All were destroyed, including the Tiger of Michael Wittmann. He and his crew were all killed. It was the same man, with a detachment of heavy tanks of SS Panzer Abteilung 101, that engaged 4th CLY at Villers Bocage on 13th June 1944.

I wanted to find John Cotton and so went in search of 'C' Squadron. "That's it, over there," said an informant when I asked where 'C' was. He nodded toward a hedge where three tanks were lined up. I found John in the turret of one of the tanks. He was surprised to see me as he thought I had "had it," as he put it, when he heard that one of the reinforcements had been killed. This was the unfortunate driver who had been killed by the second shot. We chatted away for a few moments, and it was then that he told me that he had been tempted to stay in Antwerp with a young lady in the house where he had been billeted.

'Tug' and I decided that we would like to go up onto the ridge and see if our tank was still in one piece, so after due warnings to keep off the skyline, we set off. Tom Wellbourne's tank could be seen from the valley floor, quite near the edge of the ridge. Ours was further back. We set off up a sunken track which led us up onto the ridge and from there we could see the battlefield. There were several brewed up tanks, but we could see, now, that ours was not one of them.

The tank was still in the shell-hole, canted over to the left. Tug had lost the Smith and Wesson which he had left on the top of his hatch but, as I expected, no-one had untangled my Sten from the hatch lid clip, so I was able to reclaim that. I found my shaving brush on the front mud-guard, so someone had been through the kit which was stowed in the bin on the back of the turret.

We peered inside the brewed-up tanks and then wandered downhill, tracing our flight to safety. There was still equipment lying about, including a Bren with the butt completely burned away. What had happened to the man firing that?

Tug decided that he would like to have a look at Tom Welbourne's tank, so he went forward. I stayed back, thinking about the 'no skylining' instructions. I saw Tug reach the tank and, sure enough, with the thud of distant firing and the howl of large-calibre shells, his presence had been noted by our foes. I got down in a ploughed furrow, put my hands over my ears, and kept my mouth open to minimise the effect of blast, but a shell landed to the front of the ridge where Tug was. To my relief, I saw him get up after that one and only salvo and scuttle over to join me. We walked down from the ridge again and told others about our little adventure. They, too, had heard the shells coming over and said, "We told you so!"

Later on in the day, I went up onto the ridge again and found Casey, Monahan and other enterprising individuals removing the bin from the back of the turret of our tank. It contained my best battledress and greatcoat, but also tins of food, which were the real prize. I protested at what I considered to be theft but was told that we had abandoned the tank and so it was legitimate plunder.

An examination of the front of the tank revealed a deep groove on the co-driver's side, on the curve of the hull. Looking down at the bottom of the groove I saw a hair-line crack and through it the inside of the co-driver's compartment could be seen. A lucky escape!

Replacement tanks came for us, and we prepared to move well to the rear. The tanks were loaded onto transporters, (Diamond T's) and we were able to make ourselves comfortable for the night in the large body of the vehicle, behind the driving cab. The space was filled with large blocks of wood, similar to railway sleepers, on which we spread our blankets.

So, carefree, we journeyed through the night, waking to find ourselves en route to Sonnis, in Belgium. I think that I got a short leave to Antwerp from there. We had a new CO come to us, Lt. Col. Anderson, and soon found ourselves on the transporters again, going up to the front once more.

To my surprise, we found ourselves in 'our' valley again. On the ridge skyline was the Sherman which had been Tom Wellbourne's, but it had been thrown on its side by one of the large shells and the turret had been turned so that the 75mm stuck up in the air. I had thought at first that it was an AA gun there, until a look through binoculars revealed what had happened.

There were Canadian soldiers about, and they livened up the proceedings, one giving an impromptu rodeo show by riding a heifer which was wandering around. I thought that we would see a real exhibition of Wild West expertise, but the animal bucked him off in short order, to howls of laughter from the others. Another Canadian claimed to have full-time work giving sexual satisfaction of an unusual kind to the ladies of Society in Montreal.

Reinforcements appeared and these included a very noisy young man with a ukulele. His repertoire was Formbyesque, with lewd embellishments. He was an expert scrounger and appeared one day with a small stove which he incorporated into our 'bivvy'. It certainly kept us warm and cosy during the cold nights. Unfortunately, he was a rather nervous type and one night, when Tommy Lightburn and I were on guard, a German self-propelled gun (SP) began to fire shots at random into the area. He leapt out of his blankets and hopped into the tank, where, well closed down, he refused to come out, despite our reassurances that it was quite safe.

A harmonium was produced from somewhere and Peter Smethurst gave us a tune or two, but, as I said to him, everything sounded like a revivalist meeting. Another find was a German bank-note of ludicrously high value. Obviously, a souvenir of the inflation which had plagued the country in pre-Hitler times. I was about to keep it as a souvenir, but when I turned it over, I found that it had been used for other purposes.

Hunting around, whether for stoves, harmoniums or bank-notes, could be dangerous, however, and the peace of the area was shattered one afternoon when part of a nearby farm was wrecked by a booby-trap explosion. I only hoped it had been set off deliberately by experts clearing up such devices.

Wandering along the track which lay at the foot of the ridge, I came across another small farmhouse which had been damaged by shell-fire. Beside the building was a grave and, reading the rough wooden cross, I saw that it was the grave of a woman and the date of her death was the date of our battle on the ridge. At the back of the house was a large wooden shed and, as I was examining the grave, solemn-faced toddlers came out of the shed, thumbs in mouths, and watched me with wide eyes. The father, too, came out and watched. I ceased my contemplation of the new grave and walked sadly away.

I made another trip onto the ridge with another reinforcement, Brack Brackley. By now, crosses had appeared on graves at the side of some of the tanks. We found a German rifle and proceeded to have fun with it, shooting at various targets, including an array of unbroken Kilner-type fruit jars which were standing on a shelf in the wreck of a farm. There were no spare clips of ammunition, so when we had exhausted the contents of the magazine, we threw away the rifle.

Mike Carver came to tell us that, when we got across the Rhine we would make George Patton's advances, "Look like a Funeral March!" I was interested to note his slight speech impediment and wondered that this had been no bar to his attaining high rank.

There was a crew reshuffle: I was to be gunner on a Firefly, Ken Godfrey was commander, Don Banks an operator and Desmond was the driver. I had never fired a 17-pounder, so this was to be a new experience.

The build-up for the Rhine crossing proceeded apace. Down the track from our area was a battery of heavy artillery which battered our ears from time to time, and there was a great increase in air activity. Night-time raids were common and our bombers dropped flares as they raided enemy positions on the other side of the Rhine. I remember one flare in particular which was like a great Christmas tree, lighting up the countryside for miles before slowly sinking to earth.

There was no enemy air activity, as far as we were concerned, though one sunny afternoon I saw in the far distance, in enemy territory, the vapour trails of what appeared to be V2 rockets.

There was a farm at hand and when the farmer, who was still in residence, appeared, he wore a leather moustache cover, tied behind the head. When he took it off a real 'Kaiser Bill' appeared, waxed ends and all. I wondered if his vanity extended to the wearing of corsets, too.

Somebody had an accident with a pig and a pistol, and Shorty Higham, who was a butcher in civilian life, set us to work pouring boiling water on the corpse and scraping off the bristles with sweet-tin lids. We soon had fresh pork chops and other 'piggy' delicacies to eat.

Other needs were catered for by the erection of a hessian screen in the field next to the tanks. A box was provided and the hessian screen enclosed it, enabling one to attend to the wants of nature with discretion. When one was seated, the screen extended to shoulder height and so one could both see and be seen. This was very useful as, if one was looking for someone and he was not around the tanks, it was worthwhile to have a quick check of the 'convenience' to see if the wanted head was peering over the screen.

On this Sunday morning, I was the one so concealed and I was puzzled by the behaviour of a Stirling bomber which appeared above 'our' ridge, banked and flew out of sight, only to reappear a few moments later and repeat the performance, but this time flying nearer before turning. Then I noticed a thin, dark cloud which had come into view. This soon resolved itself into the sight of aircraft and gliders. The banking Stirling had contained the radio reporter, Richard Dimbleby, who at that moment was broadcasting a description of the airborne crossing of the Rhine.

The aircraft and gliders flew overhead, and we could see flak coming up to meet them. Soon, the aircraft that had been towing the gliders began to return. One of them, a Stirling, with one engine on fire, flew over us and parachutes began to open as the crew jumped out. The canopies blossomed immediately they left the aircraft. The plane was fairly low and so I guessed that there was no time to waste. It flew along for a moment or two, then dived in a curve behind the hill. There was an enormous 'Whump!' as the plane hit the ground and exploded. A thick column of black smoke rose in the sunny air.

As the time came for our departure, the chaplain came and gave us Communion in the field next to the farmhouse.

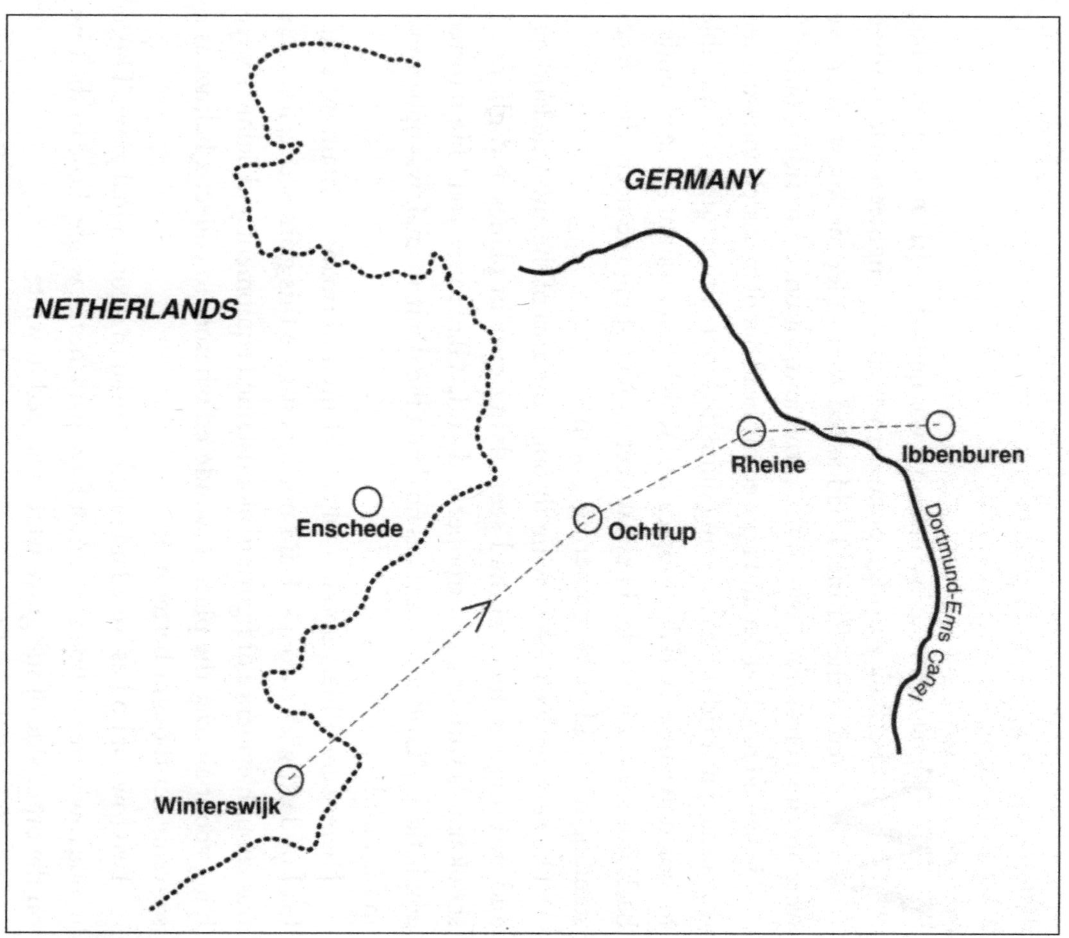

Map 6: Into Germany.

Chapter 17

Over the Rhine

We set off in the evening, so it was quite dusk when we approached the Bailey bridge pontoon which the engineers had thrown across the Rhine. I had asked Ken to let me know when we were about to cross, for I was in the turret and, for once, not riding outside.

He tapped my shoulder and I poked my head out of his hatch and surveyed the scene. The bridge was standing quite high out of the water, so I was able to look down on a Buffalo troop carrier which had brought some wounded back from the other side. They lay feet to feet along the deck, their faces standing out livid in the gathering gloom.

The next day we were moving through the area of the airborne landings and meeting the men we had seen flying over in planes and gliders. I shook hands with one paratrooper and said, "Glad to see you." He retorted emphatically, "Glad to see *you*!", as no doubt the Arnhem affair was uppermost in his mind.

There were gliders about – one, said my informant, containing a full load of dead glider troops. I did not investigate this grim scene, for there was enough evidence of fighting: bloodstained equipment and helmets were lying about all over the place. I wondered whether to collect a helmet as a souvenir but thought better of it.

Two rows of bodies were laid out for burial in a communal grave. Those in one row were wrapped in camouflage parachutes, while those in the row on the other side of the grave were wrapped in white.

A mystery that I could not explain now caught my attention. There was a slit-trench which had over it a Perspex canopy from a glider. This was what I would have expected. What I did not expect to see was, at the bottom of the slit-trench, a bed made up and, on the pillow end, a Sharpshooter's best beret, green band and cap badge, complete. How had it got there? We had only just arrived on the scene, and it was obvious that we were not going to stay on that spot, so no-one would claim a slit-trench for the night. Perhaps a paratrooper had begged a Sharpshooter beret as a souvenir of the Rhine crossing.

We remounted and drove on, hearing, over the air, instructions about not leaving the tanks to pick up parachutes as mementoes or to use as scarves when cut up.

Through my periscope, I saw more of the cost, in human terms, of the airborne landings. One particular sight stays in the memory, of a paratrooper lying beside a shell hole. The body had been cut in half and the legs, crossed, lay on one side, the torso on the other, the arms crossed in front of the face, which was at peace, but had blood running from ears and nose, dried now on the face.

We had the task of supporting the infantry, so found ourselves in a copse with a view forward over fields and hedges. The tank was concealed in the trees and, before us, right in front of the vehicle, was a slit-trench with infantrymen in it. In the distance, we could see a gun being prepared for action, with figures in field grey busying themselves around it.

We prepared to open fire and the infantry asked if they should move. Ken said that it would be alright as we would be firing armour-piercing shot. I fired twice and hit the target, but the third shot was immediately followed by an explosion in front of the turret. An anxious call from 'Sunray': "What was that?" Don had mis-heard the order to load and had loaded HE, not AP. The shell had burst on hitting the bushes in front us. Poor infantry!

I looked through my periscope and saw the disconsolate figure of an infantryman walking away from the scene. I did not know what the casualties were, except that there must have been some. I felt that we had let the 'feet' down in spite of our reassurances.

On the move again and through more woods. A truck drove from right to left along a track. We were loaded with AP and Ken said, "Traverse left!" I did the best I could, but the truck was moving too fast for me to get on target. I fired though and startled a German soldier who was running behind the truck. The shot must have gone right past his nose!

We endured a difficult time sitting on the road as the Welsh Recce Regiment investigated a road-block. As the Recce drew near the block, a carrier and one or two other vehicles were blown up by mines. This caused them to believe that they were being fired at by 88mm guns from somewhere. As Sergeant White remarked over the air, "Well, if it *is* 88s, I'm **** lucky, because I've been sitting here (in the open) all the time."

Eventually we decided to leave the road block to the Recce and took a minor road to the left, in order to get round it. We had wasted a lot of time, so it was now toward evening.

Suddenly, there was an enormous explosion and the tank heeled over to the driver's side. We had gone over a mine, perhaps connected to a larger device as it had blown off the front idler assembly completely. The only other casualty was the hood of Desmond's 'zoot suit' – it was blown off and we never found it.

The rest of the regiment began to drive past, leaving us to sit there, with night coming on. Sometimes we were nudged by others as they manoeuvred past but then the sound of the last engine and tracks died away and silence descended with the dark.

We took it in turns to sit in the turret, with the Sten handy in case anyone worried us. I must say that it was an anxious night and sense might have decreed us leaving the tank in case bazooka teams were about but, however illusory the protection of armour was against such perils, we preferred to stay inside.

Dawn brought a sense of relief and the fitters. Other members of the squadron came to join us too. There was a road-side farmhouse where we went to make our 'brew'.

A cart came down the road and on it a ladder covered with straw. This was serving as a stretcher for a German officer who had been wounded, and one of his men was leading the horse. He was brought in and laid on the kitchen floor. No doubt an ambulance was called for but, in the meantime, a painful incident. The officer had a wrist-watch and this was removed by one of us. The officer pleaded, "My watch! My watch!" Unhappily, his pleas fell on deaf ears. As the new 'owner' of the watch buckled it onto his wrist, he cheerfully observed, "They'll only take it off you further back." He was probably right but I was sorry and felt that this was unacceptable.

We must have acquired another Firefly, for I was with Ken when we were crossing a large field with a hedge running across our front some distance away. Two figures were on the other side of the hedge, hurrying along with shoulders hunched as if trying to avoid being seen. Ken had seen a gap in the hedge and saw that the two would have to dash across this. He asked me to put a shell in the gap, which I did. This should have warned the men, but they decided to make a run for it. I fired at the first one but when the second made his bid, I was groping about on the turret floor for a cigarette which I had dropped.

"Fire!" yelled Ken, so I stood on the firing button. "That was the second one," reported Ken to 'Sunray', but it would have been better to use the Browning. I am sure Jock would not approve of us wasting taxpayers' money to fire shells at individuals.

We drove through the best part of the night at one stage. Someone had picked up a man who was wearing a brand new suit of a startling brown shade. Despite his pleas that he was a forced labourer making his way back home, he was put on the back of our tank, and I rode on the back, too, keeping an eye on him. I found it rather hard to keep awake but, as I swayed on the back, he kept shaking me; had I fallen off, I expect that he would have been accused of pushing me, so it was in his interest to keep me awake. Naturally, when we had transported him through the night, back to the place from which he had started his journey, we found that his story was genuine, and his generous boss had given him the new suit to set him on his way.

Desmond left us shortly afterwards because of a silly accident. We were out of action at the time; Ken was out of the tank somewhere. The wireless was switched off, and I think that Desmond was the only other occupant, in the driving compartment. I decided that I would traverse the gun from pointing forward and swing it to the rear, where there was a clamp for the gun when it was in that position. I began to move the turret. Desmond had his drivers' hatch open and began to close it to allow the gun to move across. Unfortunately, his thumb got caught between the gun and the hatch lid. He called out, but as neither of us could hear the other properly, I thought that he was shouting to someone else. Though the gun had met some obstacle and would not traverse, it was not until I looked down at the driving compartment and saw blood dripping onto the floor that I realised something was seriously wrong. Poor Desmond had a badly squashed thumb and had to 'go sick'. Perhaps Tommy Lightburn became our driver then.

Crew changes were made several times, and I found myself as gunner to a number of crews.

We took part in a night attack at one place. I saw the silhouettes of infantrymen before a blazing farm and outbuildings. Morning revealed the sight of a dead stretcher bearer, with red crosses on his helmet and first-aid packs. He was lying sideways at an angle, caught in barbed wire, with both the soles of his boots planted firmly on the ground – an impossible position for a living man to adopt. I wondered if his ankles were broken.

A spell with Sergeant Harry Gill was notable for the manner in which we pushed on, for which Harry was commended by Peter Smethurst.

Once again it was twilight as we moved forward. Across the road was a very large tree which had been felled to impede progress. There was no way round this obstacle, as trees at the sides of the road barred our way. We were the leading tank, so Harry decided that over and through the branches of the tree was the only way. He asked me for my Sten gun in case of trouble from German infantry and we set off. I looked through my periscope and saw the rear end of a Churchill moving out of our way as we advanced on the tree. We hit the tree and, with snapping and scraping of wood, we wriggled our way forward. Harry crouched on the turret floor as branches came poking through his hatch. Then we were clear and motored to the high ground where we were to assemble. Harry gave me back my Sten gun but branches had twisted it out of shape, so that it looked like the letter 'Y' when I held it by the butt. When I asked for a new gun 'Q' asked me what I had been doing!

Peter Smethurst said that if everyone had pushed on as Harry had done, "This war would have been over long ago, Sergeant Gill!"

That night I was on guard. It was a brilliant moonlit scene with all the tanks lined up in rows. My companion was a new recruit, and I was a bit concerned for he was a very noisy young man. The night was cold and he blew on his hands to warm them, which was good enough, but he clicked his heels together to warm his feet, and the sound rang through the still night. I thought any German patrols within earshot would home in on the noise. I was glad to come off guard.

Another night attack and one of the tanks got into some kind of trouble. We heard a driver over the air say that he would go forward on foot and drive the abandoned tank, bringing it back to the others. This seemed a risky enterprise in the dark, but the tank was rescued.

Shorty Higham was my commander for a spell, and this goes down in memory as 'The Time of the Cyclists'. We were driving across fields when our attention was drawn to two figures, one tall and one short, cycling along a track crossing our front. They had 'sit up and beg' bikes. "They seem to be 'civvies'," said Shorty. Sunray said: "They should not be cycling in a battle area!" "OK, Fish," said Shorty, "Better shoot at 'em." I shot with the Browning, traversing the turret and expecting the men to take cover, as I was firing ahead of them and could see the puffs of dust where the bullets were striking. Surely, they would get off their bikes. I was willing them to do so as I fired. I thought that if I stopped traversing, they would see the strike of the bullets ahead, and that would make them stop and go to ground until we had gone. To my dismay, they rode into the cone of fire, and both came off in a tangle of legs and wheels. I stopped firing at once but, as the tracer indicated, several bullets were still in flight. I hoped that they were only wounded.

The strain of war was beginning to show for some. Our ukulele-playing friend, who had joined us before we crossed the Rhine, had lasted until he saw his first dead German soldier, then he had to be sent back. Others, with much longer active service, were beginning to find things difficult. I took the place of a gunner who had been overcome by 'nerves' and had affected the rest of his crew. There was a young officer, unknown to me, as commander of the tank and we were supporting infantry. We assembled and started off. We passed an infantry sergeant who had been wounded and was lying beside the track, waiting for the stretcher bearers. We passed in front of some farm buildings where the German soldiers were holding out. The commander wanted the tank to keep on the move, so we drove up and down in order to present a more difficult target to unfriendly fire.

He asked me to put some HE rounds into trees lining a hedgerow, thinking to liven up any German infantry who might be taking cover there. This I did but, unfortunately, the electrics packed up and neither the Browning nor the 75mm would fire. We returned to the start-line and left the rest of the squadron to push on. To my dismay, the fault had cleared itself after a few moments and we could have gone on. Ernie Riddall said how the officer had been pleased with my shooting. But it seemed an uncomplicated affair, with no 'aiming off' needed.

Peter Smethurst was a connoisseur of food and drink, and the sight of a row of German sausages hanging up in a farmhouse kitchen was enough to send him into raptures. A case of wine travelled on the engine-cover of his tank for many miles in the latter stages of our drive across Germany, but it fell off one night as we rattled on our way. This, Peter described as, "A calamity of the greatest magnitude!" Fortunately, he did not know that the 'fall' had been assisted by the proletarian boot of a member of the crew who was riding on the back.

My other memory of Peter is of a sadder event. We were on a road that ran downhill and halted right behind Peter's tank. I'm sure that I was gunner for his brother Mike again at this time. Things were not going well. One of the officers had been killed by shellfire. Hugh Stanton was coming under observed fire as he tried to get forward out of a wood and had to withdraw again.

I was watching the tank in front, where Mike Geer was operator; he was standing in the turret with Peter. Suddenly, there was a violent explosion and a great cloud of dust and smoke, in which I could see Mike climbing back into the turret. He had jumped or been blown out of it in a split second. Peter appeared at the side of our turret, obviously distressed. He seized the microphone and said, "I have been hit and my driver has been killed outright!" The unhappy driver had his hatch open and was leaning out of it. Peter's regular driver, Casey, was absent. This was something he would never have done, as he always kept closed down in times of danger.

Mike had been wounded at the back of the head but was able to wave to me as he was driven away in the passenger seat of the MO's half-track.

There was a large, modern barn at a farm where we stayed for a short while. The corner of the barn was chamfered off, and a large Crucifix had been placed there, hanging on the wall. I was surprised, as I thought that such overt religious signs would be 'verboten'.

Jack Geddes and I were examining a large cardboard box which had contained a 'Panzerfaust', or 'Tankfist', as Jack translated for me. On the front of the box there was an illustration of a giant fist descending on and crushing a small tank. We were wary of Panzerfaust men as we drove through woody areas and sprayed the bushes and verges with Browning as we went along.

There was a large house which was empty, so we took it over for our sleeping quarters. The upper floors were not carpeted and as I walked through one afternoon a series of tiny puffs of dust sprang up between all the floorboards. As I watched in disbelief, the thump of a distant explosion could be heard. Perhaps it was an ammunition dump blowing up, but it seemed to be miles away.

In the empty upper rooms of this house, we found some large wooden packing cases and something about them gave us a clue that they came from France. We set about opening the boxes and found them packed with all kinds of goodies; true enough, they had been sent from France to Germany by a member of the occupation forces. I found a pair of silk pyjamas and a damask table-cloth, as well as several pens and pencils. I stuck my head out of the window and yelled to the chaps below, "Fountain pens and propelling pencils!" and in two seconds flat, the place was full of Sharpshooters anxious to share in our find.

We strolled down to the little church. Jack Geddes and Chris Law were of the party, I remember. There was a shell-hole in the roof, and the place was covered in dust, but the organ was intact. Chris Law could play and he seated himself at the console. What about wind? On the floor near the organ was a contrivance like a plank balanced on a central pivot. By standing on this and transferring weight from one side to the other the bellows underneath were operated and Chris was able to play to us.

An officer from the Royal Artillery was seconded to us for 'battle experience'. He called everyone 'Old Fruit' so, naturally, he became known to us all as 'The Old Fruit'. I was once again gunner to Mike Smethurst, and 'The Old Fruit' occupied the co-driver's position. He wore corduroy trousers, and this caused embarrassment, once, when Bill Williams saw a battledress-trousered bottom protruding from the hatch. He gave this piece of anatomy a resounding slap, shouting, "How's that, Cliff?", under the impression that it belonged to Cliff Clifford. The red face of 'The Old Fruit' popped up. "Really, Williams," he said. He had had a change of trousers that day. That place was also notable for the incident of 'Darbyshire's Teeth'. Darbyshire had taken them out and put them on the idler wheel of the tank. Someone drove the tank forward and the teeth were squashed. Casey (was he the driver?) said that it was like looking after a child, for all Darbys food was cut up for him until new teeth appeared.

The Authorities had decreed that tank crews should be issued with two tents instead of the faithful 'bivvys' which had served since, or even from before, the beginning of the war. I shared a tent with 'The Old Fruit' and we were on guard together one night. It was pouring with rain, and we were reluctant to leave our cosy blankets as we heard the rain tippling down when we were woken to do our 'stint'. Eventually, 'The Old Fruit' said, "Well, Fisher, Old Fruit, we'd better go on guard." Next morning, Mike, who had heard all this, asked what time we had gone on guard. We had to admit that we had had a lie in. We got three extra guard duties, which was fair enough.

Next night we were walking about, doing our turn, talking of this and that as one does, when a very cross infantryman, who was concealed in a barn and was also on sentry duty, tore us off a strip for not hearing his challenge. He said that we were lucky not to be shot and it was only when he heard us talking that he realised that we were friendly.

Later on, we heard engines throbbing in the distance and there was a revving of engines and voices shouting and brilliant lights. We tried to hear what the language was but couldn't pick out the words. We trusted that it was our people moving a vehicle which had got bogged down, and not elements of the Wehrmacht making a getaway.

We were staying in the empty rooms of a large barracks at one stage. In front of this was a huge anti-tank ditch, and the contents of the rooms had been tipped into this. There was a battery of medium artillery nearby and this kept us awake at night. Other occupants of the barracks included the members of a concert party which was there to entertain the troops.

There was a film-show at one place where we stayed. The film was shown in a barn, and it was our old friend, *Alexander's Ragtime Band*. The place was so crowded that some people were sitting on the roof beams to watch.

At about this time, we heard that President Roosevelt had died.

Here, too, we found a fire-pump at the local Fire Station. Petrol was poured into the pump, and the engine was started up. Everyone was hosed down if they were unfortunate enough to be within range of the powerful jet.

Displaced persons were beginning to appear, with their goods piled on small handcarts. One party had their load sprayed with the hose, by accident I'm sure, but Ernie Riddall was very indignant about this. The owners of the cart, however, were quite good-humoured about it.

There was a scene at one place, which might have been staged for a war film, with guns hammering away at an unseen target, troops filing forward into action and civilians streaming back. One man pulling along a reluctant calf, which was terrified by all the racket and bustle.

Going through a valley, which had a large house at the top of the slope on one side, we saw a group of people waving a large bed-sheet as a sign of surrender. They were civilians, but Mike told me to put a shot over their heads as a warning. This I did and they all dropped to the ground as one when the shell flew over.

Another scene provided the awesome sight of a farmhouse, well alight, and the indignant farmer shaking his fist at us as we drove past. A railway station waiting-room was bedecked with dozens of small Nazi flags on bunting, as well as larger versions. One of these was attached to the back of a tank and trailed in the mud along the road as we drove through a small town one rainy afternoon. I was surprised to see an older woman spit on the tank in front of us as we went along.

A warm, spring day in a small village. Doc Dockerty and I were asked to escort a German woman to see the officer in charge of the place. All civilians were confined to the house, so she had to have us as escort, or she would have been arrested. It was the first time that I had spoken to any German civilian, and, to my relief, the topic was the warm weather, so that seemed a safe subject to talk about. We walked along a muddy section of the road at one stage, and I was interested to see, ground into the mud, a 'Pickelhaube' – a German spiked helmet from World War One.

Another 'souvenir' which we found on the outskirts of a village where we had halted for a moment, was an album of photographs of a child. The cover had 'Unser Kind' – 'Our Child' – on the front and Gordon Tidey was very indignant about the mindlessness of such looting.

We had listened with interest to the martial music that was being broadcast over the German radio, as a parade was held to mark the inauguration of the 'Volkssturm'. I do not think any of us expected to be attacked by Volkssturm units as we made our way through Germany in the latter stages of the conflict. Most of the civilians we encountered in the villages were women and children.

At one house, it was obvious that the women were concerned about something to do with us. It was difficult, neither group speaking the language of the other, but the women took us outside and pointed to the tank. Tom had reversed it by the side of the house, and a small tree, an apple tree I think, was bent by the rear of the tank. Tom got in and drove the tank forward and the little tree sprang upright once more. The women clapped and laughed with pleasure.

In the back garden of the next door house lay the body of a German soldier. His cap concealed his features. Why was it that corpses seemed more menacing when their eyes were covered? I always imagined that if I took off the covering, eyes would glare up accusingly at me.

A shotgun and ammunition had been found. Someone hid behind a small garden shed and hurled the German's helmet into the air. The one with the shotgun then banged away to the enjoyment of all.

I went off in search of other firearms, for there were a number of German rifles lying about. They were scattered among the bushes and rocks on rough ground, as if there had been a mass surrender. I extracted the bolts and smashed the rifles on the rocks, breaking them at the small of the butt. A number of French ex-PoWs came up to me – I suppose that there was a Prisoner of War camp nearby. We talked a little about France and the devastation in Normandy, though I do not think any of them came from that part. They asked me what I was doing and I demonstrated with a rifle. "*Pourquoi*?" they asked. I could think of no reason '*Pourquoi*' and felt rather foolish. I suppose I thought that the rifles could be put to the wrong kind of use if the civilian population rose against us.

Someone found a machine-gun, a sort of Spandau with knobs on. Incorporated in the works was a bayonet, which sprang out when something was pressed. I had never thought of the German soldier as being a 'bayonet person', unlike the accepted image of his British counterpart.

Out in the countryside again and we entered a farmyard. Against the side of a wooden shed rested a Panzerfaust, and two young German soldiers emerged, hands in the air. While they were being interrogated, I did a bit of exploring and opened a barn door. I was carrying a P 38, a sort of utility Luger pistol. I had found this when I was looking in the hedgerows near the place where we had our idler assembly blown off by the mine. I had loaded it with our 9mm ammunition and maybe this is why it was unreliable and sometimes jammed, so I was not really confident about it.

I looked round the barn. A wooden platform stood at one end, and it had a ladder leaning against it. There was a lot of straw piled up on the platform and from the pile emanated stealthy cracklings. I would have liked to say that I cocked the pistol and, in commanding tones, called upon the occupant of the platform to surrender. Instead, I sneaked out of the barn, closing the door behind me, thinking: Best of luck, if you can get away with it, Fritz, or whoever you are – if you are anybody. Then I told myself, it may just have been the straw settling – which soothed my conscience somewhat.

We stopped in a large open space to restock with petrol and ammunition and spend the night in leaguer. The bodies of two German soldiers lay in a 'scrape' they were using as cover. They had a Spandau with them. We gathered round and silently contemplated the bodies. One man was on his back, his helmet fallen forward and covering most of his face. A pathetic touch was afforded by his gloves, which were woollen and worn away at the ends. His hands were raised to shoulder height in a gesture of surrender, but I think that was just how he had fallen. I hoped so. His companion was in the undignified posture of so many dead, for his trousers had half dropped down as his body had twisted when he had fallen in death, his head and shoulders concealed in the side of the 'scrape'.

We wandered back to our tasks, and I had my one and only conversation with Olly, our squadron leader, as I unpacked the bedrolls from the back of the tank. We exchanged a brief word about the impossibility of the war going on for much longer.

Later on, as dusk gathered, a figure could be seen rummaging through the pockets of the dead. You wouldn't have got me doing that, for I was only too pleased to keep away from dead bodies. My father had said to me once when, as a boy, I ran in fright past a cemetery, "The dead will never hurt you, John. It's the living you want to watch!" True, of course, but still – Verden was the place where we were engaged in 'battling' once more before the war finished. Here we came across troops in slit-trenches, and I recall seeing tracer fly over the tops of the trenches as white handkerchiefs were waved as a token of surrender.

As we drove up to the barracks at Verden, we placed several rounds of HE under half a dozen windows to show we meant business. One of our Troop was firing his Browning across our front, and I was amazed at the rate of fire, attained, I was told, by rubbing the working parts with emery paper. I would have loved to have a gun which fired as rapidly as that.

We parked by the side of the road, just down the road from the barracks. Civilian houses were commandeered – the civilians, I presumed, staying with relatives or friends, though they were still about the house in the evening.

Tommy Lightburn said that he would like a pair of riding boots. There were bound to be some in the barracks, he thought. I set off with him up the road and, as we walked away from the tanks, a gun began to shell the area, shooting at random. We heard an explosion from the area we had just left, where the tanks were, but we were now near the barrack gates, so we turned in, passing a dead horse at the side of the road on the way.

In one of the single-storey buildings we found a store-room full of all the boots one could possibly require – both riding boots and ordinary service calf-length boots. As Tommy began to try them on the barracks were shelled. There were numerous bangs, and debris of various kinds began to patter on the roof of the store. I mentally willed Tommy to find quickly the right-sized boots, which he did, and we walked, as fast as dignity would allow, away from the barracks and back to the tanks, past the dead horse, which was just beginning to perfume the evening air. Another unforgettable smell. When we got back to the tanks, we were shown a dented bit of armour on the back of the tank where the shell we had heard as we walked away had struck. Lucky, we had gone for the boots!

Again, in the late afternoon we were beside a battery of heavy mortars. I made the discovery that if one stood behind a mortar and looked toward its target, one could see the flight of the bomb just before it landed. A strange effect, almost like the 'whizz' lines in a cartoon, appeared fora split second before it struck.

Compo rations had 'come up' and delicate negotiations were taking place about fair division of the groceries when George Ellis appeared round the side of his tank – hopping on one leg and declaring that he had just shot

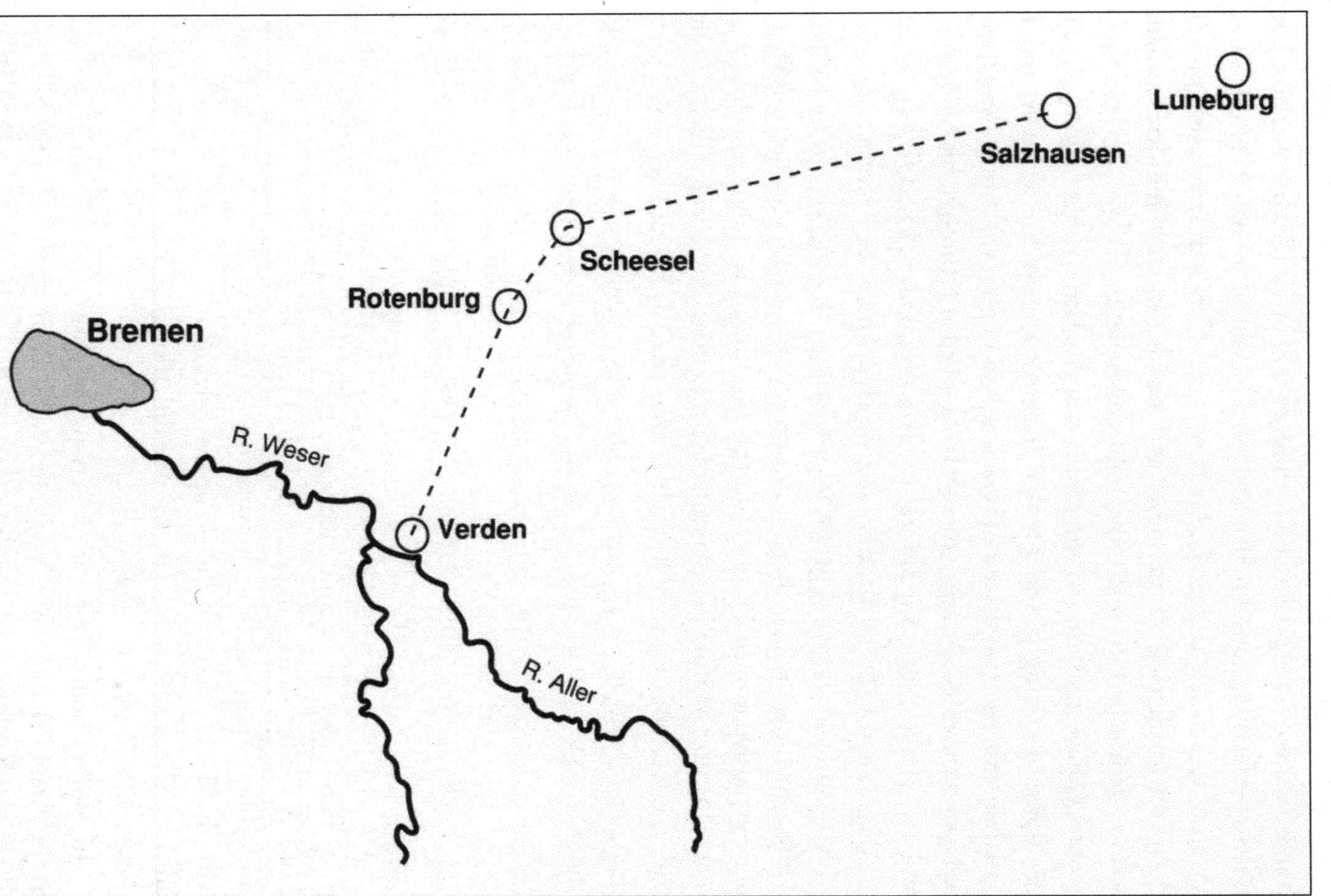

Map 7: The final days.

himself with his pistol. Everybody thought that he was having them on, but he was perfectly serious. He had accidentally cocked his pistol, a Smith and Wesson with a hair trigger, and it had gone off. His trousers were pulled down, the swollen leg was examined and the MO and the ambulance called, so George finished the war in hospital somewhere.

I recall files of infantry moving forward in the late evening to occupy their positions for the night, and a tank firing from the crest of a rise beyond. I could not quite see what kind of tank it was, though it was firing away from us beyond the ridge. At my request, Mike looked at it through his binoculars and declared it to be a Firefly and not a hostile tank as I had feared.

We came under fire from a Nebelwerfer. This was a multiple mortar which had been invented primarily for laying smoke screens – hence the name, which meant 'Fog thrower'. The weapon was also used for throwing high-explosive mortar bombs, and this was the usual mode in which we met 'Moaning Minnie'. The sound of the approaching bombs filled the air and so it was not easy to detect where they were to fall, unlike an ordinary shell, which was fairly predictable. The only sensible action was to hurl oneself on the ground until the things had exploded, hopefully a distance away. After this attack, we heard that little Taff Evans, who had driven the tank at Caen, had been wounded in the head by a splinter. Whether true or not, we also heard that the wound was so serious that his parents had been brought over to see him in hospital.

We were held up, strung along a village street which ran down to the little river. The bridge was being checked to see if it would bear the weight of tanks. A Fiesler Storch aircraft, which the Germans used for reconnaissance and artillery spotting, flew slowly across the head of the column of tanks, with the doors open and the occupants gazing at us. I suppose it seemed unfair to shoot at the plane, so no-one did, though it was a sitting duck to those at the head of the column.

In another house we received newspapers from the UK, which showed the pictures of Belsen when it was entered by our troops. One of the pictures was cut out and stuck on the front of the kitchen cabinet where it would be seen by the women of the house when they came to get crockery. Toni Pistori had written in German a brief translation of the caption accompanying the photo. The women studiously ignored the photograph even when it was pointed out to them.

There was also the Schloss where we stayed at about the same time. The family were still in residence and the Graf and Grafin were to be seen about the place. We took up residence in one room, the Graf complaining to our NCO that we were not 'gentlemen'.

The Graf, Grafin and the elderly parents of the Graf were taken to Belsen to see the horrors there at first hand. The younger couple were quite unmoved, but the parents were horrified.

A German soldier in uniform was discovered in the Schloss and was taken away sitting on the bonnet of a Jeep. An SS uniform was found in an earth privy by the members of another squadron. The owner was still hanging about so he was made to wear the uniform as it was. I must say that, after the discovery of the concentration camps, attitudes hardened sometimes.

There was a lake in the grounds of the Schloss, and a dinghy was tied up by the shore. We thought that it would be jolly to get the dinghy out of the lake and float it down the little river which ran in the valley below. We looked forward to our cruise.

We got the dinghy out of the lake and discovered how heavy it was when on dry land. We struggled over the road with it and down the grassy slope to the river. We launched away on our voyage of discovery, confident that the current would sweep us along in midstream. It was only a small river, though, and twisty, and as we had no oars, we kept ramming the bank. Alf Pitcher, who had elected to stay on the bank and watch, was convulsed with laughter at our boating antics and in the end, we abandoned the boat and let it drift away on the current.

Near disaster struck on one of my last duties on sentry before the end of hostilities. I was last sentry of the night and had the duty of waking the regimental wireless operator. We were occupying a large farm and farm buildings at the time, and the HQ Squadron was in and around a barn. The operator was sleeping on a kind of verandah and I had been shown where he was by the sentry I had relieved.

When the time came, I shook him and told him it was time to get up. He sat bolt upright, eyes staring widely and said, "Alright! Alright!" I took it that he was awake and found my own place on some straw and was soon asleep. Poor man! I had not realised that, after years of being wakened up in this way, his wide eyes and words were automatic reflexes. In fact, he was still asleep!

I was awakened by one of the sergeants kicking my instep, which hurt, and saying, "Here he is." I was able to show the place which had been occupied by the wireless operator and to describe what he and I had said. But I shuddered to think what might have happened if we had been needed to support infantry and had not been at the rendezvous on time.

We were in civvy billets again, having a cooked meal, when we heard that the Burgomeister of Hamburg had surrendered the city. At least, that was the message that came down to us. Once again, the place had only women and children living in it. We were warned about 'Fraternisation'. "You haven't been with any of these German women, have you, Fisher?" asked Mike Smethurst. "No sir!" I said. The very thought terrified me.

We had our respirators tested at this place. I had long ago had my old-fashioned respirator replaced by the new style with which the others had been issued before the Invasion. We were near a poison-gas factory, and so precautions had to be taken.

Some idiot dressed up in the uniform of a German soldier which he had found in one of the houses and his companions staged a 'capture' for our amusement. The women, too, gathered round and seemed to be quite amused by the pantomime.

On several afternoons, at about tea-time, a German fighter plane buzzed the village. We had an idea that the pilot lived here and was keeping an eye on things. Eric Shone was eager to deter this regular visitor and so, dismounting one of the Brownings, he waited for the plane to put in an appearance. Sure enough, at the appointed time, the plane appeared. In the usual manner, he flew toward the village and then dived at the houses and tanks. Eric had asked me to feed the belt for him, which I did as the plane flew away and Eric shot at it. Perhaps we gave him a fright for he did not pay another visit while we were there.

I was standing on a hill outside the village one day and a Heinkel flew over, very high. It seemed strange to hear the familiar drone of the unsynchronised engine in daylight and, moreover, to see the plane that was making the noise.

Bill Williams had wanted to fire his pistol in anger something he had not done throughout the war – so when two young Germans wanted to surrender to his tank, Bill leaned out of the driver's hatch and shot several times in the air as they ran before the tank, hands in the air. They were both all of fifteen!

We entered a barracks as we drew near Hamburg. The former occupants had left in a hurry, and cauldrons of coffee were steaming in the cookhouse kitchen. We spotted tubs of fat, which we thought would be useful for frying, so we took two or three of them.

Further exploration of the premises revealed the room of an officer or senior WO. The room was quite small and claustrophobic, for it was decorated throughout in red, including curtains, cushions and bedspread. It was a hot afternoon, so I left the stuffy atmosphere. Glancing back into the room as I closed the door, I noticed a large German Shepherd dog crouched under the bed! That was a close call, I thought, as I shut the door firmly behind me. The fitters acquired this animal, and he became a firm favourite with members of 'A' Squadron, though a declared enemy of his former masters.

Now the time came for our entry into Hamburg.

We were to rendezvous with our friends of the 'roadblock incident' the Welsh Recce, who were expected to lead us in, I understood. At the appointed hour, we drove up the road to find them still at breakfast. I was looking through my periscope and saw cooking utensils, pots and kettles emptied and thrown into vehicles in haste.

Too late! We drove past them all in a superior kind of way and left them to follow us.

Chapter 18

Hamburg and the End

Hamburg was an amazing sight. There were no whole buildings anywhere that we could see. Vast acres of devastation met our eyes as we motored along. A curtain was pulled aside, and a night-dress-clad figure peered out at us as we drove past a solitary undamaged house.

A policeman, who appeared to be on point duty, was asked to direct us and so sat on one of the vehicles at the front of the column – a Jeep, I think it was. We drove round an arm of the Alster, shining in the early-morning sun and drew up in front of a tall building where French PoWs were living. Dismounting, we mingled among them and prepared our breakfast. The tubs of fat came into their own as the eggs and bacon sizzled away but when we came to taste the fry-up it became evident that the fat was, in fact, honey. So, we breakfasted *a l'Américain*, as at Beaminster. We poured the melted honey onto an enamel plate, thinking it would come in later. When we examined it before we moved off again, we found that it had turned into a delicious toffee mixture. Needless to say, when we tried the trick again, the honey would not set. Was it something in the eggs or the salt from the bacon which had made the difference?

As I was eating my breakfast, the CO of the German guard came out and tried to make conversation. "Hello boys! Enjoying your breakfast?" he enquired cheerily. I turned my back on him, and his attempt at friendliness was met with silence. He retired to the building, no doubt hurt by his rebuff. Truth to tell, I was uncertain how to address a defeated member of the 'Master Race'.

With the French, now, we were on surer ground, for what was on their minds was *l'amour*.

They took us up to the second floor and showed us their escape route. The building itself was L-shaped and one half of the 'L' had been burned out, though the floors and stairs were still intact.

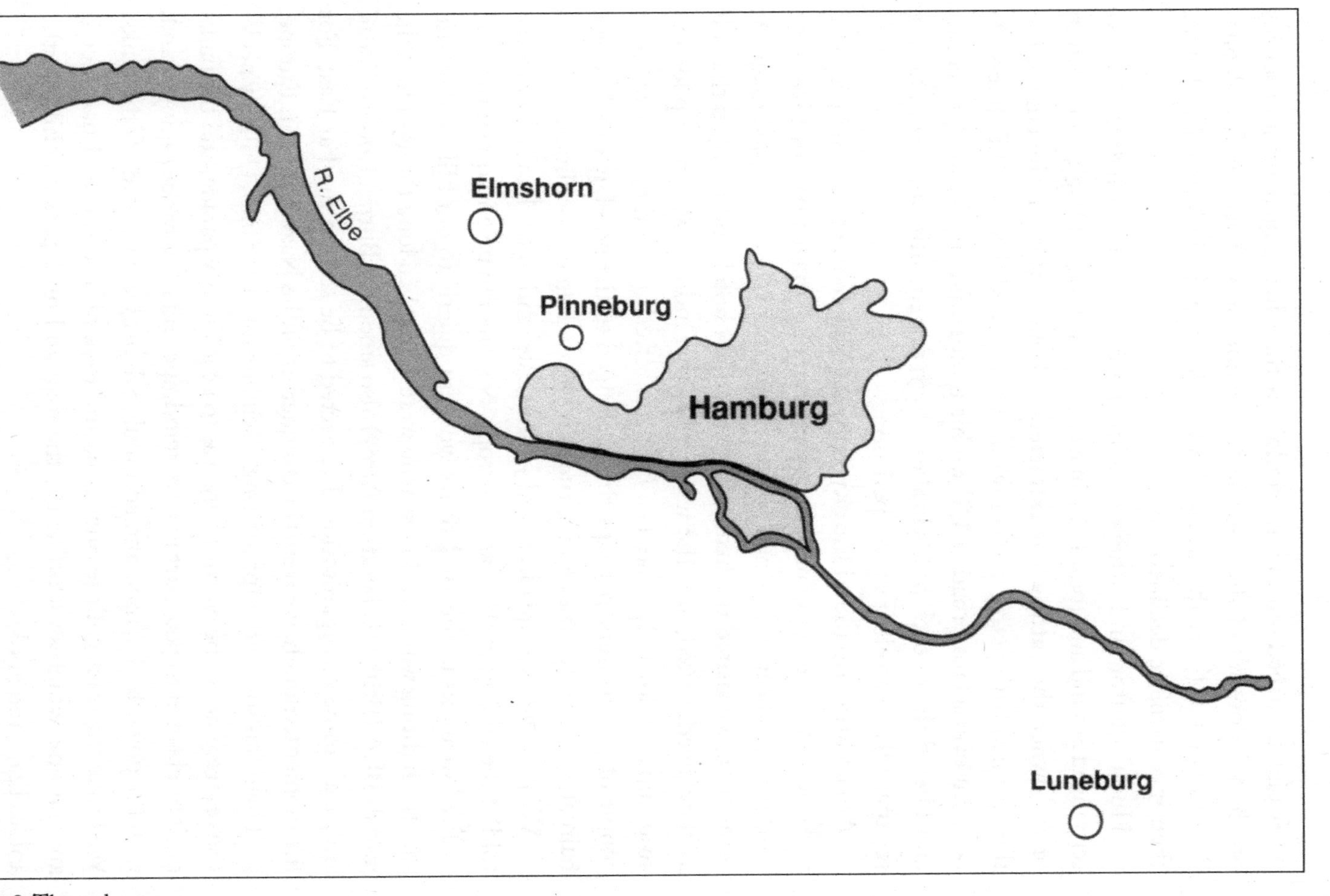

Map 8: The end.

A plank, pushed out of the window of their living quarters and resting on the window sill of the burned-out section, served as a bridge to bliss. They invited us to try this unusual way of leaving the building. Not having their incentive, we declined.

Hugh Stanton and others examined a car. It had no battery, but we scrounged around and found one in a car in a back yard. Despite the protests of the owner, the battery was extracted and put in the car; the engine was then primed with petrol and off we drove. We sped through the streets. As we went over a cross-roads a DR on his motor-bike met us at right angles and I heard the screech of his brakes. Hugh roared with laughter. "Did you see that DR?" he yelled as we sped along.

After a little trip round the city, we went back to the tanks and prepared to move to a more permanent location in an undamaged part of Hamburg. This part had been untouched by bombs and there were tree-lined roads. At some time, we visited the luxurious baths of an hotel, and I envied the lads as they dived, naked, into the water of a large indoor swimming pool and swam up and down. It looked so cool and refreshing in the green water. A couple of hairdressers, perhaps they belonged to the hotel, gave all of us a haircut, so we were clean and spruce for the ending of hostilities.

We paraded as a squadron and Jimmy Sale read to us the Orders which told of the ending of the war in Europe. No-one ran up and down the road or fired weapons in the air. I think we went quietly to our billets, thankful that the fighting was over. Those who were young had long thought that the initials BLA (British Liberation Army) also stood for Burma Looms Ahead and, after some re-organisation, I expected to be sent to the Far East. For the moment, though, we were the conquerors of the Nazi regime in Europe.

There was some attempt to bring discipline into the ranks. Unlikely neck-scarves were not to be worn. There was to be a Victory parade, and the tanks must be cleaned to take part in it. A standpipe and hose were employed and, with the powerful jet, mud and accumulated dirt were washed off the tanks. We broke the tracks of the Shermans and took off the 'spuds'. I hammered away at one, which shot off across the road and hit a passing child on the ankle. Tears and apologies.

Two ancient ladies, dressed in black from head to toe, came up and asked in carefully enunciated English, "At what o'click (sic) is curfew?" A less ancient 'lady' (one of our comrades), also dressed in black, including a pair of black civilian shoes, men's size 8 perhaps, was brought round by one of the soldiery, who introduced 'her' as "my aunt." The owner of our flat came and asked us to take care of the baby grand piano and not to ruin it. It was his wife's pride and joy, he said. The only piano player we had in our billet was Jimmy Tuckwood, but we said we would respect his wishes and treat the instrument with care.

The tanks had been spruced up in vain, for we heard no more of the Victory Parade!

I was to have another insight into Hamburg life when we were detailed to guard a small camp containing army people from Southern Europe – Yugoslavians or similar nationality. Shortly after we got there, the only German soldier in charge of the camp (he wore a black uniform, was he SS?) got word that he was to move out to a PoW camp for the German Army. He was friendly with a woman who lived in a house opposite the camp gates. She gestured to me that she wanted to speak to him. I went to his hut and stuck my head round the door. "Hey, George!" I said. To my surprise and embarrassment, he turned toward me a tear-stained face. I indicated the woman and left them to a sorrowful parting.

The prisoners, I suppose they were free now, were sitting about in the warm sunshine looking a bit dazed. One of them had been immobile for a long time and his thin Belsen-like legs were unable to bear his weight.

For one prisoner, freedom had come too late and his funeral was held one afternoon. The coffin and escort drove out of the camp on the way to the cemetery and Sergeant Ruby Ayres paraded the guard and saluted as the cortège drove past.

An officer from the Engineers came to the camp and took charge of things. He brought a radio with him, and we listened to the broadcasts from London. I remember the King speaking, because he had trouble with saying 'Vicissitudes'. The engineer officer came to the salute as we heard 'God Save the King', and some of the PoWs saluted too.

We were relieved by an infantry detachment, some of whom, if I understood them correctly, had only just arrived in Germany. Then back to the squadron, as we were to move to Elmshorn, a town about 20 kilometres outside Hamburg.

The large houses which were to be our billets were divided into flats, but we occupied the whole house. The occupants had been bundled out in short order, as items of wrung-out washing still on the end of the bath indicated. The houses backed onto a small river which provided interest, though I think it also served as a drain for the houses. The flats were comfortable and I shared with a ginger-haired lad who had recently joined us.

We settled into a new regime. We had a new squadron leader. Olly Woods had gone to take up the reins of civilian life once more; we now had a major seconded from a Regular Army unit. The rumour was that he was a renowned rider of horses and had broken every bone in his body. This was Major Renton.

The tanks were taken away and sprayed a grey colour, coming back bright and shiny. The tank-park was in a small field opposite our house. There was a hard tennis court, a playing field, the river, and summer was well on its way.

In the town itself, about five minutes' walk away, was the White House. So called because it was painted white and not out of deference to our gallant allies. Here the guard was mounted every day, and the place was a scene of much activity as civilians came with all kinds of problems, and applications for permission to do this or that. Prisoners were held in a dreadful cellar which had a small, barred opening in the door, and a noisome bucket. Here, too, were brought curfew breakers.

One evening, as dusk fell, we heard singing in the distance but drawing nearer. We looked out of the windows onto the road. An orderly procession of people, many in night attire, marched down the road toward us. They had been pulled in by our patrol for being outside after curfew. I wondered if standing on the doorstep could be termed as being 'outside', for I couldn't imagine people walking the streets in pyjamas and nightdresses. There they were, marching along. "Sing!" shouted the Major, who was driving alongside the column in a Jeep, "Sing!", and sing they did: but it was defiant singing – a marching song – and each one singing his or her part as they tramped on their way to the White House.

We heard next day that the curfew breakers had all been made to have a cold bath when they reached the White House. There was a rumour that the first woman prisoner had refused the treatment and had been plonked bodily in the bath, night-dress and all. True or not, when I was on guard next day, a soaking-wet night-dress was to be seen on the bathroom floor.

Although we now look back on those days with misgiving, at the time it seemed the only way we could show that we would stand no nonsense. I don't know whether we thought that the populace would rise up and engage us in guerrilla warfare, but we, or at least the 'Higher Ups' under whose orders we were, seemed to want no-one, soldier or civilian, to be under any illusion about who were the conquerors and who the conquered. We later heard that the local populace named us the 'Zwarte Rat Panzer SS'.

The street next to the White House had borne the name of a Nazi leader. That had been removed and the name 'Allitsen Street' put up in its place. When I was on guard one day, an elderly, upright, white-moustached gentleman approached me. "Ah!" he said, "Allitsen is one of your generals, no?" I said, "Er – well, no, actually. It is the name of a road in St John's Wood in London, where the barracks are." He walked away rather baffled, I thought.

Mike Carver came to speak to us on the matter of 'fraternisation'. He said that he was horrified at the way in which other units (not under his command, of course) were breaking the 'No fraternisation' order. He was sure that we, with our experience of years of fighting, would not break the rules. Well, true, but I think that the bond of common humanity which holds men and women together prevailed sometimes, despite the wishes of those set over us.

Of course, there was no such ban on making the acquaintance of the Lithuanian girls who lived in a house near the tennis courts. I was walking along one day when the voice of Toni Pistori rang out from their rooms: "Left, right, left, right – ", and he began to drill me for some minutes as I entered into the spirit of the thing, to the amusement of the girls.

On the road a short distance from our billet, a road block had been set up. Here we vetted people before allowing them to proceed into town. Peter Smethurst dressed up in female attire and tried to bluff his way past the sentries on one notable occasion.

Ernie and I escorted a young German Panzer soldier into town as he had to go to the hospital, right next to the White House, for a wounded hand to be treated. The wound was healing up quite well and he told us that he had sustained it during an attack by aircraft. "Kameraden!" he said, as we, too, were Panzers. "You're no comrade of mine!" growled Ernie, which I thought was a bit ungracious.

Sergeant Piet van Beuren was a tower of strength at the White House, for he knew how to interrogate prisoners and suspected Nazis. Off he would go in a Jeep and bring back to the White House the unfortunate person who had been reported to him. After the prisoner's interrogation, he was held in the cell below stairs, before being moved on elsewhere.

One day a German was brought in and was made to stand at attention, thumbs under the armpits, hands spread on the chest, while Piet got to work. His voice went up a notch in tone, and a torrent of abuse, accusation and questions were poured out on the suspect. I think that this way of speaking is called 'sprechstimmer' and it is supposed to intimidate the one to whom it is being directed. To quote the Duke of Wellington, "By God, it frightened me!"

What was special about a young man who was kept upstairs in one of the rooms, and not in the cell, I do not know. He was what one might call a typical Aryan, blond and handsome. We had to wake him every hour during the night and take him to the bathroom for the cold bath treatment. When it was time, I went up with the orderly officer and brought him down. He took off his shorts and got into the bath and stood there. There was a shower attachment, and the officer told me to play this shower on his back, but it was more than I could do. Soon the officer took the shower spray and did it himself.

As I expected, our prisoner did not twitch an eyebrow at this treatment, and I thought that it was a bit pointless. I found that I did not like to degrade anyone, even an enemy.

A Belgian lad from Antwerp attached himself to us for a week or two. He, too, was an interpreter and was on hand to sort out any problems which arose. He went off to collect and bring in a Russian who was making a nuisance of himself in town. He came back in the Jeep, bringing the very drunken Russian, who was three times his size. Undeterred, he joined the drunk in singing and they both made their way up the stairs, carousing away until the door of a room was locked on the man and he was left to sleep it off.

An officer in the Royal Air Force stopped his Jeep at the entrance to the White House when I was on guard one day. He congratulated us on our smart appearance. We were still wearing the white webbing, skeleton order for this duty. Certainly, we were smart, marching through town to mount guard, though the effect was spoilt one day by Arnold Jones, who had a stiff knee which was bandaged up. On their return from guard, the whole squad, as one man, suddenly developed stiff knees, and peg-legged along the road like a crazy comedy act.

Two girls, who had been walking up and down in front of the guard and making rude remarks in German, were pulled in and confined to one of the upstairs rooms. They waited there while their parents were called in to read them the riot act and take them away. Cowboy Rogers (so called because he played the guitar) gave them a packet of cigarettes with strict instructions, in pantomime, to throw the packet out of the window if an officer came into the room.

On the last duty of the guard with Eric Shone, we heard footsteps from the top of the road where there was a T junction. "I've had enough of this", said Eric, and went off to find out who these people were who were so blatantly breaking curfew. Unfortunately, he came back with a protesting policeman in tow. He, of course, was exempt from the regulations about staying indoors. Later on, when we had cleared up that little difficulty, a civilian was dragged past us by two policemen. He appealed to us in pitiful tones as he tried to get taken into our custody. He seemed to be in a state of fear. What had he done? We watched as he was taken away up the road, for this was presumably a civil matter and we could not interfere.

The billet where we lived seemed to belong to a painter. In the bookcase I found a book of original water colour studies of troops in action on the Eastern Front. There was a particularly good water colour of a Nebelwerfer in action in the snow.

On the wall hung a plaster cast of a face. Of course, the face soon acquired a moustache and the owner seemed quite amused when he came into the flat one day.

One night I came into the room and found that a red silk scarf had been put over the lamp. When I switched on the light the room was bathed in a red glow. Looking at the bed, I saw a human form lying there. Had the lads bribed a fraulein to seduce me? Closer inspection revealed that the face on the pillow was that of our moustached plaster friend!

I found a very poor German uniform made of inferior material in the cellar and put it on, though it was a tight fit. A coal-scuttle helmet completed the outfit, and Charlie Spiller took a photograph of me standing in the garden.

We paddled up and down the little river in a canoe that we had found. Once, four of us got in and paddled in unison, singing that canoe-paddling sang from '*Sanders of the River*'. We worked up quite a speed in our canoe, though with little freeboard it was a wonder we did not sink. I had difficulty in coming to terms with another river incident. Three women had been bathing in the river, well away from the houses, and some of our people had discovered them. As two of us paddled up in our canoe, we found a traffic jam of boats as the soldiers looked at the women getting dressed. The word 'gawping' comes to mind. This was an unedifying scene, I thought, and though the women seemed quite unperturbed, the expression in their eyes showed their contempt at such behaviour.

We had an interesting detail one day, and once again a river featured in the proceedings. A large quantity of weapons had accumulated at the White House, and we had the job of disposing of the store. There was everything from Panzerfaust rocket heads to a big 0.45 Colt automatic, which looked as if it fired a bullet big enough to stop an elephant. We loaded the stuff onto a three-tonner and drove off in search of a suitable river where we could dump the weapons. We found a bridge, where the river seemed deep, and there was a cobbled area beside it where the three-tonner could stand while we threw the arms into the water. We set to work, extracting bolts and working parts and hurling in the bits. Darby startled me by pressing the release gear on the Panzerfaust he was handling and the bomb, oilskin fins extended now, rattled out and onto the cobbles. I expected an explosion at any minute!

As the waters engulfed the weapons, we thought we had done a good job. How the locals must have smiled as they watched us, for as we motored past later in the week, we saw most of the weapons stuck on a mud bank. Either the river was tidal, being only a few miles from the Elbe, or someone had opened a sluice-gate.

We paraded for a service at the church at Pinneburg. It was to give thanks for the end of the war in Europe. As we sat down in the church, which was a very large one, I noticed that all round the walls were three rows of small black wreaths. Each one had the name of a German serviceman written in Gothic script inside it. On some, as well as a name, there was a place mentioned – in Africa, for instance, or France – but the vast majority just had the stark words: 'Im Ost Gefallen', (Fallen in the East) and it seemed as if a vast army had just vanished into nothingness. As we rightly gave thanks for our own victory, I became conscious of the total cost of the last years to the nations and to humanity.

The time came for us to move on, and we found ourselves in the Kiel area.

Raisdorf was a small village just outside Kiel. We were split up into squadrons now and so 'A' Squadron was in sole occupancy of the village, taking over small but spacious houses beside the road.

Initially, we drove the tanks and parked them opposite our billets, and there the wireless operators asked permission to close down. The clear, high voice of the regimental wireless operator gave permission. I was alone in the tank, the others staking their claim to rooms in the house opposite, so it fell to me to ask permission. I waited as long as I dared, for I wanted to be last to go off the air! After a long silence, I made my request and was allowed to close down. I switched off the wireless, the sound of the generator died away, and I thought that now the war was really over in Europe!

The upstairs rooms were all occupied by the time I got my belongings into our house, so I had a downstairs room, being the only occupant, which suited me. There were three downstairs rooms and a kitchen with corresponding rooms upstairs. The washing and other facilities were in an outhouse at the back. I admired the planning of the houses, for though they were small, there seemed to be plenty of room inside.

In the front room there was a sideboard and, stuck on the top, a message in English stating that the occupant had not been a Nazi. Hanging on the wall was a print of action in the Boxer rebellion in China, which showed British troops cheering on an advancing line of German Marines. Underneath was the caption, 'Forward the Germans'. I wondered if this masterpiece had been looked out specially to remind us of former alliances against the 'Yellow Peril', for the war against the Japanese was not yet over.

As far as I could see, Raisdorf was just one string of buildings along the road between Kiel and Preetz. At the Kiel end of the road lay a small railway station and a yard that was used as the tank-park. Near the tank park was a large house (the new 'White House') which did duty as the guard room.

Between this and our houses was a level-crossing, and beyond the level crossing was the village restaurant and hall, where we met for meals. There was a cookhouse at the back, and a bar was incorporated in the building. A large double-fronted house was next, and here was the squadron office, 'Q' stores and squadron leader's office. There was a flagpole in front of this, and the Union flag fluttered there between dawn and dusk.

As soon as we arrived, we announced our presence by a curfew raid on an area of Kiel. We arrived there in a three-tonner. Once again, devastation met our eyes. The area was on the outskirts of town and there was a small farm, utterly wrecked. The cow-shed had been burned out and the carbonised skeletons of cows lay, still chained, in the stalls. Such was the concentration of bombs which had fallen in this place that the craters joined each other.

The people who lived in this area were still wandering about, though curfew-time had passed. They were rounded up and put in the three-tonner, Mike Smethurst chasing one unfortunate and firing his Naval Luger into the air to hurry him on.

All these people were put into the guard house at Raisdorf, identity cards were produced, men and women separated and kept overnight. I think that there was a statutory time limit for keeping people in custody without food; after that time, a meal had to be provided. It was customary to keep detainees for up to about an hour before the time allowed and then release them.

When we had been in Elmshorn, someone had discovered the wife of a naval officer, and her son, a boy, trying to hide arms in the garden of her house. She was duly pulled in and at Raisdorf she was still with us and, I think, her son, too. At night they were kept in detention in the guard house, but we allowed them to sit on the patch of grass in front of the building in the daytime. I remember her talking to Jack Geddes and telling him that we ought to leave Germany and go home. "What then?" said Jack, in German, "Ein undere Hitler?"

At Raisdorf again, two girls must have lived nearby for they could be seen knocking about the place. They were always ready to engage in banter. One was comely, the other decidedly not. They over-reached themselves when they got into one of the houses, put on uniforms, and began holding up traffic on the road!

There was also 'The Girl with the Million-Dollar Legs' – not because they were anything like the legs of the renowned pin-up girl, Miss Betty Grable, but because they were rather like pipe cleaners, both in colour and shape.

Because we were not in barracks, contact between civilians and soldiers was inevitable. We used cigarettes as currency, and we, with our abundant supplies, were the source of trade in this commodity. We could even have cigarettes sent to us from the UK, in addition to our canteen supplies. I once went home on leave with a soldier who had bought a German plastics factory by this trade and was taking home a kit-bag of combs as samples for buyers! It was, in short, a racket and it was very sad to see aged German men around the billets selling wedding rings and family possessions for cigarettes.

In course of time, our own currency, British Armed Forces Service Vouchers, was introduced but I well remember walking into Preetz with someone who said he would buy me a meal. I was astounded when he produced a roll of Marks which he had obtained by means of the cigarette trade.

Even here in Raisdorf there were the traces of war. Next to our row of houses was a field, and close by the hedge was the burned-out chassis of a lorry. Around this spot was the unmistakable smell of decaying flesh, but a search revealed nothing. Perhaps a corpse had been buried, but not very deeply.

Just down the road on the way to Preetz was a wood and we were sent there under the direction of an ancient forester to fell trees for fuel for the coming winter. To see this old man at work was an education, for tree-felling had been his life. The economy of his movements and the ease with which trees fell to his expertly wielded axe were a lesson to me. He asked one day if we would like to see a man in the woods. We said "Yes!" Who would it be? A hermit, perhaps, or a refugee, or a fugitive German soldier? We set off and found that it was none of these things. In a little clearing lay a skeleton, wearing a pair of brown riding boots. These were the remains of the owner of a local saw-mill, who had Polish labour working for him. He had not treated them kindly, we understood, so when the war ended, they took him out into the woods and shot him!

His wife had identified him by his boots, we were told, but why had she not arranged for the remains to be buried? Perhaps it was an indication of the chaotic times. At the entrance to the woods was another burned-out vehicle and after we had been there a few months, a grave appeared at the side of this. Someone had found something to bury, among the debris.

A group of us went to Kiel to be taken round the harbour by German naval personnel. We went round by water first of all, passing the upturned hull of a pocket battleship. Could it have been the 'Hipper'? Ashore again, we looked round the rest of the establishment. Another pocket battleship was in dry dock, smoke still drifting from a large hole in the deck at the bows. Some brave souls got up into the superstructure above the bridge, but that was too dizzy-making for me to ascend to those heights.

I climbed into a one-man submarine, which was suspended on a platform ready to be lowered into the water. Though I was not averse to confined spaces, I found the wealth of pipes and valves too claustrophobic and the thought of being under water in the vessel quite frightening. Brave men to tackle a job like that, in whichever Navy!

Huge concrete bunkers housed some more submarines, and we were to come across prefabricated sections of hulls ready to assemble.

We had to do escort and guard duty at Plön, which was a Headquarters town. Here was the court of the Military Government and a morning sitting in the courtroom revealed more of the disrupted society of the times. Displaced and displeased persons appeared for all kinds of misdemeanours.

Toni Pistori came with a story about the KRR Band which had accompanied the Changing of the Guard when their regiment took over from us. One of the KRR marches they played was Lutzows 'Wild Hunt', and the schoolchildren who were watching knew this tune. They were fascinated by a British Regiment having a German tune as a march.

The 'Black Rat Club' in Preetz was a good place to get a meal and hear good music, too. There was a small band of expert musicians playing cymbalum, piano and two violins. I think the gentlemen of the band were Hungarian. They had a large and tuneful repertoire and were very good indeed. On one occasion, one of the lads brought in an ATS girl from some military establishment in the town. The couple were very embarrassed when the lead violinist played some 'hearts and flowers' stuff as he hovered round their table.

Behind the club was a lake where one could row a boat. Two small boys played with a metal aeroplane beside the jetty, plunging it into the water and saying, "Das ist ein Englander!", as children at home would say: "This is a Jerry," under similar circumstances.

The canteen and bar at Raisdorf were scenes, now, of parties for those who were getting demobilised. The departure of each group of people became the excuse for a rowdy session, ending as a rule, with the departing officers and ORs, being hoisted shoulder-high and carried outdoors to cries of "Throw 'em out! Throw 'em out!" Even the squadron leader received this good-humoured treatment as he went, having made a speech in which he recalled our welcome to him as a 'Regular', even though we were a Territorial Army regiment. One can visualise the atmosphere at these 'do's' if I relate that I saw someone holding an earnest conversation whilst balancing a large ashtray on his head. As he spoke, a geranium, without its pot, hurtled across the room and neatly removed the ash-tray, crashing into the wall in a shower of earth. The conversation never faltered.

There was sometimes a small band, which really played for the amusement of its members. Cowboy Rogers played the guitar, there was also a pianist, and drums and trombone. I was once asked to accompany the group in a Latin American rhythm, tapping on a hollowed-out bit of wood. I had not realised how one had to concentrate on timing and was soon asked, rather tetchily, by 'Cowboy' to stop.

In the house next door to our billet, I spotted a starting pistol in one of the wardrobes, and shortly afterwards an officer came round to ask if we had seen it, and pointing out that, if so, it should have been reported as a weapon. If the lads in the billet, who all knew it was there, had not reported it, I didn't see why I should. Ted Dunn, now our squadron leader, was having none of this and we were all marched into his office. There was silence in answer to his questions and then my conscience began to prick me. After all, he had been a jolly good tank commander when we had first met, so I admitted seeing the pistol and, as it was only a starting pistol, said I hadn't thought it worth reporting. I apologised to the officer who had first asked about it. Next day, I was marched in before Ted again, together with several others – this time for each of us to be promoted to Lance Corporal, or, as Bill Williams put it 'Lance Comical'. Talk about the wheel of fortune!

Someone had found a large and lethal-looking motor cycle which had a huge tank and a sort of bucket saddle in red leather. He rode this down the road one day with other members of the squadron clinging to him. One of the officers rang up the rider's billet to tell him that "This was not a bloody circus!" I think two of the extra riders were Casey and Monahan, who were full of ingenious ways of making life amusing.

When Harry Gill left his shoes in the orderly room, this delightful duo nailed them to the floor. When Harry was demobilised, they promised to come and see him at his pub in Hull. "Not both together! Not both together!" Harry pleaded, almost on his knees. A scheme which they had worked out involved one of them engaging in conversation with someone who was waiting for the truck to take him to the station for demob. The other would then sneak up and cut off the tie of the 'demobee', just below the knot. If the latter had another tie, it was usually packed up with his kit, so he had to go off with this mutilated thing round his neck.

A detachment was sent to a small village beside a lake which must have been in the area of Plön. We took over a house which was still occupied by young German ladies. I had a bedroom which had a small window, facing east, and I remember thinking about the poem which began: 'I remember, I remember the house where I was born', and that bit about the 'little window where the sun came creeping in at dawn'.

We were under the command of Sergeant Ruby Ayres and lived happily, with the minimum of fuss. I don't know why we were there, unless it was to show the flag in the more remote parts of the countryside.

There was great excitement one night, when a Polish gentleman was discovered trying to break into a house opposite. The night watchman of the place blew a great horn, which looked as if it had originated on the head of a beast like the Highland cattle at home. The would-be burglar shot off on a bike, but we had no transport and there was none in the village, so he was able to vanish into the night.

In the daytime, my ginger-headed friend and I went for a walk round the lake. It was very large, so we only got part way. He decided to have a dip and stripped off, wading naked into the water. We heard female voices in the distance, however, so he splashed out of the water and dried himself in haste, as best he could. Somewhat damp though he was, we continued round the shores and came across a large Schloss. More of our lads were in occupation here so we had a good look round.

There was a gigantic stuffed grizzly bear in the hall. I remember that the Guards had been in occupation before us, and on bedroom door's upstairs were little labels in Gothic print stating that the bedroom was that of Major the Lord So-and-So, or Captain the Honourable Blank. Inside the bedrooms were four-posters straight out of a Hollywood epic about the Three Musketeers, and in the main bedroom a canopy which could have graced a bedroom in Buckingham Palace.

There was a huge attic consisting of a series of rooms at the top of the Schloss. In these was a veritable Aladdin's Cave of stuff – exotic costumes for grown-up parties, small uniforms for boys to attire themselves as helmeted Prussians – all that kind of thing. There were also sealed diplomatic trunks from the capitals of the world. What secrets did these hold?

We had strayed into the land of the aristocracy and felt suitably awed.

Before the detachment was withdrawn from the village I was called back to go on agricultural leave.

It was harvest-time in the UK and so I asked a farmer friend if he would apply for me to work on his farm, which was just up the road from where my parents lived. I spent a month on the farm and then reported back to Harwich, to be told that those who wished to do so could apply for a further month's leave. So, much to the surprise of everyone, I appeared at home again on the evening of the day I had supposedly left for Germany.

When I got back to the squadron, I found that I had missed some excitement and drama. Perhaps all would have been well, had not Joe Holway, the RSM, decided to have a little fire-drill in the early morning. He had appeared on the waste ground behind the cookhouse and lit a pile of petrol-soaked cotton waste. Stirring it with his stick, he shouted "Fire!" to Trooper Jock Gordon, who was stirring the breakfast porridge and could be seen through an open window. Jock pointed out that he was, at that very moment making porridge for breakfast. That a Scot was making the porridge gave added importance to the operation and Jock pointed out that he was not leaving this delicate operation to attend to a fire started by the RSM, or anybody else, for that matter.

Joe gave up and went back to RHQ.

On the next night, Eric Shone, who lived in one of the rooms above the cookhouse, canteen and mess-hall, had occasion to get up in the middle of the night. He smelt something burning and, as he opened the door, clouds of black smoke enveloped him. He plunged through the clouds and ran down the corridor shouting "Fire!" People thought that this was Joe up to his tricks again and took no notice. Someone did get up after a while and soon added his voice to the alarm. People began to come out of rooms and discovered the smoke billowing about and getting thicker.

One of the chaps rang Ted Yeates, who was guard commander. "Ted, there's a fire in the canteen." "Oh dear!" said Ted, "I'd better ring the fire picquet, then!" Meanwhile, another keen type had rushed out to the front of the squadron office, where a shell-case hung as a fire alarm. Beating this soundly, he woke up someone in the office, who thought that it was a nasty German making a drunken nuisance of himself. Seizing a pistol, he fired a round in the direction of the dimly-seen figure, which took to its heels. The keeper of the peace then rushed out into the road and loosed off several shots after the fleeing form. The fire picquet, running up the road, found bullets whistling past them in the darkness and took appropriate cover, making their way cautiously up the road to the canteen when firing had ceased.

It was inevitable that the fire picquet should have as two members Casey and Monahan. To get to the fire, they had to pass through a room where there was a table-tennis table. The sight was too much to resist, so they decided to have a quick 'knock up' before tackling the fire. The orderly officer appeared and organised the fire-fighting team, which disappeared upstairs to tackle the blaze. A bucket of water was thrown at the seat of the fire in the approved manner. The seat of the fire had now become a hole in the floor and ceiling, and the orderly officer, who was standing looking up at the fire, got the full force of the water.

The fire was put out without more ado (and I must say that Peter Randall denied all of this story, but this is what I heard on my return). It so happened that the formidable Brigadier, Michael Carver, was to inspect the squadron on the following day. The hole was patched up, 'surplus' transport was driven off into the countryside, and the drivers told not to return until it was safe to do so. An engine, also surplus to requirements, was sunk in a nearby lake. It seems, from the Regimental Diary which I read in later years, as if we didn't really come up to the exacting standards set by the Brigadier.

Nearby was a displaced persons camp that was under our jurisdiction. When a farmer complained that a cow of his was missing, a team was sent to the camp to investigate. In the early morning the team descended on the camp, looking for the missing cow. Huts were entered and, as it was summer, some of the ladies were sleeping 'au naturel', which provided a diversion. No cow was found in the camp, but a group of men were discovered carrying half of the animal back to it later on in the morning.

A sadder incident concerned a pig farmer who was periodically having his livestock stolen. A guard was mounted at the farm and, one dark night, footsteps were heard approaching. On being challenged, the approaching people ran away, or at least one of them did. The sergeant in charge of the guard opened fire with a Sten gun and hit one of them, killing him. The intruders turned out to be policemen who were also checking on the farm. At the subsequent enquiry the widow agreed that, had the man not run away, all would have been well. The policemen were under the impression that they had run into a band of armed raiders.

I heard about all this when I came back from agricultural leave and was sorry to have missed out on some of the excitement.

Winter was coming closer and the nights were getting darker, but there was work to be done on some nearby gunnery ranges and to get there we had to drive through Area 'F'. In this area was a vast camp of German PoWs who were waiting to be processed for demobilisation. The men had made their preparations for winter and had constructed mud and wattle huts which had stoves inside and looked weather-proof and cosy. I wondered if they had learned the skill of hut-making in Russia.

The weather deteriorated as we began work on the ranges. When it was my turn to fire the 17-pounder, a sea fret was blowing up the range. When the gun fired, the muzzle blast always kicked up a great cloud of dust in dry weather; now, dust was mixed with the sea fret and made a sticky cloud which was blown back onto the tank gunner's telescope. After the first shot it was impossible to see the target. I told Ernie Riddall that it was hopeless, but he insisted that I fire the shot. I fired and the shot went into the sea, nowhere near the target. I was cross about being asked to shoot in such hopeless conditions and told all and sundry so!

On our way back to Raisdorf, our tank driver was one of the 4th CLY people who had been captured at Villers Bocage. As he still had a little time to serve, he had elected to come and be with 'his' regiment in Germany until the time of his discharge. I heard later on that some of the crew of Hugh Stanton's tank, which had been brewed up at Nederweert, had met the German gunner who had fired the shot. This was an interesting story, but I was unable to find out the truth of the matter.

Back at Raisdorf, being on guard brought its own excitements. Two naval officers stopped their German car at the level crossing and began to fill up with petrol. Some fuel fell onto the red-hot exhaust pipe and the car caught fire. Several of us rushed up to the tank park and got extinguishers from the tanks, but we could not save the car, and it became a burnt-out wreck.

I was on guard with Chris Law one night when a train was signalled and the level-crossing barrier was lowered. Chris thought that it would be a good idea if we sat on the end of the barrier, thereby preventing the man in the signal box from raising it again when the train had passed. We carried out this operation, but the gearing must have been very good, because the man wound up the barrier with no difficulty at all and we were both tipped off.

We had a visit from an army chaplain who had opened a Retreat House in Preetz. This was in a complex which had been a convent for unmarried daughters of wealthy families in former times. We listened to what the chaplain said about Retreats, and their purpose, and I and several others put our names down take part. The chaplain's name was John Lance, and he had served with distinction as chaplain to the Inns of Court Regiment. He had wangled himself on a detachment which was to get out of the invasion bridgehead on D-Day and demolish bridges. This risky project had to be abandoned when the LCT carrying the detachment's vehicles was blown up by a mine before landing.

I joined a driving course on a three-tonner. Because there was no pressure on me, I enjoyed driving the vehicle, not like the course at the Training Regiment. I looked out of the back of the truck one morning and saw a dispatch rider overtaking us. To my surprise, he was one of the Troop at the Training Regiment and, though I didn't know it then, was in the East Riding Yeomanry. We were to meet again.

Unfortunately, just as I was getting more confident, someone else drove the truck into the back of another vehicle and bashed in the radiator. The truck was taken off the road, and our driving lessons came to an end. There was some attempt to give us instruction in maintenance, and I remember 'grinding in' some valves, but no more driving came my way. If we had been able to gain certificates, then we could have had driving licences when we were discharged.

To my surprise, I was made intelligence corporal and had a load of maps dumped on me. They bore no relation to each other and were just odd maps of bits of north-west Europe, but I found a large wooden box, which was not on the inventory of the house furnishings, and decided to keep them in that.

Winter came, and snow. We walked back from Preetz one night and came across a van which had slid into a ditch at the roadside. We were poking round it to see if there was anyone in the driving cab when the driver appeared from inside the back. There was nothing we could do to help him, so we left him a few cigarettes and walked on.

On guard, I watched as a DR approached in the dark. His machine slipped on the ice and careered toward us on its side. We skipped out of the way and helped him get it upright again. I didn't fancy riding a motor bike in those conditions.

Jack Geddes and I were on guard one snowy night and very late, after curfew, we heard the sound of approaching voices. A group of Poles came along so; to keep them under observation, we walked on the opposite side of the road. We approached the guard room and Jack told them to stop where they were; he then went inside to make sure that it was alright for them to proceed. They had been to a party to provide music, I think. As Jack left me, he said, "Keep them covered!" I did but what I would have done had they made a break for it, I don't know. They went on their way after that slight delay.

On another occasion I was on guard with Brackley, my companion of the Udem ridge. We walked up to the tank park where there was something that Brack wanted. At the end of the park were the burnt-out ruins of a workshop of some kind. Brack grubbed about among the wreckage and emerged with two weights – round spheres with handles on them. He drew a length of rope from his greatcoat pocket and tied this onto the weights. "Why do you want these, Brack?" I asked. "They'll come in," was his reply, so we set off through the snow with the weights bumping and sliding over it as we walked back to his billet. This made me remember that, during the summer, an inspection of billets took place; a case was discovered under Brack's bed. "Whose is that?" asked the inspecting officer. "Mine, sir." "Let's have a look inside," and look he did, at a collection of rusty saws, chisels and other metal junk of all kinds. Brack was a scrap dealer in the making.

Chapter 19

Schleswig – Schloss Gottorf

As intelligence corporal I was given the job of producing a plan of the squadron accommodation at the Schloss Gottorf, which was to be our home. The Schloss itself was built round a central courtyard, into which sunlight barely entered, at least in winter. Snow was still on the ground, and I remember Joe Holway giving some men foot drill and seeing the straight lines worn in the snow by the feet of the men. "That'll please Joe," somebody said as we admired the pattern.

Snow was also responsible for us getting an unusual supper one night, for a lady of the Control Commission was making her way back from Denmark, when her car skidded into the ditch. Our fitters got her out of the ditch, and she appeared at the guard room to thank us. She had on board a tray or two of delicious open sandwiches that she was bringing back with her. We were invited to tuck in, which we did, scorning the bits of bread and cheese which we were usually given.

We heard from the Retreat House at Preetz, so those of us who had put down our names went there for a week. It was an instructive time and John Lance, the retreat conductor, had a remarkable presence. I had certainly never met anyone like him, and we were to meet again in the 1970s when he was Archdeacon of Wells and I came under his Archidiaconal eye as one of his parish priests.

We wandered into Preetz one dark night to see if any other unit had taken over the old 'Black Rat', but all was darkness and the place was shut. By coincidence, in that party was a lad in the RASC, who had seen the Focke Wulf shot down by the Bofors in Normandy!

On another occasion, we were taken up into the roof of the church and had to walk along a narrow plank, with only a flimsy hand-rail on one side and the fan vaulting roof swooping away below our feet. I declined the offer to get up into the little cupola that stood above the roof and admire the scenery.

Back at Schleswig, new tanks arrived. They were Comets, and we had only seen one before, when we gathered round one when it drove through Elmshorn. I did not realise that they had been used in action at the end of the campaign. We wished that we had landed with them instead of Cromwells. Up-gunned and with thicker armour, we might have then been able to give a better account of ourselves in encounters with the enemy.

Because of demobilisation, our personnel numbers had run down considerably, despite some reinforcements joining us, so we were brought up to strength again by a big group of officers and men from the East Riding Yeomanry – including the dispatch rider I had seen from the back of the truck at Preetz. It is always a difficult time, as we knew from our own experience, when regiments are broken up and sent to other units. The amalgamation of 3rd and 4th CLY was easier, for we were sister regiments, but ERY had a different way of doing things and many of the men who joined us were conscious of the fact that their regiment had vanished into suspended animation. Had we been in their shoes, I think we would have been resentful.

In CLY, when an NCO asked someone to give a hand with a task, it was done without any official 'detailing'. Now, we found, this would not do and personnel had to be detailed to do work in a new 'regimental' way. The new SSM did not make himself popular by telling us that we would have to learn to be soldiers! But a little cameo comes to the memory.

Scene: a parade. All lined up except a CLY chap, who appears a little late.

SSM: "Where have you been?"

CLY Trooper looks at his row of medal ribbons and indicates with finger: "Oh! Africa, Italy, France, and so on. Where have you been?"

SSM: "Get fell in!"

I was orderly corporal one night, when the canteen barman called me over. One of the new men had refused to remove his beret in the canteen, as was our custom. I managed to persuade him that it would be a good idea if he conformed with everyone else; his reluctance to do so was another sign of the times.

I had spotted an advertisement in the "Soldier" magazine, which was for an audition as a broadcaster on the British Forces Network radio based in Hamburg. Richard Dipple had also seen the advertisement so we both set off to the broadcasting studio one day in a 15-cwt driven by Eric Shone. When we got there the officer who saw us explained that the deadline for applications had closed. Nevertheless, he would give us each a test.

Richard entered the studio first and I could hear his voice unfalteringly reading the test material. I was sure that his was the kind of voice they were looking for. Then it was my turn and I also went into the studio. I had never been in such a place before and I was taken aback by the large number of reel curtains draped around. This was to kill resonance and aid the sound of the voice of the broadcaster. I read my piece, and then a previously unseen news item about the repatriation of PoWs from the Far East, among whom (I read) "Beri-beri is rife." Richard, listening outside, was sure that mine was the kind of voice they were looking for. The officer thanked us for coming. He didn't actually say "Don't ring us, we'll ring you," but we gathered that neither of us had The Voice! I believe a chap called Michelmore got the job!

The drive back in the dark was hair-raising, as Eric wanted to get back quickly. We found ourselves driving through a park at one stage and saw a man run behind a tree to get out of our way.

A dance was held in the Schloss Barracks – officers only – but I saw a lad who I had met at the Preetz Retreat House. He had come with the dance band that was made up of personnel from the Rifle Brigade band. Even if it had been an 'All Ranks' affair, I had never learnt to dance and so would not have gone. Later, some of the lads went dancing with the WAAF personnel from the airfield nearby. The girls called us 'The Lineshooters', of course.

The SSM, whom I later discovered had not such a confident character as the one he presented to us, agreed to take us for riding instruction. I had only sat on a horse once or twice and found the distance from the ground, when I was 'up', terrifying. After a few lessons in the Riding School attached to the barracks, I decided that it was not for me.

As the summer came, we made another move, this time to Hamm, in the Ruhr.

Everyone had heard of Hamm, for it was a regular target for RAF bombers in their many attacks on the industrial heartland of Germany. The barracks were untouched by bombs, though there was a wrecked house opposite the barrack gates. A near miss?

One of our first jobs as we occupied the barracks was the demolishing of a large wooden-surrounded earth latrine which stood on the edge of the barrack square. The woodwork was soon dismantled and then the other matter had to be dealt with. Spades and shovels came to the fore and, as someone remarked, the Sharpshooters really did live up to their alliterative nick-name!

The summer days went past and there was quite a lot of spare time. A coco-matting cricket pitch was set up on the square, but I was not a cricketer, though I was pulled into the Troop team, only to be run out when a young officer called for a run, having touched the ball to one of the fielders. He did have the grace to apologise.

Casey and Monahan were still going strong, becoming enthusiastic about unarmed combat. Bodies flew through the air and crashed onto mats in the gym.

A cabaret was laid on for our entertainment. We went to a hall outside the barracks and heard musical items of various kinds. The nubile young acrobat was what I remember, and someone getting her some soap, as her hands had become grubby on the hall floor. I hoped that he had let her keep the soap. There was a cafe in town, and I think the artistes came from there. I went once or twice with some friends – Noel Parr, Eddie Robinson, Alec Keen and co. – but there were endless jokes told in German and so it was a bit boring.

On a sadder note, one of our DRs ran into the back of an unlit trailer parked on the road and was killed. His body lay in our barrack block, and Ted Dunn decreed that we should not play our radios or make unnecessary noise, as a mark of respect. We saw the bike afterwards, and the handlebars had been pushed right over the petrol tank.

The funeral took place in a military cemetery where there were several Service graves. On a sunny afternoon, the squadron was taken in three-tonners – best BD of course. The coffin was on another three-tonner, from which the canvas cover had been removed. The squadron sergeants were bearers and accompanied the coffin.

The body having been lowered into the grave, we all saluted – Ted Dunn with an earth shaking 'Guards' salute. Next to the cemetery there was a school. The children crowded up to the fence to watch the funeral, and, as they were supervised by Sisters, I guessed that it was a Roman Catholic infants school.

Chapter 20

Winterbourne Gunner

To my surprise, I was to be sent on a six-week course at the Army School of Chemical Warfare on Salisbury Plain. After a welcome weekend at home, I reported to the school. There was a mixture of NCOs from all regiments, and I soon struck up an acquaintanceship with a lad from the Royal West Kents and an RTR corporal named Bull, from Nottingham.

Also on the course, for the second time, as they were on a twelve-week stay, were Maltese artillery men who were all jolly and, with one or two exceptions, somewhat rotund.

The course itself was very interesting, if you liked playing round with poison gas and fire! There was chemical warfare theory, of course, and, at the end, we were invited to give a lecture on flame-throwers. Using napalm, we 'flamed' targets from Bren carriers and also from back-packs. More efficient ways of killing people were coming into vogue, however, and the latest back-pack flame-thrower had a system of cartridges arranged round the nozzle, like the bullets in a revolver, each igniting in turn, so you got a number of shots.

We were also shown the latest in equipment for the foot soldier. The uniform was green and all the packs were suspended from the waist. There was a small hat, and the 'model' carried an Enfield Mark 5 rifle, which was short, like a carbine, and had a bayonet that could be used as a fighting knife if one was unfortunate enough to be close to the enemy. All this equipment had been designed for fighting in the Far East and a 'poncho' ground sheet, with a hole in its middle for the head, had been also designed, as a protection against monsoon rains.

I stayed in the camp one weekend and went into Salisbury with my Royal West Kent friend. I do not remember anything about the cathedral, but I do remember going into a tea shop and clumping over highly polished oak floorboards in my army boots and listening in fascination to two very English ladies talking in very loud voices. It was the first time that I had come across this affectation and thought it quite extraordinary.

From the top of the bus taking us back to camp, we saw one of our Maltese friends under a street lamp, talking animatedly to two other people. Over his shoulder, in a fireman's lift, was draped the senseless body of a young lady!

My female company was limited to having the odd word with the ATS cooks on the camp. They seemed to be predatory young ladies, and I was a bit afraid of them. Being cooks, they were mostly of 'cookly' proportions, and they seemed to speak of things which had veiled sexual connotations. Or was that just me?

I spent my 21st birthday at Winterbourne Gunner and got one or two cards from home. There was the usual final dance for all those who had been on the course. Several ATS girls came to this, and amongst them was a dazzling blonde. One of our number, a Welsh Guardsman, had imbibed more drink than was good for him, so my pal and I escorted him back to the barrack hut, where we plunged his head into cold water. As he came up for air, he spluttered that he wanted to see Blondie! We all wanted to see Blondie!

Back at the dance, things were going with a swing, and my abiding memory is of the cooks doing the 'Hokey-Cokey'. 'You put your whole self in – !'

When the dance was over, I went to the barrack hut and found a tearful girl leaning in through a window in conversation with one of the infantry sergeants who had been on the course. He, too, was half-seas over and his friends had put him to bed, from whence he declared that he was, "Alright!" to the girl, who was concerned for his welfare. Some relationships seemed to have got out of hand.

At the dance was a Sharpshooter officer who wore a dark blue uniform jacket and green overalls, with a double yellow stripe down the leg. I had not seen him at the camp and gathered that he had been on a separate course for officers.

Back, then, to Hamm and travelling on the same train as the officer. I was always amused to note that, when we stopped for refreshments on the journey across Europe, ORs were instructed to 'Proceed' to the mess-hall, but officers were asked to 'Make their way'.

At Hamm railway station, the officer demanded the attentions of a porter. An ancient came up with a four-wheeled trolley and the officer put on it one small bag, declaring that he wanted to "keep the Germans in their place!" I didn't want to play that game and so carried my own kit.

When the time came for us to move from Hamm, I was to be in charge of the train that took our heavier equipment and other impedimenta to Lüneburg, which was our next, and, as it turned out, our last posting as a regiment.

The night before the move to Lüneburg I put in an early call, and soon found myself, together with the members of a small guard which was travelling with me, on the train rattling through the countryside, in the hands of the German train crew.

The next night, we disposed ourselves to sleep on seats or on the floor of the passenger carriage allotted to us. I was awakened by the train guard, who called me to the carriage door. The train had stopped and, looking down the train, I saw figures in silhouette pouring sand on an axle-box that had burst into flames. Hoping that it was not an ammunition truck, we watched until the fire was put out. That truck had to be left behind and so I was taken across to a railway hut at the side of the track and found myself talking to the RTO at the nearest station. A disembodied voice assured me that it would be in order to shed the truck and leave it there, so after much shunting and banging of buffers, we went on our way.

Dawn saw us drawing into Lüneburg, shunted into a siding away from the station. There was an aircraft engine half buried beside the railway track. A remnant of some bombing raid. We mounted guard for the rest of the day and were relieved. I reported the loss of a truck on the way but that caused no upset.

Our new barracks were three-storied, next to those housing our comrades of long standing, the Royal Scots Greys. Further out along the road was an airfield, where gliders could be seen taking to the air on calm days.

Over the entrance to our block, a stony-faced warrior gazed out over the barrack square, his expression somewhat marred by the red nose which some disrespectful soldier had painted there.

Lüneburg was a pleasant town with several amenities for troops. There was a Red Shield Club, which had a dance-hall attached, a cinema, a theatre and (Oh, luxury!) an ice-cream parlour.

An amusing story circulated about a member of the 'Greys' who had a dram and got into a horse-drawn carriage which plied for trade in the town. "Sing '*Fahren Gegen Engeland*!'," he roared at the aged driver.

"*Nien! – Das ist verboten. The English* – !"

"'The English? The English?' I'm a Scot!! Sing '*Fahren Gegen Engeland*'!!!"

The poor German driver obliged, quaveringly.

Because there were ATS in town, we sometimes had the opportunity to escort them to the cinema or a show. A companion and I once managed to persuade two girls to go with us to the theatre. It was one of the shows where the 'link' between the acts was provided by one of our soldiers. The acts themselves were foreign – acrobats and so on. Before we went to the show, we went for tea in the ice cream parlour. My companion, who was ex-ERY, had been mentioned in Dispatches, as he had pulled a wounded companion out of a blazing tank. We were surprised when one of the girls asked why he had a small oak leaf sewn on his medal ribbon. "Mentioned in Dispatches," he growled, rather embarrassed, but didn't elaborate on his award. Later on, he explained to me as we walked back to barracks, that his face had been badly burned and his hair had been allowed to grow in consequence. Once, he had been standing at a bus stop in England when a heavy hand fell on his shoulder and a military policeman began to berate him about the length of his hair. When my friend turned round and revealed the extent of his facial injuries, the MP was full of apologies.

One entertainment landmark was a 'Big Band' show in one of the hangars at the RAF station up the road. There was a female vocalist who sang to us the popular numbers of the day. The song that won all hearts was *Don't sit under the Apple Tree with anyone else but me*, because she implored her lover not to 'Share his joystick with anyone else but me.' Roars of laughter and approval from the audience.

I was helping Monahan, now a corporal, at the cinema in town. The film of the week was *The Wicked Lady*, with Margaret Lockwood, Patricia Roc, James Mason and Michael Rennie. I saw this masterpiece about fourteen times in all and could repeat whole chunks of dialogue, aided by Noel Parr, who I coached in his part.

Accompanying the film there was a newsreel in which one saw an atom bomb being exploded. After which Professor Joad told the audience that "all scientists should be put in a bag and dropped into the ocean!"

One day we were honoured by the presence of a high-ranking staff officer, with red tabs galore. He emerged from the cinema in high dudgeon, for two ATS girls in the sparse audience had not stood for the National Anthem. He told us to put them both on a charge and he would check later on to see that we had done so. We had a word with the girls, who had kicked off their shoes for greater comfort and hadn't had time to put them on again before the Anthem. We decided that we would take a chance on retribution from On High and would not charge them. Needless to say, we heard no more.

There were six people in our barrack room. Amongst these were Lofty Long, who was always last in and always opened the door with a great crash hoping to wake us all up. I found this habit rather tiresome but feigned sleep, as did everyone else; Alec Kean, who was a rotund Scot from Edinburgh; Noel Parr, a friend of long standing; and Eddie Robinson, a gentle sheep farmer from the north of England.

Eddie and I went to Brussels together on a short leave. Somehow or other he had got in with a Belgian family who had some good friends in Lüneburg. We were to call in at the Brussels address, in the Marché au Charbon, and return to Germany with goodies which they would pack for us. We agreed to pick up the goods on the day we returned to Germany. In the meantime, Brussels and sight seeing. We saw a sentry outside the Royal Palace, standing with fixed bayonet. "Do you think he'll move if we walk straight at him?" I asked. Unfairly, we did just that and he pulled his rifle out of our way!

A tall, white-haired, upright gentleman stopped to talk to us. He had observed our 'Sharpshooter' shoulder titles. He himself, he said, had shot (demonstration with walking-stick) in the Belgian Congo. I think that he thought we were a specialist sniper regiment. Another elderly upright gentleman we saw had on his arm a beautiful young lady. Uncharitably, we drew our own conclusions about this.

I remember being in bed in the Red Shield Club, where we were staying, when the cleaning ladies came in. One sat on my bottom, as I lay face down, and shouted: "*Levez vous! Levez vous!*", joining in the laughter of the other ladies and the chaps who were still in bed. I thought that this was very 'Belgian' behaviour. "C'était impossible, Madame!" I cried, and indeed it was. The lady was no lightweight.

We visited the Belgian friends and were given two large cardboard boxes for the German family at Lüneburg. Returning from Brussels, as the train moved off, MPs came down thc carriage, so we closed our eyes and pretended to be asleep, avoiding questions about the contents of the boxes.

We took part in an exercise on Lüneburg Heath – I and several others with the supply column. Chris Law, I remember, was one of the party and for much of the time we just sat around yarning. The SSM was driven up in a Jeep one morning, for first aid. A plastic grenade had gone off, and his face was pitted with fragments. Fortunately, the damage was superficial. Either then or on some subsequent occasion, he was talking about himself and his work as SSM. "Usually," he said, "the Sergeant Major is regarded with awe, but they see me coming and say, 'Now what does the bloody fool want?' But, of course, not to me." I was surprised at this revelation from one who was outwardly confident and brusque in his manner.

A new quartermaster was in charge of our supply column. He was a newcomer and I thought him a rather vulgar man, for he related stories of his service in Egypt, and they were of a very unedifying nature. Sleep, however, was once again to be my downfall. I was sitting on a box of rations, dozing away in the afternoon sun, when 'Q' came up and shook me. "Are you OK?" he asked. I said "Yes," and dozed off again. When I came to, everyone had vanished, trucks and all, to replenish the tanks, which had finished for the day and were now in leaguer. I was the one who was detailed to record the returns of fuel that would be needed on the following day. I rushed around and found a three-tonner which was still parked in another part of the area. I commandeered it and we found the tanks and trucks. I had to go round and check how much petrol each tank had used.

There was excitement one summer evening as I walked into town over a long wooden bridge which was for pedestrians only. A crowd of civilians was on the bank of the river, watching the members of the Lüneburg fire brigade at work. How odd, incidentally, to see someone wearing the 'coal scuttle' helmet again. Floating in the River Lüne was what appeared to be a body – that of a young woman with long blonde hair and wearing a red and white check dress. The firemen were trying to grab this dress with long poles as the body floated past and then out into the middle of the river again. When at last they managed to grab the dress, screams arose from the women on the bank and children dung to their mothers in apprehension.

As the body was dragged nearer to the bank, we could see that the 'victim' was just a red and white check mattress, and the long blonde hair was yellow straw, trailing in the water.

The wheels of reorganisation were turning, and it was decreed that the regiment should go into suspended animation.

Those of us who still had some time to serve were asked to which regiment we would like to be posted. A queue formed up outside the orderly room, as those who did not make a decision about a unit would be posted to the Royal Scots Greys. I toyed briefly with the idea of joining the Greys, for my maternal grandmother was a Scot and I felt that I had some affiliation with Scotland.

Events, however, were to take another turn and guide me out of regimental life for a time.

I had seen in Part One Orders a mention of a course for training clerks. This was run by Royal Engineers and was a course of six weeks duration. Called 'Quill', the course was held at Bad Oeynhausen and seemed a useful one to take. Several other Sharpshooters put their names down for it and so I would have some company.

The night before I was due to leave Lüneburg I had a very pleasant surprise. Charlie Spiller, who had months ago gone on a mechanics course in London, his home, came back to the regiment. I was pleased to see him, as he was a comrade from war-time and we had knocked about together in Preetz and Raisdorf.

Now I was off to new things and we lost touch again.

First of all, to a holding unit, then to the RE and RASC barracks for the training course.

Chapter 21

Clerk's Course, 'Quill'

My companions and I travelled to the large barracks where the course was to be held. There was a cosmopolitan crowd of personnel from all branches of the Army and all kinds of regiments, not all on our course, some being engaged on other duties at the barracks and awaiting postings, too.

At that time, there were difficulties in Palestine as the Jewish people struggled to carve out a homeland and build a future for the nation after the terrors of Europe. Naturally, British personnel were involved in these struggles, and some servicemen and women died at the hands of the Stern Gang and Irgun Zvei Leumi.

Some units, therefore, were posting Jewish personnel away and several of them came on the 'Quill' course. One, I remember, was a well-built lad named Kalmanowski. He said he had been a traveller in ladies' underwear, and I remember him having a furious argument with somebody about what cami-knickers were.

But to the course. We had typing instruction and tuition on office administration; I have forgotten all the administration instructions except the directive to: "Open a File on it if a new subject comes up." Of course you've got to remember to actually file the stuff afterwards.

As usual, there was the problem of command – who was to 'get this lot fell in' and march them to the NAAFI and to meals etc. There were 26 on the course, including me, and one of them was another lance corporal. As he had been promoted after me (he said) I had the job of seeing that everybody was in the right place at the right time. All the lads played the game and there was no skiving but there was one little difficulty with two members of the Durham Light Infantry. As soon as the squad was brought to a halt, these two instantly stood at ease, as was their long-established custom. As they only did this when we were on our own, and not when senior NCOs or officers were about, I allowed them to continue doing this, and there were no disputes.

The course was easily managed, once we had got into the rhythm of typing, first of all to the beat of music played on a gramophone and then 'touch typing' with expert fingers. Knowing why the DAQMG at Brigade was always a major (if I remember rightly) was a little more difficult. We had a talent concert, and I performed my 'Wicked Lady' extracts, including James Mason's speech from the gallows.

Mid-week, we marched down to the sports field to watch football. I had a cough – "too much smoking," my mother had said when I last went on leave, and as we marched along, I felt a lump come up in my groin. I knew it was a hernia and scrounged a lift on a truck going back to barracks. Next day I went sick and the MO said, "Would you like to be operated on now, or would you like to complete the course?" I knew that I would have to begin the course again if I had the operation done right away so I elected to complete it. My fellow lance corporal now had charge of the squad, and I tagged along with hand in trouser pocket holding in 'the lump'. Not once was I pulled up for walking about in this unsoldierly manner. Perhaps the word had got round!

Back to the holding unit, then, and so to hospital.

I reported in to reception, having been taken in an ambulance to the hospital. "What is your demob number?" I was asked. "54!" I said, much to the surprise of the ATS clerk who was also in reception. I expect she thought I had just come over to Germany.

I was examined by the MO, who said: "Right, we'll do it tomorrow!", which was a bit of a shock, but didn't give me time to brood over the prospect. I apologised for not having had a bath, for all the water in the showers at the holding unit was frozen in the bitter weather. However, I was able to use the Ward bathroom and was then shaved by a medical orderly wielding a cut-throat razor.

In the morning, I was given my pre-med and then wheeled off to the theatre. I was given a very painful spinal injection and the operation proceeded apace. I could feel intense pain as it proceeded but could do nothing about it, of course. I think that the anaesthetist was just keeping me under and I was bumping along between going under and nearly coming round again. I woke to find myself back in the Ward but spent a very restless night and woke up with the top sheet wrapped round my neck. Sister was most displeased.

The next afternoon, I felt very seedy and asked one of the lads to see if the radio could be turned down as it was making my head ache so much. He asked how I felt and then said, "You don't look very well!" and went to fetch Sister. She came with an Irish nurse, a VAD. They looked at me and then the Sister pressed her thumb into the palm of my hand. "Do you feel that?" she asked. I didn't and said so. By this time, I was beginning to feel so ill I just prayed "O God, if this is death, let it be quick." I felt very sick and said so to Paddy, the VAD. She held a pint mug for me, but I filled that with fresh blood and splashed her apron and the floor. (I sneaked a look at my notes later on and 'fresh blood' it was). I was told to lie down flat with no pillow, and a Very Senior Medical Officer came to look at me. "Keep him flat," he said, "Fluids only!" This seemed to do the trick, and I felt really better as Christmas approached. In fact, I ate someone else's Christmas Pudding. I kept awake on purpose to see the New Year in and watched as Verey lights and other pyrotechnics were fired into the air from surrounding units.

Soon, I was able to get up and move around the Ward and help a little by taking meals to those still confined to bed. The Ward became a very lively place, inevitably, I suppose, with young nurses and young men knocking about. I got to take meals to other Wards, but I surprised one young lady, who was not expecting to have her breakfast brought to her by a man and was combing her hair, rather like a mermaid.

Orderly duties ceased forthwith.

I learned that I was to be sent to a British Red Cross convalescent home in Berlin, so I packed my kit ready to go there.

I was taken to the train and put, to my surprise, in a sleeping compartment with an officer. I had expected to be sitting up all night. We introduced ourselves and I said that I had just had an operation. He suggested that I should occupy the bottom bunk, which I gratefully did. We travelled across Germany through the Russian Zone and dawn brought Berlin and a journey through the ruined city to the convalescent home in Spandau.

The convalescent home was at a house which, we were told, had belonged to the Minister of Education. The house was spacious and built on a hill, above a large lake, with views through the trees to the frozen water far below. The 'Con' home was well heated, of course, so we were warm and comfortable. There was a sergeant major in charge of a small staff of army personnel, drivers and so on. The Red Cross ladies looked after our medical needs, and I was taken aside each morning and examined to see if my scar was healing satisfactorily. The German staff waited on us at meal times and brought us coffee or tea in between whiles.

There were a number of men and women recovering from spells in hospital and I was pleased to meet George Hardy, who lived a few miles away from my own home, though I had not known him before.

The atmosphere at the 'Con' home was relaxed, as the idea was that we should recover from our operations and illnesses as speedily as possible, so there was the minimum of discipline. Girls from a local ATS unit came in to a dance during the first week but then more young women were admitted as convalescents, and we were able to stage our own dances. Among the new arrivals was the young lady who was to become my wife!

Berlin was not a romantic place, though, in those immediate post-war times. Huddled figures could be seen on the thickly iced-over lake, fishing through holes in the ice, just like Eskimos. The litter of war still lay round in the snow. Amongst Russian helmets and other items of equipment and vehicles, I remember seeing a truck of about 15-cwt size, completely burnt out, and with a load of typewriters in the back.

There was large NAAFI in town, to which we aften went to have a cup of tea, and sometimes a small orchestra played for dancing. We went to see a ballet in one of the theatres. It was called 'Potiphar's Wife', and one striking scene was when Mrs. Potiphar (bright red long-haired wig) tore off Joseph's coat, leaving him, wearing only a G-string, to climb a flight of stairs in a most balletic way. Tod Slaughter came to the theatre and did his melodramatic best as William Corder in 'Maria Martin and the Reel Barn'. After the performance, he stood at the footlights and told us that the record of the trial of William Corder was in a volume bound with the murderer's own skin. "And," he said, "I have held the book with my very own hands" – holding them out to the audience. All the girls said, "Ooooh!"

We were taken to the Olympic Stadium to play badminton and other indoor sports. A physical training instructor, who was attached to the 'Con' home, took me on at badminton, but it was far too fast a game for me. I wondered at the stamina of an aunt, the smallest of my mother's sisters, who played regularly in winter (tennis in summer, of course).

A tooth that had been worrying me became painful, so I went to the dentist, who whipped it out without more ado. I was pacing up and down nursing my aching jaw when one of the German ladies on the staff noticed me. When I explained what the dentist had done, she said, "Oh! German dentists never take out teeth!" I thought this rather surprising in view of the rows of gleaming gold teeth one saw everywhere.

My scar was pronounced 'fit for duty' and so I returned to the holding unit. Soon, a posting came through, telling me to report to the College of the Rhine Army at Göttingen, south of Brunswick. The college was running month-long courses for teachers who were returning to civilian life, but anyone nearing demobilisation could apply, as there were facilities for students in this university town.

Another, younger lad – an infantryman – was on the same posting to CORA and so we travelled together. It was early morning and quite dark when we set off on the train, and I looked forward to a relaxing nap. My companion, however, was a talker and, as he had only just arrived in Germany, was full of questions about life in the army of occupation. As a result, we spent a few wakeful hours together before arriving in Göttingen.

Chapter 22

The College of the Rhine Army

We were duly installed in a barracks outside the town and awaited an interview with the CO, a seemingly vague, scholarly colonel who habitually rode a 'sit up and beg' bike, which creaked along as he pedalled.

The time of our interview was near, so my companion, who had let his hair grow, was literally chased to the barbers. Shorn and out of breath he joined me in a 15-cwt, and we were taken to the CO. "That'll have to come down," said the CSM, indicating my single stripe, so I reverted to Trooper once more.

I imagined myself being installed in an office but, instead, found myself helping to run the college petrol station, which was at the bottom of the road leading to the barracks. Here, together with another member of the staff, I dealt with customers from the college, and other people authorised to draw petrol. A Military Police Jeep drew up once, I recall, and one of the policemen turned out to be a lad named Bull, who had been with us in CLY at Raisdorf. I remember when he was posted to the MPs, at his own request, we looked down our noses a bit.

There were night callers too. Once, an attractive young lady came seeking her soldier friend who had gone away on demobilisation. I had taken his place, but she seemed unmoved by his departure and chatted away to one of my companions, who had known him. She leaned over me, for I had gone to bed, and scrounged a light for her cigarette. It will be observed that not only was I smoking but I was smoking in bed – both practices that I now deplore.

A brisk, large German knocked imperiously on the door one night. "I must have petrol!" he demanded in firm tones. Before I could make a suitable reply, my companion leapt in, saying to me, "It's the colonel's driver." How was I to know? I learned later on that he had been a fighter pilot, but I didn't think that this entitled him to throw his weight about. However, as my companion dealt with him, a scene was averted.

The owner of the petrol station still lived 'over the shop'. He had served on the Eastern Front and had made his way back home by devious means when the war had ended. His wife had given him up for lost in the final Russian onslaught on Germany. He told us about the winter-time habits of the Russian people who, in the poorer houses, slept all together on the large stoves.

From the garage windows, one could see across snow-covered fields and, on the road into town, the civilian population, muffled up against the cold, trudged past a tree, in the branches of which was wedged a German rifle, as if pointing the way to some forgotten battle.

My presence was required at the barracks. At last, I thought that I might get to see a typewriter, but no! I was put in charge of the gun-store, which was in the cells in the guard room.

I was happily oiling the weapons, locked in for security reasons, when my name was called. Going to the bars in the corridor which led to the cells, I found the sergeant who had run the 'Quill' course. I had written to him to tell him about my posting to the college, and he had now come on a course, prior to demobilisation. "I got quite a shock when they brought me to the cells to see you!" he said. Afterwards, whenever we met, we exchanged a friendly word, and he came to see me before he went away.

Another pleasure was meeting Sharpshooters who came on the courses. John Stoddart was one of these and we spent a lot of spare time together in town, talking about The Meaning of Life, and so on. Another Sharpshooter who appeared told me about the last night at Lüneburg. He described how Richard Dipple and another reveller had tried to get a large wooden CLY badge, which had been made by the carpenters, out of an upstairs window. I could imagine the scenes and the thick heads that abounded the next morning.

So that was the end of the Sharpshooters in Germany! Numerous clerical and other staff had billets in town, but a decree was later issued, directing them to live in the barracks. They were not very pleased about this change in their fortunes, and we who were already in barracks felt that they were working out their displeasure on us. There was the physical training instructor, for instance, who tried to start early morning runs. I, together with the other two in my room (the talkative infantryman and a Grenadier who had come on the scene) once stayed in bed and were put on a charge by him. We spent three evenings cleaning the showers and bathrooms. There was a slight contretemps between the infantryman and the CSM, when the lad asked if he could be excused the punishment that evening, as it was his birthday!

The chief clerk, a staff sergeant, also had a brush with me about Orders. By now I was installed in one of the offices and my duties involved typing out the Orders for the Day. These were written in a book, which was then taken to the officer in charge, for his perusal and signature. I had typed Orders for the following day and had included instructions for people who were setting out on a trip in a three-tonner. I had typed that they would 'catch' the transport at 08.30 hours, or whatever the time was.

The staff sergeant came into the office almost foaming at the mouth. "Who typed the Orders?" he demanded. "Me, sir" (I suppose it should have been "I, sir"). "You don't say 'catch' the 'bus!" he shouted, "You say Take the 'bus! Take the 'bus!" I should have gone to the officer, taking the written copy with me and asked him if that was his signature. I might, perhaps, then have been in the clear. It wasn't my fault that the staff sergeant had lost his 'civvy' billet – for that, I suspected was the reason for his outburst. The early morning runs had faded into oblivion by now and so the other members of the staff were becoming reconciled to living in barracks with the common soldiery.

When I had been 'in the cells', as gun storeman, I had noticed on the wall of one of the cells abusive comments, in German, about the German warrant officer in charge of the German drivers in the transport pool. Evidently, he was not a popular man, and he had the culprit banged up for some misdemeanour. To our surprise, he was fired and a gentler, older German was promoted into his place. We were pleased about this, for the replacement was a much easier man to deal with.

The snow melted and spring drew near. A trip into the Hartz mountains was arranged for members of the staff. This was an impressive part of the country, and we spent an enjoyable day beside a small river and had our meal in a large wooden building.

A football was kicked about and, naturally, it was kicked into the river.

One of our more eccentric members plunged in to rescue it and then had to be dried out in the hut, so there must have been a stove or open fire. When his uniform was dry, he was persuaded to do his 'Act'. This was a convincing imitation of 'The Hunchback of Notre Dame'. The lad had a head start, for he was by no means handsome to begin with. I had seen him in this guise before but had no idea how he did it. He took off his pullover and stuffed it up the back of his battledress blouse. This was the 'hunch'. He tore up bits of cardboard to pad out his cheeks and, as a final touch, rolled up small tubes of cardboard to stuff up his nostrils. His nose was flattened by this process, and he now breathed only with difficulty. Dragging one leg, and hissing away, he limped about and was a terrifying figure.

He made himself up as this character one Sunday morning and woke up my friend the infantryman, who was still in bed. One glance at this threatening apparition and there was an car-splitting yell and the terrified sleeper rushed into the WC, locking himself in and refusing to come out until assured that the 'Hunchback' was back to normal.

I had gone into town to see a film and called at the NAAFI to have a 'char and wad'. There was an American sergeant there who was sitting at a table but, while I was there, he moved to where two ATS girls were seated and fell into conversation with them. I was fascinated by his accent, which I recognised as Brooklyn, but had only heard on screen through the lips of actors like William Bendix. Now here he was, a Brooklyner in the flesh.

Later on, as I was booking in at the guard room, an MP appeared, with the American in tow. We had a company of the Northamptonshire Regiment at the barracks, for security, and two members of the Northants had got into conversation with the American, left the NAAFI and stolen his Jeep. I wondered whether they were still fighting the American War of Independence, for the backing to the Northants cap-badge was a square of dark red cloth, which commemorated the Battle of Brandywine in that war. I really think our transatlantic friend would have been better advised not to speak to the ATS girls!

I remember the orderly officer, who was in the guard room at the time, grumbling that we could only provide an MP, whereas, he thought, if it had been the American Sector and it was a British soldier who had had his Jeep stolen, all hell would have broken loose and the US Army would have pulled out all the stops to retrieve our man's stolen transport.

Somewhere along the way, at any rate between going into hospital and coming to CORA, my demob number had been changed. At the hospital, I had been Demob Group 54. Now I discovered that I was Group 55. How the mistake had taken place, I never knew, but the increase in number was to have unfortunate consequences.

On the staff notice board one day, in Part One Orders, appeared the directive that all personnel in Demob Group 55 and over were to return to their units. I was dismayed, for I had no unit to return to; the Sharpshooters had gone and I was an orphan with no 'family'. I and the companion who had come to the college with me were interviewed by the second-in-command. "You are not being posted for anything you have or have not done," he said. But I wondered about that staff sergeant!

I had an argument, finally, about what kind of weapon I should take with me. I was given a rifle, but I insisted that, as I had come with a pistol, I was going to leave with one. My pistol was duly issued, and the infantryman and I set off for the holding unit once more.

This time my journey was much more tranquil, for I and my travelling companion (the lad who had joined CORA with me) had become so much more friendly that I was able to tell him how tiresome he had been when we had first met, and we laughed together about the experience.

I had applied to go on leave to Asten, to our Dutch family. Permission had been granted but the time for the leave was drawing near and it was going to be difficult if I was going to be between units.

We arrived again at the holding unit and settled in once more among a crowd of anonymous soldiery. To my surprise, the regimental police sergeant, who must have got used to my presence at various times in between postings, asked if I would like to join him in his duties. "Promotion to sergeant right away," he said. Not for the first time I thought that maybe the Sharpshooter colours on the shoulders and the distinctive green band round the beret made one stand out from other Army personnel. I decided that I did not want to spend the rest of my army career dealing with unattached personnel who had no regimental loyalties and were only intent, it seemed, on looking after number one when waiting to be posted elsewhere.

My posting came within a day or two of my leave, and so I could see no way of going to the family at Asten. I wrote to tell them of my disappointment and prepared to join the 13/18th Hussars at Wolfenbüttel near Brunswick. My main concern was for the ATS friend whom I had met at the 'Con' home, and who was now stationed at Hamburg. After an exchange of numerous letters, we had arranged that we should go on leave together to Asten and spend a short holiday with the family. Now she would have to go alone.

Chapter 23

The Lillywhites – 13/18th Hussars

Once again, I travelled overnight and arrived at Brunswick station at 05.30 hours.

I reported to the RTO, who contacted the barracks for me. Several times during the day he saw me waiting for transport, until, on coming back from lunch, he saw me again – still waiting. "Are you still here?" he said, in astonishment, and rang up the regiment yet again, as he had done several times during the morning.

At 14.30 hours a 15-cwt truck arrived to pick me up. I flung my kit on board and expected to be whisked off, but we spent the next half-hour pushing the thing round Brunswick, to make it go. I was not impressed!

The Hussars were unknown to me, though I did know that they had swum ashore on D-Day with DD Sherman tanks. I wondered whether they would be a replica of the 15/19th Hussars and, in some ways, they were, as I was to find out.

When an individual arrived at CLY, someone carried his kit, settled him into his billet and made sure he felt welcome and at home. On arriving at the Hussars, however, I was told that I was being placed in HQ Squadron and then had to find my own way to my room in the barracks. The lads there seemed pleasant enough and I awaited an interview in the morning with the squadron leader. I presented my documentation to a corporal in the outer office. On the front of the file was a hand-written note of commendation from the CLY. The corporal tore it off and threw it in the wastepaper basket without so much as a glance. I then went in to see the squadron leader, who welcomed me to the regiment. I explained about my intended leave to Asten and was granted permission to go. I took a train from Brunswick and arrived at Weert on the morning of the next day. The first part of my journey was by lorry, in which I hitched a lift. To my astonishment, we turned a corner and there was Hugh Stanton's Sherman, now sunk in the ground a little. We were at Nederweert.

I was then able to get a lift in a car to Asten and was able to renew my acquaintance with the van der Zanden family. To my delight, Doreen had made her way from Hamburg, arriving at the van der Zanden home on the evening before my arrival. We were able to spend a very happy leave together; our stay being made all the more memorable when we decided to become engaged.

Piet took us back to Nederweert to view Hugh's tank again, and there we found two men preparing to cut up the hull with oxy-acetylene cutting equipment. Piet was quite annoyed with them, for they were quite indifferent to my uniform and the fact that I was in the regiment to which the tank belonged.

An amusing note was struck when the mail came. Marie looked at one letter and then said, "This is from you, John, to tell us that you are not able to come!"

Back to Wolfenbüttel and the Hussars, with our holiday ended, we rejoined our units. We spent our time in the corridor of the train talking to each other until the parting of the ways at Hanover when Doreen went on to Hamburg and I to Wolfenbüttel via Brunswick.

I had promised the staff at CORA that I would return and take part in a course, but when I asked at the orderly room at the barracks, they told me that I was too late, the application forms had gone in while I was away on leave.

At first, I was just a spare 'bod' in the squadron. My typing skills were not required, which was disappointing, and there was little work for us to do.

The nearest thing to excitement was guard duty. This was a very 'Regimental' affair with a 'stick man', picked out as being the smartest man on parade; he was then excused guard duties and had only to bring supper to the guard room later in the evening. I knew the gun storeman and borrowed his kit when I was detailed for guard. And behold, I got the 'stick'!

An additional squad, which paraded behind the guard in the evening, was a Polish contingent that had the job of guarding a local airfield. They wore dark-blue uniforms like the civil defence people in the UK. They carried no weapons, but I imagine that they had pick-handles back at the airfield for their sentry duties.

There was a mysterious figure in the guard room cells. Mysterious, because when he emerged from his cell, he was handcuffed and blindfolded. Naturally, the rumour was that he was a spy. We were not far from the border between ourselves and our Soviet 'allies', and woods which could be seen in the distance were in their zone of Germany.

The guard were issued with the Enfield No. 5. Bayonets were fixed, of course, when one was 'on sentry'. The tip of the short bayonet was just above waist height. The main gate was plagued by mosquitoes, and the tendency was to flap at them. Two or three sentries had 'pronged' themselves quite badly on the bayonet tips, so it was deemed wiser to 'stand and be still' and risk being eaten alive.

I was at my post one evening, as darkness fell, when a figure approached my fellow sentry at the other side of the entrance gate. The voice of the shadowy figure was familiar, so I called across: "Is that Peter Knight?" (Peter had been one of my squad on the 'Quill' course). "Is that you, John?" he said, as he walked across to me. "What are you doing here?" So, I explained about 'All Demob Groups 55 and over', a directive of which he had not heard. He was just spending the night in his old barracks (he was 13/18th Hussars) before going back to clerkly duties on detachment. I never saw him again.

We went to the ranges at Bergen-Belsen to shoot our guns. In those days, the regiment was equipped with armoured cars which carried quite small-calibre (37mm) weapons. I kept a low profile and was not called upon to fire.

I got a surprise one day as I saw a 15-cwt bowling along one of the roads in camp. Driving the truck, right arm leaning on the driver's door as usual, was Lofty Long, now a sergeant and in full Sharpshooter regalia! He stopped and we had a chat about the Hussars and recalled our days in the CLY.

Meanwhile, to my delight, back at the barracks I was promoted to gun storeman, as the lad who had lent me his equipment for guard duty had gone to be demobbed. The post just suited me, as I was able to sleep in the arms store and the duties were light, consisting of issuing arms for the guard and receiving them after duty, and keeping the weapons clean and oiled.

Days passed and the time for my discharge came. Off we went to Brunswick and the train. As we journeyed through Germany, I bumped into another 'Quill' clerk. This was 'Wee Jock', once again someone with a much higher group number than I had. This lucky lad was going to join a battlefield research unit in Belgium! I would have given a lot for a job like that.

We sailed from the Hook of Holland to Harwich and then took the train to the demobilisation centre at York.

There, a sergeant had the unenviable task of asking all of us if anyone would like to 'Sign on'. Amid a chorus of 'Boo's!' he explained that a good leave and a posting to the unit of our choice would be ours. Despite these added inducements, there were no volunteers. I think that we were all champing at the bit to leave the Army.

We proceeded on our journey to 'Civvy Street', by way of the MO, the people who issued ration books for everything, and the tailor who addressed me as "Sir!" when I made my choice of a suit. ("Light grey with chalk stripe, Sir?").

All my new clothes were packed into a large cardboard box and, carrying this and my kit-bag, I boarded the Nottingham train from York.

As we waited for the train to leave the station, I took off my white lanyard and all my Hussar insignia (beret and collar badges) and dropped them out of the carriage window onto the track. I had a battledress blouse with all the titles and badges of the Sharpshooters at home, so if I were to wear uniform again, I would appear as a Sharpshooter once more. That was the Regiment to which I really belonged.

Appendices

Appendix I

The Sharpshooters

In 1900, Lord Dunraven was given permission to raise a squadron of troops who could both shoot and ride well, for service in the war in South Africa. They were given the official title of 'Sharpshooters' and numbers expanded rapidly, two battalions eventually serving until they returned home in 1902.

In 1901, official notice was given of the formation of the 3rd County of London Yeomanry (Sharpshooters) Imperial Yeomanry, and as 3rd CLY the Regiment served in the 1914-18 war in Egypt, Gallipoli, Macedonia, Palestine and, towards the end of the war, in France and Flanders.

In 1938, the Sharpshooters were instructed to form two regiments and as a result the 4th CLY came into being. Both regiments served in North Africa from 1941. The 3rd CLY took part in the invasion of Sicily and both 3rd and 4th CLY fought in Italy until withdrawn to take part in the allied invasion of France on 7th June 1944 – 4th CLY in 7th Armoured Division and 3rd CLY in 4th Armoured Brigade.

Heavy losses in Normandy brought about the disbandment and amalgamation of several units and 3rd and 4th CLY received orders to reduce to one regiment. The 3/4th CLY then came into being as part of 4th Armoured Brigade and was in Hamburg when the war ended. It stayed there as part of the occupying army until September 1946, when the Regiment was suspended. Early in 1947 the TA was restored and the Sharpshooters began to recruit again as part of the Territorial Army.

After many roles and changes of title, the Regiment still exists in the form of The Kent and Sharpshooters Yeomanry, as part of the TAVR.

Appendix II

Kruishoutem – The Belgian Account

This extract is taken from the Flemish book Gent, September '44, *by Jean-Paul Marchal (Ed J. Verbeke – Gent – Belgium) and translated by Liz Fincham.*

'A little later, 3 Troop, B Squadron 11th Hussars came to reconnoitre Kruishoutem.

After a short time of fighting in the street, 4 Germans are killed and 40 taken prisoner.

One hour later the tanks of the 3/4th County of London Yeomanry take position on the roads leading out of the town. However, they are due for a warm reception, as our witness R. D'Huyvetter records.

One Sherman was positioned on the Market – gun pointing to Waregem. However, the tanks driving up the Waregemsesteenweg collided near 'de Warande' with an important German contingent. Two Shermans were destroyed, one by the residence of K. de Ketele and the other one a little further up the road by the then 'Den Haas' Inn.

V. Brent was found by the destroyed tank by the 'Den Haas' Inn and his fellow crew member, E. Pinch, in the surrounding field. Corporal R. Brown was found dead in the Sherman by the residence of K. de Ketele.

Because of the shortage of infantry, the tanks retreated in the direction of Oudenarde.

The Germans retake Kruishoutem for the umpteenth time and celebrate their victory by taking revenge on the innocent civilians (primarily those from Waregemsesteenweg). Nine innocent civilians are killed in cold blood.

The German 'infiltrations' naturally result in regular interruptions of the roads and gradually the point of the Ghent Force are being cut off from the rest of the Division.

The situation along the central route is not a lot better!'

Appendix III

The 'Sharpshooters' Centre Line

The main route of advance of the 4th and 3rd/4th COUNTY OF LONDON YEOMANRY through North-West Europe from D-Day to V.E. Day and afterwards. Compiled by Jim Webber, 4th CLY Recce Troop, and given to Peter Symes in 1984.

High Ash Camp, near Brandon and the Stanford Battle Training area of Norfolk.

Orwell Embarkation Camp, near Ipswich, Felixstowe, for embarkation in Tank Landing Craft of the 7th Armoured Division assault convoy – Thames Estuary – The English Channel – Off the Isle of Wight – GOLD Beach on the Normandy coast at le Hamel, near Arromanches.

Sommervieu – Ryes – Bayeux 7th Armoured Divisional thrust to enlarge the Operation OVERLORD bridgehead – Tilly-sur-Seulles – la Belle Epine – Villers Bocage: worst tank battle of operations in France, in which 4th CLY suffered heavy losses at the hands of the crack German SS Panzer Heavy Battalion 101 with SS-Haupsturmfuhrer Michael Wittman, who was, with more than 100 tank kills to his credit in Russia and the West Front, the 'Richthofen' of the German Panzer armies.

Douvres – Benouville – Caen – Ifs and Bras: the battle for Borguebus Ridge.

[1]Carpiquet Airfield: the amalgamation of 3rd and 4th CLY into a composite regiment, made necessary by the heavy losses of tanks and personnel.

Le Beny Bocage – Vire – Thury-Harcourt bridgehead over the River Orne – The Falaise Gap – Trun – Gace – Bernay – Beaumont le Roger – le Neubourg – St. Etienne du Vouvray (West Rouen) – Louviers – Les Andelys and the crossing of the River Seine – Gournay en Bray – Formerie – Picquigny and the crossing of the River Somme – Flixecourt – Ailly-le

1 Transfer from 7th Armoured Division to 4th Independent Armoured Brigade.

Haut Clocher – St. Riquier – Auxi le Chateau – The V1 firing bases parallel to the Channel coastline.

St. Pol – Through the battlefields of World War One – Outskirts of Lille – Pecq and the frontier of France and Belgium – Oudenarde – The road to Ghent and the breakthrough with fuel for the stranded 7th Armoured Division.

Dendermonde – Boom – Antwerp – Hoboken and the Docks area – Westerloo – Hasselt – Genk – Budel – Crossing from Belgium into Holland – Weert The Wessem Canal assault crossing – Eindhoven – Nijmegen – Elst: at the extreme tip of the sixty-miles deep Allied salient towards Arnhem Bridge – Tilburg – Asten – Venraij – Wanssum and the German assault over the Maas.

Into Germany: The Battle of the Reichswald Forest – Kleve – Goch Kevelaer – Amen Corner near Udem – The Hochwald Forest – The link-up with the Americans of US Ninth Army.

Return to Bourg Leopold in Belgium for re-equipment for the Rhine Crossing – Udem in Germany again – Xanten – Rhine Crossing – Dingden – Bocholt – Through a corner of eastern Holland: Winterswijk and Enschede – Back into Germany – Ochtrup – Rheine – The Dortmund-Ems Canal – Ibbenburen and the battle with the fanatical young Nazi officer cadets – Nienburg and the crossing of the River Weser – Verden and the crossing of the River Aller – Bremen.

Rotenburg – Schleesel – The liberation of the Allied prisoners-of-war at Fallingbostel Camp and Munsterlager Camp on Lüneburg Heath – Soltau Salzhausen – Lüneburg and the crossing of the River Elbe.

Geesthacht and the last shots of World War Two – Hamburg occupied – Blankenese – Elmshorn – Preetz and Plon, where Area 'F', a vast concentration of German PoW encamped in fields, had to be policed – Selenter See – Schleswig and the Schloss Gottorf – Transfer to Hamm, on the fringe of the bomb-shattered Ruhr industrial area of Westphalia – Back to Lüneburg and final disbandment in 1946.

Appendix IV

Wireless Operator's Alphabet

Wireless Operator's Daily Check List

A	-	Petrol in gallons				
B	-	Oil				
C	-	Ammo				
	1	75 H.E				
	2	75 A.P				
	3	75 Smoke				
	4	17 H.E				
	5	17 A.P				
	6	17 Sabot				
	7	Browning boxes				
	8	37 H.E				
	9	37 A.P				
D	-	Strength				
E	-	Casualties				
	X	Killed				
	Y	Wounded				
	Z	Missing				
F	-	P.W.				
	1.	Officers				
	2.	O.R's				
G	E.	Sherman	A.	B.	C	D.
	F.	Firefly	Fit	Fitters	W/shops	K.O.
	J.	Stuart				
	X.	S. Car				
	Y	O.P.				

Wireless Operator's Code

Copied from the back of an old photograph

COMMDR.	SUNRAY
G. STAFF.	SEAGULL
H.Q.	MOLAR.
Sigs.	PRONTO
R.A.	SHELLDRAKE
R.E.	HOLDFAST
Sup. Trans.	PLAYTIME.
Medics.	STARLIGHT
Ord.	RICKSHAW
REME.	BLUEBELL (SPIDERS BOYS)

Wireless Operator's Alphabet

A	Able	N	Nan
B	Baker	O	Oboe
C	Charlie	P	Peter
D	Dog	Q	Queen
E	Easy	R	Roger
F	Fox	S	Sugar
G	George	T	Tare
H	How	U	Uncle
I	Item	V	Victor
J	Jig	W	William
K	King	X	X-ray
L	Love	Y	Yoke
M	Mike	Z	Zebra

Bibliography

Graham, Andrew, *Sharpshooters at War*, 1964
Mollo, Boris, *The Sharpshooters*, 1970
Collier, Richard, *Ten Thousand Eyes*, 1958
Myatt, Frederick, *The British Infantry 1660-1945*, 1983
D'Este, Carlo: *Decision in Normandy*
Hastings, Max: *Victory in Europe*, 1985
Lefevre, Eric, *Panzers in Normandy-Then and Now*, 1983
Richardson, Charles, *Flashback*
Buffetant, Yves, *D-Day Ships*, 1994
Tout, Ken, '*Tank!*'
Tout, Ken, '*Tanks Advance!*', 1987